How Can the Human Mind Occur in the Physical Universe?

OXFORD SERIES ON
COGNITIVE MODELS AND ARCHITECTURES

How Can the Human Mind Occur in the Physical Universe?

John R. Anderson

OXFORD
UNIVERSITY PRESS

2007

OXFORD
UNIVERSITY PRESS

Oxford University Press, Inc., publishes works that further
Oxford University's objective of excellence
in research, scholarship, and education.

Oxford   New York

Auckland   Cape Town   Dar es Salaam   Hong Kong   Karachi
Kuala Lumpur   Madrid   Melbourne   Mexico City   Nairobi
New Delhi   Shanghai   Taipei   Toronto

With offices in
Argentina   Austria   Brazil   Chile   Czech Republic   France   Greece
Guatemala   Hungary   Italy   Japan Poland   Portugal   Singapore
South Korea   Switzerland   Thailand   Turkey   Ukraine   Vietnam

Published by Oxford University Press, Inc.
198 Madison Avenue, New York, New York 10016
www.oup.com

Oxford is a registered trademark of Oxford University Press

Library of Congress Cataloging-in-Publication Data
Anderson, John R. (John Robert), 1947–
  How can the human mind occur in the physical universe? / John R. Anderson.
     p. cm. — (Oxford series on cognitive models and architectures ; 3)
  Includes bibliographical references and index.
  ISBN 978-0-19-532425-9
  1. Cognition. 2. Newell, Allen. I. Title.
  BF311.A5897 2007
  153—dc22   2007003533

1 3 5 7 9 8 6 4 2

Printed in the United States of America
on acid-free paper

In memory of Allen Newell and Herbert Simon,
who made so much possible for so many

Preface

I set out to write this book as a modern statement of the ACT-R theory and to show how it relates to what we know about the human brain. I wanted this to be a succinct and accessible statement that got at the essence of the matter. Early on, struggling with these goals, I was drawn to the last lecture of Allen Newell by my memories of a few minutes from that lecture that were particularly inspiring for me. I found the recording of this lecture and reaffirmed my memories of those minutes. The first chapter discusses what Newell said during those few minutes. However, I listened to the whole lecture, and I would recommend that everyone who aspires to contribute to cognitive science do the same. The spirit of that lecture has managed to guide me through this book, and the book has become more than just a succinct and accessible recounting of the ACT-R theory. Constantly having Newell's voice in the back of my mind has helped me focus, not on ACT-R, but rather on what Newell identified as one of the ultimate questions of science. This is the title of the book. At times I shift from this central question to the supporting details that Newell loved, but I hope the reader will be able to come away from this book with the sense that we are beginning to understand how the human mind can occur in the physical world.

Many individuals have helped me in various ways in the writing of this book. At the highest level, this book reflects the work of the whole field, the countless conversations I have had with many cognitive scientists, and the many papers I have read. Much of what the book reports are contributions of members of the ACT-R community. My own research group at Carnegie Mellon University has heard me talk about these ideas many times and has given me feedback at many levels. In September 2006 I gave a series of five Heineken Lectures[1] in the Netherlands to different groups based on the five major chapters of this book. Their feedback was valuable and did much to complete my image for the book. My colleague Niels Taatgen, in addition to all of his intellectual contributions, contributed the cover of the book, which was the art piece chosen by Heineken Award committee.

The book also reflects the products of the generous funding of science, particularly in the United States. Different aspects of my own research described in this book have been funded at different times by DARPA, ONR, NASA, NIE, NIMH, and NSF.[2] The long-standing and steady support for the development of ACT-R has come from ONR. Susan Chipman, who ran the Cognitive Science program there for many years, has done so much to support the establishment of a firm theoretical foundation for our field.

Many people read the complete book and gave me blunt feedback on its content: Erik Altmann, Stuart Card, Jonathan Cohen, Stanislas Dehaene, Gary Marcus, Alex Petrov, Frank Ritter, and Josh Tenenbaum. A number of people have commented on specific chapters: Scott Douglass, Jon Fincham, Wayne Gray, Joshua Gross, Yvonne Kao, Sue Kase, Jong Kim, Christian Lebiere, Rick Lewis, Julian Pine, Lynne Reder, Lael Schooler, and Andrea Stocco. Catharine Carlin at Oxford University Press has been a great editor, dealing with all my concerns about creating a contract that would enable maximal dissemination of the ideas, arranging for many of these reviews, and shepherding the book through the publication process. Nicholas Liu, also at Oxford, has also been of great help, particularly in the later stages of getting this book out. Last but not least, I thank my research associate Jennifer Ferris, who has read the book over many times, kept track of figures and permissions, and managed the references and the many other things that are needed in getting this book out.

1. I received the first Heineken Award in Cognitive Science in 2006. This was really given in recognition of the work done by everyone in the ACT-R community.

2. For those for whom these American acronyms are not just common words: Defense Advanced Research Projects Agency, Office of Naval Research, National Aeronautics and Space Administration, National Institute of Education, National Institute of Mental Health, and National Science Foundation.

Contents

How Can the Human Mind
Occur in the Physical Universe?

1

Cognitive Architecture

Newell's Ultimate Scientific Question

On December 4, 1991, Allen Newell delivered his last lecture, knowing that he was dying. Fortunately, it was recorded.[1] I recommend it to anyone who wants to hear a great scientist explaining the simple but deep truths about his life as a scientist. For different people, different gems stand out from that talk, but the thing that stuck with me was his statement of the question that drove him. He set the context:

> You need to realize, if you haven't before, that there is this collection of ultimate scientific questions, and if you are lucky to get grabbed by one of these, that will just do you for the rest of your life. Why does the universe exist? When did it start? What's the nature of life? All of these are questions of a depth about the nature of our universe that they can hold you for an entire life and you are just a little ways into them.

Within this context, he announced that he had been so blessed by such a scientific question:

> The question for me is, how can the human mind occur in the physical universe? We now know that the world is governed by

---

1. The portion of the lecture in question is available at our website: act-r.psy.cmu.edu. The entire lecture is available in video form (Newell, 1993) and at wean1.ulib.org/cgi-bin/meta-vid.pl?target=Lectures/Distinguished%20Lectures/1991.

physics. We now understand the way biology nestles comfortably within that. The issue is, how will the mind do that as well? The answer must have the details. I have got to know how the gears clank and how the pistons go and all the rest of that detail. My question leads me down to worry about the architecture.

When I heard these remarks from Newell, I heard what drove me as a cognitive scientist stated more clearly than I had ever been able to articulate it myself. As Newell said, this question can hold you for a lifetime, and you can only progress a little way toward the answer, but it is a fabulous journey. While Newell spent much in his lifetime making progress on the answer, I think he would be surprised by the developments since his death. For instance, we are now in a position where biology can really begin to inform our understanding of the mind. I can just see that enormous smile consuming his face if he had learned about the details of these developments. The purpose of this book is to report on some of the progress that has come from taking a variety of perspectives, including the biological.

Although Newell did not come up with a final answer to his question, he was at the center of developing an understanding of what that answer would be like: It would be a specification of a *cognitive architecture*—"how the gears clank and how the pistons go and all the rest of that detail." The idea of a cognitive architecture did not exist when Newell entered the field, but it was well appreciated by the time he died. Because Newell did more than anyone else to develop it, it is really his idea. It constitutes a great idea of science commensurate to the ultimate question of science that it addresses.

The purpose of this chapter is to describe what a cognitive architecture is, how the idea came to be, and what the (failed) alternatives are, and to introduce the cognitive architecture around which the discussions in chapters 2–6 are organized.

What Is a Cognitive Architecture?

"Cognitive architecture" is a term used with some frequency in modern cognitive science—it is one of the official topics in the journal *Cognitive Science*—but that does not mean that what it implies is obvious to everyone. Newell introduced the term "cognitive architecture" into cognitive science through an analogy to computer architecture (Bell and Newell,

1971), which Fred Brooks (1962) introduced into computer science through an analogy to the architecture of buildings.[2]

When acting in his or her craft, the architect neither builds nor lives in the house, but rather is concerned with how the structure (the domain of the builder) achieves the function (the domain of the dweller). Architecture is the art of specifying the structure of the building at a level of abstraction sufficient to assure that the builder will achieve the functions desired by the user. As indicated by Brooks's remarks at the beginning of his chapter "Architectural Philosophy" in *Planning a Computer System*, this seems to be the idea that he had in mind: "Computer architecture, like other architecture, is the art of determining the needs of the user of a structure and then designing to meet those needs as effectively as possible within economic and technological constraints" (p. 5).

In this passage, Brooks is using "architecture" to mean the activity of design; when people use "architecture" this is usually what they mean. However, computer architecture has come to mean the product of the design rather than the activity of design. This was the way Bell and Newell used it and, as can be seen in his 1990 definition, this is also the meaning Newell used when he referred to the "cognitive architecture": "The fixed (or slowly varying) structure that forms the framework for the immediate processes of cognitive performance and learning" (p. 111).[3]

This conception of cognitive architecture is found in a number of other definitions in the field: "The functional architecture includes the basic operations provided by the biological substrate, say, for storing and retrieving symbols, comparing them, treating them differently" (Pylyshyn, 1984, p. 30). Or my own rather meager definition: "A theory of the basic principles of operation built into the cognitive system"[4] (Anderson, 1983, p. ix).

---

2. Brooks managed the development of the IBM 360, which at the time was a revolution in the computer world. His perspective on computer architecture came from his experiences at IBM leading up to and including this development.

3. Elsewhere, reflecting the history that led to this definition, Newell describes cognitive architecture as follows:

> What is fixed mechanism (hardware) and what is content (software) at the symbol level is described by the description of the system at the register-transfer level. . . . To state the matter in general: given a symbol level, the architecture is the description of the system in whatever system-description scheme exists next below the symbol level. (Newell, 1990, p. 81)

4. Although my quoted definition predates the Newell definition, I know I got the term from discussions with him.

Architecture

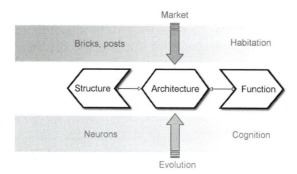

Figure 1.1. An illustration of the analogy between physical architecture and cognitive architecture. (Thanks to Andrea Stocco.)

It is worth reflecting on the relationship between the original sense of architecture involving buildings and this sense involving cognition. Figure 1.1 illustrates that relationship. Both senses of architecture involve relating a structure to a function:

Structure: The building's structure involves its physical components —its posts, fixtures, and so on. None of the above definitions of cognitive architecture actually mentions its physical component—the brain—although Pylyshyn's hints at it. While it would be strange to talk about a building's architecture at such a level of abstraction that one ignores its physical reality—the building itself —one frequently finds discussions of cognitive architecture that simply do not mention the brain. The definition at the end of this section, however, makes explicit reference to the brain.

Function: The function of building architecture is to enable the habitation, and the function of cognitive architectures is to enable cognition. Both habitation and cognition are behaviors of beings, but there is a difference in how they relate to their given structures. In the case of a building, its function involves another agent: the dweller. In the case of a cognitive architecture (or computer architecture), the structure is the agent.[5] Thus, there is a functional shift from construction being designed to enable

5. One could get Platonic here and argue that "knowledge" is the agent occupying the cognitive architecture; then the analogy to physical architecture would be even closer.

the activity of another to construction enabling its own activity. Except for this shift, however, there is still the same structure–function relationship: the function of the structure is to enable the behavior. In both cases, an important measure of function is the success of the resulting behavior—building architecture is constrained to achieve successful habitation; cognitive architecture is constrained to achieve successful cognition.[6]

Before the idea of cognitive architecture emerged, a scientist interested in cognition seemed to have two options: Either focus on structure and get lost in the endless details of the human brain (a structure of approximately 100 billion neurons), or focus on function and get lost in the endless details of human behavior. To understand the mind, we need an abstraction that gets at its essence. The cognitive architecture movement reflects the realization that this abstraction lies in understanding the relationship between structure and function rather than focusing on either individually. Of course, just stating the category of the answer in this way does not give the answer. Moreover, everyone does not agree on which type of abstraction will provide the best answers. There are major debates in cognitive science about what the best abstractions are for specifying a cognitive architecture.

With all this in mind, here is a definition of cognitive architecture for the purposes of this book:

> A *cognitive architecture* is a specification of the structure of the brain at a level of abstraction that explains how it achieves the function of the mind.

Like any definition, this one relates one term, in this case cognitive architecture, to other terms. I suspect readers are going to wonder more about what the term "function of the mind" means in this definition than what the term "structure of the brain" means. The goal of a cognitive architecture is to provide the explanatory structure for better understanding both of these terms. However, before specifying such an architecture—and as some protection against misunderstanding—I note here that the "function of the mind" can be roughly interpreted as referring to human cognition in all of its complexity.

---

6. However, in one case the constraint is created by the marketplace and in the other case by evolution. I am aware that this discussion ignores aesthetic issues that influence the architecture of buildings.

Alternatives to Cognitive Architectures

The type of architectural program that I have in mind requires paying attention to three things: brain, mind (functional cognition), and the architectural abstractions that link them. The history of cognitive science since the cognitive revolution has seen a number of approaches that tried to get by with less; and so they can be viewed as shortcuts to understanding. This chapter examines three of the more prominent instances of such shortcuts, discusses what they can accomplish, and notes where they fall short of being able to answer Newell's question. By looking at these shortcuts and what their problems are, we can better appreciate what the cognitive architecture program contributes when it attends to all three components.

Shortcut 1. Classic Information-Processing Psychology:
Ignore the Brain

The first shortcut is the classic information-processing psychology that ignored the brain.[7] It was strongly associated with Allen Newell and Herbert Simon, and one can argue that Newell never fully appreciated the importance of the brain in an architectural specification. In the decades immediately after cognitive psychology broke off from behaviorism, many argued that a successful cognitive theory should be at a level of abstraction that ignored the brain. Rather than cite someone else for this bias, I will quote myself, although I was just parroting the standard party line:

> Why not simply inspect people's brains and determine what goes
> on there when they are solving mathematics problems? Serious
> technical obstacles must be overcome, however, before the physi-
> ological basis of behavior could be studied in this way. But, even
> assuming that these obstacles could be properly handled, the level
> of analysis is simply too detailed to be useful. The brain is com-
> posed of more than 10 billion nerve cells.[8] Millions are involved

7. The modifier "classic" is appended because "information processing" is used in many different senses in the field, and I do not want this characterization to seem to apply to all senses of the term.
8. This number has also experienced some revision.

in solving a mathematics problem. Suppose we had a listing that explained the role of each cell in solving the problem. Since the listing would have to describe the behavior of individual cells, it would not offer a very satisfactory explanation for how the problem was solved. A neural explanation is too complex and detailed to adequately describe sophisticated human behavior. We need a level of analysis that is more abstract. (Anderson, 1980, pp. 10–11)

The problem with this classic information-processing account is that it is like a specification of a building's architecture that ignores what the building is made of. Nonetheless, this type of account was very successful during the 1960s and 1970s. For example, the Sternberg task, and Saul Sternberg's (1966) model of it, were held up to my generation of graduate students as the prototype of a successful information-processing approach. In the prototypical Sternberg paradigm, participants are shown a small number of digits, such as "3 9 7," that they must keep in mind. They are then asked to answer—as quickly as they can—whether a particular probe digit is in this memory set. Sternberg varied the number of digits in the memory set and looked at the speed with which participants could make this judgment. Figure 1.2a illustrates his results. He found a nearly linear relationship between the size of the memory set and the judgment time, with each additional item adding 35–40 ms to the time. Sternberg also developed a very influential model of how participants make these judgments that exemplifies what an abstract information-processing model is like. Sternberg assumed that when participants saw a probe stimulus such as a 9, they went through the series of information-processing stages that are illustrated in figure 1.2b. The stimulus first has to be encoded and then compared to each digit in the memory set. He assumed that it took 35–40 ms to complete each of these comparisons. Sternberg was able to show that this model accounted for the millisecond behavior of participants under a variety of manipulations. Like many of those who created the early information-processing theories, Sternberg reached for the computer metaphor to help motivate his theory: "When the scanner is being operated by the central processor it delivers memory representations to the comparator. If and when a match occurs a signal is delivered to the match register" (Sternberg, 1966, p. 444).

From its inception, there were expressions of discontent with the classic information-processing doctrine. With respect to the Sternberg model itself, James Anderson wrote a 1973 *Psychological Review* article protesting

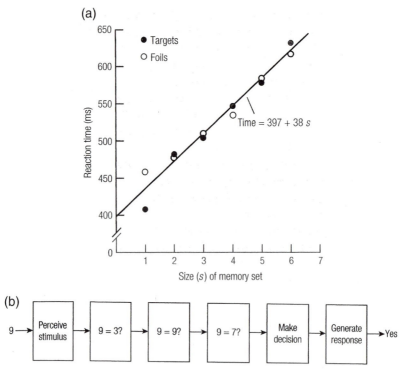

Figure 1.2. (a) The results from a Sternberg experiment and the predictions of the model; (b) Sternberg's analysis of the sequence of information-processing stages in his task that generate the predictions in (a). From Sternberg (1969). Reprinted by permission of the publisher. Copyright by *American Scientist*.

that this model was biologically implausible in assuming that comparisons could be completed in 35 ms. It became increasingly apparent that the computer-inspired model of discrete serial search failed to capture many nuances of the data (e.g., Glass, 1984; Van Zandt and Townsend, 1993). Such criticisms, however, were largely ignored until connectionism arose in the 1980s. Connectionism's proponents added many examples bolstering Anderson's general claim that processing in the brain is very different from processing in the typical computer. The connectionists argued that processing was different in brains and computers because a brain consists of millions of units operating in parallel, but slowly, whereas the typical computer rapidly executes a sequence of actions, and because computers are discrete in their actions whereas neurons in the brain are continuous. The early connectionist successes, such as the Rumelhart and

McClelland (1986) past-tense model, which is described below, illustrated how much insight could be gained from taking brain processing seriously.

The rise of neural imaging in the 1990s has further showed the importance of understanding the brain as the structure underlying cognition. Initially, researchers were simply fascinated by their newfound ability to see where cognition played out in the brain. More recently, however, brain-imaging research has strongly influenced theories of cognitive architecture. In this book I describe a number of examples of this influence. It has become increasingly apparent that cognition is not so abstract that our understanding of it can be totally divorced from our understanding of its physical reality.

Shortcut 2. Eliminative Connectionism: Ignore the Mind

As noted above, one reason for dissatisfaction with the information-processing approach was the rise of connectionism and its success in accounting for human cognition by paying attention to the brain. Eliminative connectionism[9] is a type of connectionism that holds that all we have to do is pay attention to the brain—just describe what is happening in the brain at some level of abstraction. This approach ignores mental function as a constraint and just provides an abstract characterization of brain structure. Of course, that brain structure will generate the behavior of humans, and that behavior is functional. However, maybe it is just enough to describe the brain and get functional behavior for free from that description.

Eliminative connectionism is like claiming that we can understand a house just in terms of boards and bricks without understanding the function of these parts. Other metaphors reinforce skepticism, for example, trying to understand what a computer is doing solely in terms of the activity of its circuitry without trying to understand the program that the circuitry is implementing, or indeed, trying to understand the other parts of the body just in terms of the properties of their cells without trying to understand their function. Despite the reasons for skepticism, this is just the approach of eliminative connectionism and it has had its successes. Its goal is to come up with an abstract description of the computational properties of the brain—so-called "neurally inspired" computation—and then

9. This term was introduced by Pinker and Prince (1988) to describe connectionist efforts that eliminate symbols as useful explanations of cognitive processes, although here I am really using it to refer to efforts that ignore functional organization (how the pieces are put together).

use this description to explain various behavioral phenomena. Eliminative connectionism is not concerned with how the system might be organized to achieve functional cognition. Rather, it assumes that cognition is whatever emerges from the brain's responses to the tasks it is presented and that any functionality comes for free—the house is what results from the boards and the carpenters, and if we can live in it, so much the better.

Eliminative connectionism has enjoyed many notable successes over the past two decades. The past-tense model of Rumelhart and McClelland (1986) is one such success; I describe it here as an exemplary case. Children show an interesting history in dealing with irregular past tenses (R. Brown, 1973). For instance, the past tense of "sing" is "sang." First, children will use the irregular correctly, generating sang; then they will overgeneralize the past-tense rule and generate "singed"; finally, they will get it right for good and return to "sang." The existence of this intermediate stage of overgeneralization has been used to argue for the existence of rules, since it is argued that the child could not have learned from direct experience to inflect "sing" with "ed." Rather, children must be overgeneralizing a rule that has been learned. Until Rumelhart and McClelland, this was the conventional wisdom (e.g., R. Brown, 1973), but it was a bit of a "just so story," as no one produced a running model that worked in this way.[10]

Rumelhart and McClelland (1986) not only challenged the conventional wisdom but also implemented a system that approximated the empirical phenomena by simulating a neural network, illustrated in figure 1.3, that learned the past tenses of verbs. Their model was trained with a set of 420 pairs of root verbs with their past tenses. One inputs the root form of a verb (e.g., "kick," "sing") as an activated set of feature units in the first layer of figure 1.3. After passing through a number of layers of association, the past-tense form (e.g., "kicked," "sang") should appear as another activated set of feature units. A simple neural learning system was used to learn the mapping between the feature representation of the root and the feature representation of the past tense. Thus, their model might learn (momentarily, incorrectly) that words beginning with "s" are associated with past tense endings of "ed," thus leading to the "singed" overgeneralization (but things

---

10. Actually, this statement is a bit ungenerous to me. I produced a simulation model that embodied this conventional wisdom in Anderson (1983), but it was in no way put into serious correspondence with the data. Although the subsequent past-tense models are still deficient in various aspects of their empirical support, they do reflect a more serious attempt to ground the theories in empirical facts.

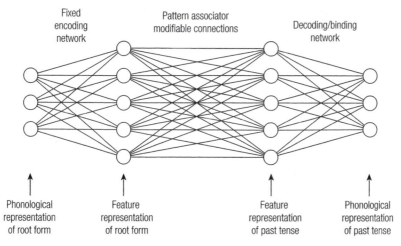

Fixed encoding network

Pattern associator modifiable connections

Decoding/binding network

Phonological representation of root form

Feature representation of root form

Feature representation of past tense

Phonological representation of past tense

Figure 1.3. The Rumelhart and McClelland (1986) model for past-tense generation. The phonological representation of the root is converted into a distributed feature representation. This representation is converted into a distributed feature representation of the past tense, which is then mapped into a phonological representation of the past tense. From Rumelhart, D. E., & McClelland, J. L. In *Parallel Distributed Processing: Explorations in the Microstructure of Cognition, Volume 2: Psychological and Biological Models.* Copyright 1986 by MIT Press.

can be much more complex in such neural nets). The model mirrored the standard developmental sequence of children: first generating correct irregulars, then overgeneralizing, and finally getting it right. It went through the intermediate stage of generating past-tense forms such as "singed" because of generalization from regular past-tense forms. With enough practice, the model, in effect, memorized the past-tense forms and was not using generalization. Rumelhart and McClelland (1986) concluded:

> We have, we believe, provided a distinct alternative to the view that children learn the rules of English past-tense formation in any explicit sense. We have shown that a reasonable account of the acquisition of past tense can be provided without recourse to the notion of a "rule" as anything more than a description of the language. We have shown that, for this case, there is no induction problem. The child need not figure out what the rules are, nor even that there are rules. (p. 267)

Thus, they claim to have achieved the function of a rule without ever having to consider rules in their explanation. The argument is that one can understand function by just studying structure.[11] The rule-like function of the past tense inflection just emerges from low-level neural computations that were not particularly designed to achieve this function. This original model is 20 years old and had shortcomings that were largely repaired by more adequate models that have been developed since (e.g., Plunkett and Juola, 1999; Plunkett and Marchman, 1993). Many of these later models are still quite true to the spirit of the original. This is still an area of lively debate, and chapter 4 describes our contribution to that debate.

The whole enterprise, however, rests on a sleight of hand. This is not often noted, perhaps because many other models in cognitive science depend on this same sleight of hand.[12] The sleight of hand becomes apparent if we register what the model is actually doing: mapping activation patterns onto activation patterns. It is not in fact engaged in anything resembling human speech production. Viewed in a quite generous light, the model is just a system that blurts out past tenses whenever it hears present tenses, which is not a common human behavior. That is, the model does not explain how, in a functioning system, the activation-input patterns get there, or what happens to the output patterns to yield parts of coherent speech. The same system could have been tasked with mapping past tenses onto present tenses—which might be useful, but for a different function. The model seems to work only because we are able to imagine how it could serve a useful function in a larger system, or because we hook it into a larger system that actually does something useful. In either case, the functionality is not achieved by a connectionist system; it is achieved by our generous imaginations or by an ancillary system we have provided. So, basically in either case, we provide the function for the model, but we are not there to provide the function for the child. The child's mind must put together the various pieces required for a functioning cognitive system.

The above criticism is not a criticism of connectionist modeling per se, but rather a criticism of modeling efforts that ignore the overall architecture and its function. Connectionism is more prone to this error because its more fine-grained focus can lead to myopic approaches. Nonetheless,

11. "Structure" here refers to more than just the network of connections; it also includes the neural computations and learning mechanisms that operate on this network.

12. Our own ACT-R model of past tense (Taatgen and Anderson, 2002) is guilty of the same sleight of hand. It is possible to build such ACT-R simulations that are not end-to-end simulations but simply models of a step along the way. However, such fragmentary models are becoming less common in the ACT-R community.

there are connectionist efforts that are concerned with full functioning systems (Smolensky and Legendre, 2006) and strive to capture more of the overall flow of information processing in the brain (O'Reilly and Munakata, 2000). Particularly in the Smolensky and Legendre case, this reflects a conscious decision not to ignore function.

Shortcut 3. Rational Analysis: Ignore the Architecture

Another shortcut starts from the observation that a constraint on how the brain achieves the mind is that both the brain and the mind have to survive in the real world: rather than focus on architecture as the key abstraction, focus on adaptation to the environment. I called this approach rational analysis when I tried practicing it (Anderson, 1990), but it has been called other things when practiced by such notables as Egon Brunwik (1955; "probabilistic functionalism"), James Gibson (1966; "ecological psychology"), David Marr (1982; "computation level"), and Roger Shepard (1984, 1987; "evolutionary psychology"). More recent research in this spirit includes that of Nick Chater and Mike Oaksford (1999), Gerd Gigerenzer and colleagues (1999), and Josh Tenenbaum and Tom Griffiths (2001). My application of this approach was basically Bayesian, and more recent approaches have become even more Bayesian. Indeed, the Bayesian statistical methodology that accompanies much of this research has almost become a new Zeitgeist for understanding human cognition. Briefly, the Bayesian approach claims the following:

1. We have a set of prior constraints about the nature of the world we occupy. These priors reflect the statistical regularities in the world that we have acquired either through evolution or experience. For instance, physical objects in the universe tend to have certain shapes, reflectance properties, and paths of motion, and our visual system has these priors built into it.
2. Given various experiences, one can calculate the conditional probability that various states of the world gave rise to them. For instance, we can calculate the conditional probability of what falls on our retina given different states of affairs in the world.
3. Given the input, one can calculate the posterior probabilities from the priors (1) and conditional probabilities (2). For instance, one can calculate what state of affairs in the world most likely corresponds to what falls on our retina.

4. After making this calculation, one engages in Bayesian decision making and takes the action that optimizes our expected utilities (or minimizes our expected costs). For instance, we might duck if we detect information that is consistent with an object coming at our head. Anderson (1990) suggested that at this stage, knowledge of the structure of the brain could come into play in computing the biological costs of doing something.

The Bayesian argument claims neither that people explicitly know the priors or the conditional probabilities nor that they do the math explicitly. Rather, we don't have to worry about how people do it; we can predict their cognition and behavior just from knowing that they do it somehow. Thus, the Bayesian calculus comes to take the place of the cognitive architecture.

I regard the work I did with Lael Schooler on memory as one of the success stories of this approach (Anderson and Schooler, 1991; Schooler and Anderson, 1997). We looked at how various statistics about the appearance of information in the environment predicted whether we would need to know the information in the future. Figure 1.4 shows an example related to the retention function (how memories are lost with the passage of time). Figure 1.4a shows how the probability that I will receive an email message from someone on a given day varies as a function of how long it has been since I last received an email from that person. For example, if I received an email message from someone yesterday, the probability is about 30% that I will receive one from that person today. However, if it has been 100 days since I received an email message from that person, the probability is only about 1% that I will receive one from him or her today. Figure 1.4a shows a rapid dropoff, indicating that if I have not heard from someone for a while, it becomes very unlikely that I will again. Anderson and Schooler found that this same sort of function showed up for repetition of information in all sorts of environments. It reflects the demand that the world makes on our memory. For instance, when I receive an email message, it is a demand on my memory to remember the person who sent it.

If the brain chose which memories to make most available, it would make sense to choose the memories that are most likely to be needed. Figure 1.4a indicates that time since a memory was last used is an important determinant of whether the memory will be needed now. Anderson and Schooler did the Bayesian math to show that this temporal determinant implied that retention functions should show the same

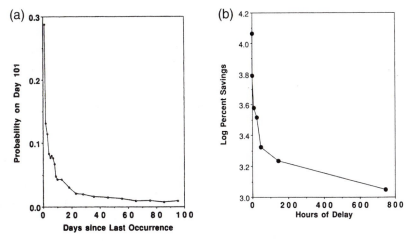

Figure 1.4. (a) Probability that an email message is sent from a source as a function of the number of days since a message was received from that source (Anderson and Schooler, 1991); (b) saving in relearning as a function of delay (Ebbinghaus, 1885/1913). From Anderson, J. R., & Schooler, L. J. (1991). Reprinted by permission of the publisher. Copyright 1991 by *Psychological Science*, Blackwell Publishing.

form as environment functions such as figure 1.4a. And they do, as figure 1.4b shows in the classic retention function obtained by Ebbinghaus (1885/1913). Thus, a memory for something diminishes in proportion to how likely people are to need that memory. We showed that this was true not only for retention functions but also for practice functions, for the interaction between practice and retention, for spacing effects, for associative priming effects, and so on. Human memory turned out to mirror the statistical relationship in the environment in every case. As described in chapter 3, we discovered a relationship in human memory between retention and priming in the environment that had never been tested. Schooler did the experiment, and sure enough, it was true of human memory (Schooler and Anderson, 1997). Thus, the argument goes, one does not need a description of how memory works, which is what an architecture gives; rather, one just needs to focus on how memory solves the problems it encounters. Similar analyses have been applied to vision (Karklin and Lewicki, 2005), categorization (Anderson, 1991b; Tenenbaum, 1997; Sanborn et al., 2006), causal inference (Griffiths and Tenenbaum, 2005), language (Pickering and Crocker, 1996), decision making (Bogacz et al., 2006), and reasoning (Oaksford and Chater, 1994).

While I was an advocate of this approach, I started to realize (e.g., Anderson, 1991a) that it would never answer the question of how the human mind can occur in the physical universe. This is because the human mind is not just the sum of core competences such as memory, or categorization, or reasoning. It is about how all these pieces and other pieces work together to produce cognition. All the pieces might be adapted to the regularities in the world, but understanding their individual adaptations does not address how they are put together.

In many cases, the rational analyses (e.g., vision, memory, categorization, causal inference) have characterized features of the environment that all primates (and perhaps all mammals) experience.[13] Actually, many of these adaptive analyses were inspired by research on optimal foraging theory (Stephens and Krebs, 1986), which is explicitly pan-species in its approach. The universal nature of these features raises the question of what enables the human mind in particular.[14] Humans share much with other creatures (primates in particular), so these analyses have much to contribute to understanding humans, but something is missing if we stop with them. There is a great cognitive gulf between humans and other species, and we need to understand the nature of that gulf. What distinguishes humans is their ability to bring the pieces together, and this unique ability is just what adaptive analyses do not address, and just what a cognitive architecture is about. As Newell said, you have to know how the gears clank, and how the pistons go, and all the rest of that detail.

ACT-R: A Cognitive Architecture

It was basically a rhetorical ploy to have postponed giving an instance of a cognitive architecture until now. Many instances of cognitive architecture exist, including connectionist architectures.[15] Newell was very committed to an architecture called Soar, which has continued to evolve and grow since his death (Newell, 1990; for current developments in Soar, see sitemaker.umich.edu/soar).

13. Schooler has done unpublished analyses of primate environments.
14. While there have been some interesting analyses of how the statistics of the language affect language learning and language use (e. g., Newport and Aslin, 2004), exposing a nonhuman primate to these statistics does not result in language processing capability.
15. You can see this by searching Google for "connectionist architecture."

A different book could have included a comparison of different cognitive architectures, but such comparisons are already abundant in the literature (e.g., Pew and Mavor, 1998; Ritter et al., 2003; Taatgen and Anderson, in press). The goal of this book is not to split hairs about the differences among architectures, but to use one to try to convey what we have learned about the human mind. For this purpose, I will use the ACT-R architecture (Anderson, Bothell et al., 2004) because I know it best. However, this book is not about ACT-R; rather, I am using ACT-R as a tool to describe the mind. Just as the architect's drawings are tools to connect structure and function, the ACT-R models in this book are used as tools to connect brain and mind. We may be proud of our ACT-R models and think they are better than others in the same way that architects are proud of their specifications, but we try not to loose track of the fact that they are just a way of describing what is really of interest.

ACT-R has a history (discussed in appendix 1.1) going back 30 years to the HAM theory and early ACT theories. ACT-R emerged in 1993 (Anderson, 1993) when I realized the inadequacy of rational analysis, but the R stands for "rational" to reflect the influence of rational analysis. Today ACT-R is the product of a community of researchers who use it to theorize about cognitive processes. There is an ACT-R website (act-r.psy.cmu.edu) that you can visit to read about example models or to consult the user manual and tutorial for the simulation system, which specify the details of the architecture. (A computer simulation of the architecture has been developed that allows us to work out precisely what ACT-R models predict about human cognition.) Having this documentation on the Web allows this book to focus on core ideas about human cognition. The goals of the remainder of this chapter are to briefly describe ACT-R as an illustration of a cognitive architecture, to show how an architecture can be connected to the results of brain imaging, and to use ACT-R as a context for discussing contentious issues regarding the status of symbols in cognitive science.

ACT-R's Modular Organization

Figure 1.5 illustrates the ACT-R architecture as it appeared in Anderson (2005a). In this architecture, cognition emerges through the interaction of a number of independent modules. Anderson (2005a) was concerned with how the ACT-R system applies to the learning of a small fragment

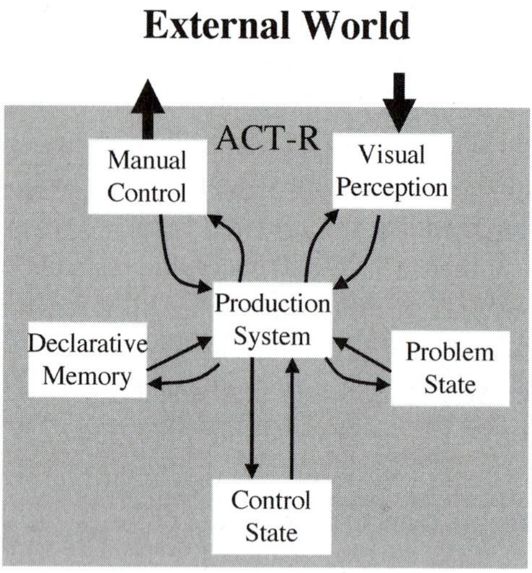

External World

Figure 1.5. The interconnections among modules in ACT-R 5.0. From Anderson (2005a). Reprinted by permission of the publisher. Copyright 2005 by Cognitive Science Society, Inc.

of algebra. The five modules in figure 1.5 were those used in the model I developed of algebra learning:[16]

1. A visual module that might hold the representation of an equation such as "$3x - 5 = 7$"
2. A problem state module (sometimes called an imaginal module) that holds a current mental representation of the problem; for example, the student might have converted the original equation into a mental image of "$3x = 12$"
3. A control module (sometimes called a goal module) that keeps track of one's current intentions in solving the problem; for example, one might be trying to perform an algebraic transformation
4. A declarative module that retrieves critical information from declarative memory, such as that $7 + 5 = 12$
5. A manual module that programs the output, such as "$x = 4$"

Each of these modules is associated with specific brain regions; ACT-R contains elaborate theories about the internal processes of these modules.

16. Chapter 2 discusses all eight modules that are currently part of ACT-R.

Later chapters explore the specifics of some of these modules, which must communicate among each other, and they do so by placing information in small-capacity buffers associated with them. A central procedural system (a sixth module) can recognize patterns of information in the buffers and respond by sending requests to the modules. These recognize–act tendencies of the central procedural module are characterized by production rules. For example, the following is a description of a possible production rule in the context of solving algebraic equations such as $3x - 5 = 7$:

> If the goal is to solve an equation,
>> And the equation is of the form "expression – number1
>> = number2,"
> Then write "expression = number2 + number1,"[17]

where the first line refers to the goal buffer, the second line to the visual buffer, and the third line to a manual action.

Anderson (2005a) describes a detailed model of learning to solve simple linear equations (e.g., $3x - 5 = 7$) that was used to understand the data from an experiment (Qin et al., 2004) involving children 11–14 years of age. They were proficient in the middle-school prerequisites for algebra, but they had never before solved equations. During the experiment, they practiced solving such equations for one hour per day for six days. The first day (day 0) they were given private tutoring on solving equations; on the remaining five days, they practiced solving three classes of equations on a computer:

0-step: e.g., $1x + 0 = 4$
1-step: e.g., $3x + 0 = 12$, $1x + 8 = 12$
2-step: e.g., $7x + 1 = 29$

Figure 1.6 shows how the time required by the children to process these equations decreased over the course of the experiment.

Figure 1.6 also illustrates the predictions of a model implemented in the ACT-R architecture. The model is not programmed to do the task; instead, it starts with declarative representations of the instructions that the children receive and has general production rules for following any set of instructions. It also has a virtue that can be achieved by a system built in a full cognitive architecture: It does the entire task, from the appearance of the equation on the screen to the pressing of the keystroke

---

17. This rule is hypothetical, used for illustration; consult Anderson (2005a) for more accurate details.

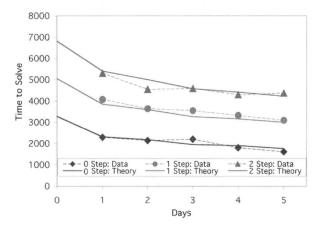

Figure 1.6. Mean solution times (and predictions of the ACT-R model) for three types of equations as a function of delay. Although the data were not collected, the predicted times are presented for the practice session of the experiment (day 0). From Anderson (2005a). Reprinted by permission of the publisher. Copyright 2005 by Cognitive Science Society, Inc.

(unlike past-tense models, which model a small fraction of the task and leave to the imagination how that fraction results in functional behavior). We sometimes call this a model of *end-to-end behavior*.

The model, like the children, took longer with more complex equations because it had to go through more cognitive steps. More interesting, it improved gradually in task performance at the same rate as children: the effect of six days of practice was to make a two-step equation like a one-step equation in terms of difficulty (as measured by solution time) and a one-step equation like a zero-step equation; Anderson (2005a) describes the detailed processing. The critical factors in learning to solve equations are considered in chapter 5. However, for current purposes, Figure 1.7 illustrates the detailed processing involved in solving the two-step equation $7x + 3 = 38$ on the first day (part a) and fifth day (part b) of the experiment. In the figure, the passage of time moves from top to bottom, and different columns represent the points in time at which different modules were active. This can be seen

Figure 1.7 (*facing page*). Comparison of the module activity in ACT-R during the solution of a two-step equation on day 1 (a) with a two-step equation on day 5 (b). In both cases the equation being solved is $7 * x + 3 = 38$. From Anderson (2005a). Reprinted by permission of the publisher. Copyright 2005 by Cognitive Science Society, Inc.

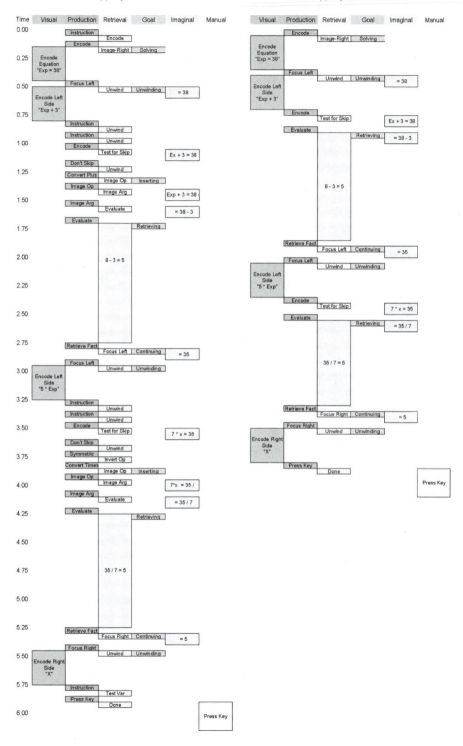

(a) Day 1   (b) Day 5

as just a great elaboration of the Sternberg stage model (figure 1.2b) in which stages include activities in multiple modules that can be active simultaneously. The primary reason the model requires less time on day 5 than on day 1 is a reduction in the amount of information the declarative module is called upon to retrieve. This becomes clear when one compares the amounts of activity in the retrieval columns in figure 1.7 on Day 1 versus Day 5. As elaborated in chapters 3 and 4, there is less retrieval activity on Day 5 both because of the increased speed of individual retrievals and because retrieval of instructions is replaced by production rules specific to algebra.

Brain Imaging Data and the Problem of Identifiability

The complexity of figure 1.7 compared with the simplicity of the behavioral data in figure 1.6 reflects a deep problem that has seriously hampered efforts to develop cognitive architectures. A very complicated set of information-processing steps is required to go from instruction on algebra and the presentation of an algebraic equation to the actual execution of an answer. No matter how one tries to do it, if the attempt is detailed and faithful to the task, the resulting picture is complicated, as in figure 1.7. However, although we know the process is complicated, it does not necessarily follow that those complicated steps are anything like those represented in figure 1.7 in terms of the modules involved or the sequences of operations. Working with standard behavioral data, the only way cognitive modelers had of determining whether their models were correct was to find whether the models matched data such as those in figure 1.6. But such data do not justify all of this detail.

In Anderson (1990), I showed that given any set and any amount of behavioral data, there would always be multiple different theories of the internal process that produce those data. I concluded, "It is just not possible to use behavioral data to develop a theory of the implementation level in the concrete and specific terms to which we have aspired" (p. 24). This was part of my motivation for developing the rational approach. In 1990, a diagram such as figure 1.7 would have been as much fantasy on my part about what was going on as it would have been fact. However, I did acknowledge that physiological data would get us out of this identifiability dilemma. I claimed that "the right kind of physiological data to obtain is that which traces out the states of computation of the brain," because this would provide us with "one-to-one tracing of the implementation level" (p. 25). I noted the progress that the pioneers of brain imaging had already made by 1990.

While the field is still not altogether there yet in 2007, it is much closer to having what is needed to base a diagram such as figure 1.7 on fact rather than fantasy. In my lab, we have been mainly working with fMRI (functional magnet resonance imaging) brain imaging data. Chapter 2 includes an up-to-date report of the connections we have made between modules of ACT-R and activity in specific brain regions. This chapter provides a preview of these ideas, illustrating that it is possible to map some of the detail in figure 1.7 onto precise predictions about brain regions.

The children whose behavioral data are reported in figure 1.6 were scanned on days 1 and 5 in an fMRI scanner. The details of the study and derivation of predictions from figure 1.7 are available in Anderson (2005a); figure 1.8 summarizes the predictions and results for five brain regions. These regions are not cherry-picked for this one study; rather they are the same regions examined in study after study because they are associated with specific modules in the ACT-R theory.

Predicting the BOLD Response in Different Brain Regions

Figure 1.8a illustrates the simplest case: the manual module. The representation of the hand along the motor strip is well known, and there is just a single use of this module on each trial to program the response. The x-axis presents time from the onset of the trial.[18] The data in figure 1.8 show the increase from baseline in the BOLD (blood oxygen level–dependent) response in this region. The top graphs show the BOLD response for different numbers of operations (averaging over days). The three BOLD functions are lagged about 2 s apart, just as the actual motor responses are in the three conditions. However, as typical of BOLD functions, they slowly rise and fall, reaching a peak 4–5 s after the key press. The bottom graphs compare the BOLD response on days 1 and 5 (averaging over the number of transformations). Basically, the response shifts a little forward in time from day 1 to day 5, reflecting the speed increase. The predictions are displayed as solid lines in the figure and provide a good match to the data. As detailed in chapter 2,

18. The first 1.2 s involved presentation of a warning signal before the equation was presented. The data in figure 1.6 are from the presentation of the equation.

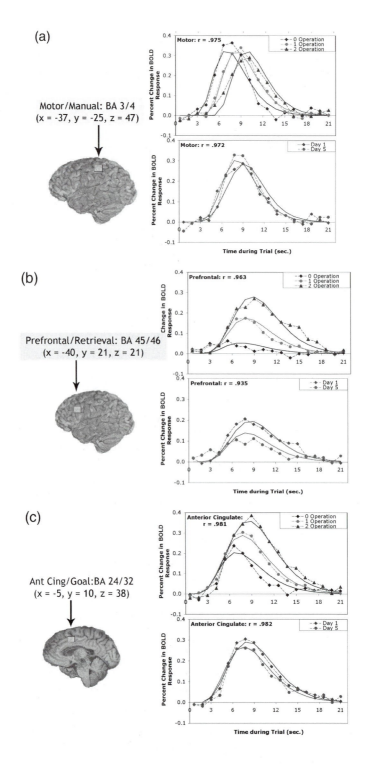

(a)

Motor/Manual: BA 3/4
(x = -37, y = -25, z = 47)

(b)

Prefrontal/Retrieval: BA 45/46
(x = -40, y = 21, z = 21)

(c)

Ant Cing/Goal:BA 24/32
(x = -5, y = 10, z = 38)

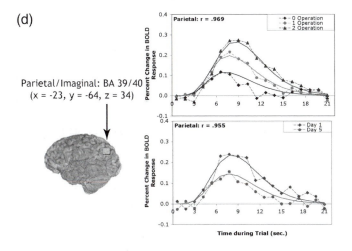

(d)

Parietal/Imaginal: BA 39/40
(x = -23, y = -64, z = 34)

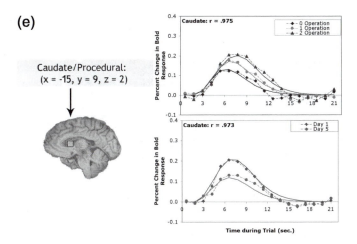

(e)

Caudate/Procedural:
(x = -15, y = 9, z = 2)

Figure 1.8. Use of module behavior to predict BOLD (blood oxygen level–dependent) response in various regions: (a) manual module predicts motor region; (b) declarative module predicts prefrontal region; (c) control/goal module predicts anterior cingulate region; (d) imaginal/problem state module predicts parietal region; (e) procedural module (production system) predicts caudate region. The top graphs show the effect of number of operations averaging over days, and the bottom graphs show the effect of days averaging over operations. The actual data are connected by dashed lines, and the predictions are the solid lines. From Anderson (2005a). Reprinted by permission of the publisher. Copyright 2005 by Cognitive Science Society, Inc.

these predictions are generated according to when the module is active. Whenever a module is active, it creates extra metabolic demand in its associated brain region, which drives a larger BOLD signal. In the case of the manual module, the activity and metabolic demand happen at the end of the charts in figure 1.7. Figure 1.8a illustrates the ability of this methodology to track one component in an overall task.

Unlike the manual module, which is just used at the end of the problem, the other modules are used sporadically through the solution of the problem (see figure 1.7). Because the BOLD response tends to smear together closely occurring events, it is not possible in this experiment to track the timing of a specific step in these other modules. Nonetheless, we can generate and test distinct predictions for these regions.

We have associated a prefrontal region (see figure 1.8b) with retrieval from the declarative module. In contrast to the motor region, in this prefrontal region there are very different magnitudes of response for different numbers of operations, as shown in the top graph. These differences are predicted because more transformations mean that more instructions and mathematical facts need to be retrieved to solve the equation. A distinguishing feature of this region is the very weak response it generates in the case of 0 steps. According to the model, this case involves some brief retrievals of instructions but no retrieval of numerical facts, which is why the response is so weak. As noted above, the major reason for the speed increase across days is that the number of retrievals decreases and the time per retrieval speeds up. Therefore, in the bottom graph in figure 1.8b the reduction is predicted in the BOLD response in going from day 1 to day 5.

We have associated a region of the anterior cingulate cortex (see figure 1.8c) with the control function of the goal module. As in the prefrontal region, there is a large effect of the number of operations, as shown in the top graph, because the model has to go through more control states when there are more transformations. In contrast to the prefrontal region, however, in the anterior cingulate cortex there is a robust response even in the zero-step case, because it is still necessary to go through the control states governing the encoding of the equation and the generation of the response. The striking feature of the anterior cingulate is that there is almost no effect of learning, as shown in the bottom graph. The effect of practice is largely to move the model more rapidly through the same control-state changes, and so there is little effect of number of days on number of control-state changes.

For the sake of brevity, I skip discussion of the other two regions (the parietal in figure 1.8d associated with the imaginal module, and the caudate in figure 1.8e associated with the procedural module), except to note that they display patterns similar to one another but different from that of any of the other regions. Details can again be found in Anderson (2005a), as well as evidence of just how good the statistical match is between prediction and data. Our ability to obtain and predict four different patterns of activation across the same conditions demonstrates that imaging has the power to go beyond the latency data displayed in figure 1.6.

The rest of the book is concerned in great detail with the properties of these specific regions and their associations with ACT-R modules. I discuss the similarities and differences between the ACT-R interpretation of these regions and other interpretations in the literature. Unless you are quite familiar with this research, the similarities among the theories will seem much greater than the differences. There is convergence in the literature on the interpretation of the functions of these various brain regions.

Summary

For the purposes of this chapter, consider how the ACT-R architecture avoids the pitfalls of the shortcuts reviewed above:

1. Unlike the classic information-processing approach, the architecture is directly concerned with data about the brain. Although brain imaging data have played a particularly important role in my laboratory, data about the brain have been more generally influential in the development of ACT-R.
2. Unlike eliminative connectionism, an architectural approach also focuses on how a fully functioning system can be achieved. Within the ACT-R community, the primary functional concern has been with the mathematical-technical competences that define modern society.[19] Chapter 5 elaborates extensively on what algebra problem solving reveals as unique in the human mind.
3. Unlike the rational approach and some connectionist approaches, ACT-R does not ignore issues about how the

---

19. However, the reader should not think this is all that has been worked on. The ACT-R website displays the full range of topics on which ACT-R models have been developed.

components of the architecture are integrated. Indeed, ACT-R
is more a theory about that integration than anything else.

Symbols Versus Connections in a Cognitive Architecture

The Debate

There is a great debate in cognitive science between architectures that are
called symbolic and those that are called connectionist, and ACT-R has
been reluctantly placed on one side of this debate. I would rather skip that
to get on with the story, but the debate is too notorious to just ignore.[20]
While it is not a commonly held characterization among members of the
ACT-R community, many members of the larger cognitive science community tend to regard ACT-R as an instance of a symbolic architecture.[21]
The connectionist past-tense models described above did not garner so
much attention simply because they accomplished what had not been
done before. They were magnets for attention in the cognitive science
community because of statements their creators made claiming that they
had done away with symbols. They claimed to have shown fundamental
inadequacies in "symbolic" architectures such as ACT-R. There has been
no lack of people willing to join the debate on the symbolic side (e.g.,
Fodor and Pylyshyn, 1988; Pinker and Prince, 1988; Marcus, 2001). It was
a particular virtue of Newell that he never engaged in this debate, even
though others had placed him on the symbolic side of the world (and he
certainly did believe in symbols).

Some fraction of the controversy is really a debate about the language
used to describe cognition, rather than about scientific claims. This debate
turns on the word "symbol"—a word that enjoyed a happy existence in
the English language until the advent of cognitive science. In the good
old days, symbols were physical objects (usually visual representations,
e.g., the cross as the symbol for Christianity) that were used to stand for
or designate something else. There were good symbols and bad symbols
(in many senses of the words "good" and "bad"), but nobody would have
thought to debate whether symbols per se were good or bad. Among these

---

20. Perhaps this is why I put this off to the last topic in the chapter.

21. I received the Rumelhart prize in 2005 as "the leading proponent of the symbolic
modeling framework." While I was very honored by the prize, I have to confess the characterization stuck in my craw.

symbols were those used by mathematicians and logicians. Among these mathematicians and logicians were people such as Church, Turing, Goedel, Post, and von Neumann, who noted that computation could be achieved by operations on such symbols—hence the idea of symbol manipulation emerged. With the appearance of real computers, individuals such as McCarthy who were heavily influenced by this logical background created symbol manipulation languages such as LISP that formed the backbone of early artificial intelligence. By this time, the "symbol" in cognitive science retained only a loose connection to its original meaning.

There is a lack of consensus about whether symbols in cognitive science maintain the referential feature of original symbols—that is, whether they stand for something. Newell and Simon (1976) explicitly state that symbols designate other things. Nonetheless, they extend the notion of symbols to pointers in data structures, which can have no reference to anything outside of the data structure itself. Pointers really derive their meaning from the structures and processes in which they participate; they do not have external reference. Nonetheless, the idea that symbols have reference continues in discussions. For instance, Vera and Simon (1993) assert that "we call patterns symbols when they can designate or denote" (p. 9). On the other hand, one finds people such as Searle (1980) and Lakoff (1988) talking about "meaningless symbol manipulation." Searle, focusing on their physical appearance, refers to them as "meaningless squiggles." Harnad (1990), in describing what he calls the symbol-grounding problem, asks, "How can the meanings of the meaningless symbol tokens, manipulated solely on the basis of their (arbitrary) shapes, be grounded in anything but other meaningless symbols?"

Given this lack of agreement on what symbols are, it should come as no surprise that there is no consensus about what role symbols play in an explanation of the mind and how they should be coordinated with our knowledge of brain processing. The various positions can be classified according to whether they give an explanatory role to symbols or connections. These positions are enumerated below with a "+" to indicate an explanatory role and a "–" a nonexplanatory role:

1. +Symbols, –Connections: The classic symbol manipulation position holds that the principles by which the mind operates involve transformations of the structural properties of symbolic representations. This is the position that symbols are like the symbols that appear in LISP (which are basically pointers and, as noted above, can be almost devoid of any sense of external reference). The claim is that, while the mind is not a LISP program, symbols play the same critical role in the explanation of mind as they do in a LISP program. There are two subtraditions—the linguistic tradition, represented by linguist Noam Chomsky and by philosopher Jerry Fodor, and the information-processing tradition, represented by Newell and Simon. The latter position has threads in common with the information-processing shortcut described above and tends to regard as unimportant the physical processes that realize these symbols.

2. *–Symbols, +Connections:*   This position is called eliminative connectionism because it seeks to eliminate symbols in the explanation of cognition. It views symbols much like elements in explicitly stated rules ("If the verb ends in d or t, add ed") and regards such assertions about the mind as, at best, good approximate descriptions of brain computations and, at worst, misleading. This position is called eliminative connectionism because it seeks to eliminate symbols in the explanation of cognition. This position sees no explanatory role for symbols, just as the classic position sees no explanatory role for the brain.

3. *+Symbols, +Connections:*   Implementational connectionism believes that connectionist computations are organized to achieve symbolic results and that both connectionist and symbolic characterizations play an important explanatory role (e.g., Shastri and Ajjanagadde, 1993; Smolensky, 1995). One way or another, this view assumes that connectionist computations implement symbolic computations. For instance, in Smolensky and Legendre's (2006) Integrated Connectionist/Symbolic (ICS) architecture, connectionist calculations can serve to enforce a hierarchy of symbolic constraints on grammatical selections. For Smolensky and Legendre, with their emphasis on linguistic applications, the symbols are basically the kinds of terms that appear in classic linguistic models such as "verb phrase" or "stressed."

4. *–Symbols, –Connections:*   Some researchers have rejected both symbols and connections as explanations. In their place, other explanatory devices are offered, or the possibility of explaining the human mind is simply rejected. Historically, functionalism and some varieties of behaviorism, such as that of behaviorist B. F. Skinner, have had this characteristic. More recently, some versions of adaptive explanations (see above discussion of rational analysis) have argued that the explanation resides completely in

the environment. Differing slightly in their emphasis, some versions of situated cognition (e.g., Lave, 1988; Lave and Wenger, 1991; Greeno et al., 1992) have also emphasized that the explanation resides in what is outside the human.[22]

In my opinion, debates among these positions have the character of jousting with windmills. Because there is not even agreement about what symbols mean, these debates are a waste of time.

The Symbolic–Subsymbolic Distinction

I cannot, however, simply reject all discussion of symbols and use the ACT-R architecture, because that architecture makes a distinction between what it calls "symbolic" and "subsymbolic" levels.[23] These terms bear only partial relationships to the terms of the debate about symbols versus connections. The symbolic level in ACT-R is an abstract characterization of how brain structures encode knowledge. The subsymbolic level is an abstract characterization of the role of neural computation in making that knowledge available. The following discussion of symbols from Newell (1990) captures the essence of the symbolic level as we use it in ACT-R and sets the context for also understanding ACT-R's subsymbolic level:

> Symbols provide distal access to knowledge-bearing structures that are located physically elsewhere within the system. The requirement for distal access is a constraint on computing systems that arises from action always being physically local, coupled with only a finite amount of knowledge being encodable within a finite volume of space, coupled with the human mind's containing vast amounts of knowledge. Hence encoded knowledge must be spread out in space, whence it must be continually transported from where it is stored to where processing requires it. Symbols are the means that accomplish the required distal access. (p. 427)

---

22. One might also include dynamical systems (e.g., Thelen and Smith, 1994; van Gelder, 1998) in this category, as Clark (1997) suggests. However, at least some practitioners of this approach (e.g., Smith and Samuelson, 2003) have argued that their battle with the greater common enemy (the classic symbol manipulation approach) means that the connectionist and dynamic systems approach are really complementary.

23. An apology is in order for having introduced these terms into the theory, I suppose. It happened as Christian Lebiere and I attempted to describe an important distinction in a way that we thought would be meaningful to the cognitive science community. We were not thinking deeply about what the words meant to us or what they really meant (or did not mean) in the cognitive science community.

Newell identifies the critical role of symbols as knowledge access; there is neither a mention in this quote of the popular image of symbol manipulation with its juggling of symbols, nor is there any commitment to whether symbols refer. He notes that most computation is local (true of the brain with its hypercolumns and the like), but information must be brought from other locations to influence the local processing (again, true of the brain with its fiber tracks). Symbols for Newell provide this distal access. This is also exactly what they do in ACT-R; one might identify them with fiber tracks in the brain.

If symbols provide distal access so that information can be brought from one location to another, there is then the question of just what information will be brought and how quickly that information will appear. This is what the subsymbolic level is about. Symbolic structures have subsymbolic quantities associated with them that control how fast the structures are processed and which structural units get processed at which choice points.[24] This symbolic–subsymbolic relationship reflects a very general theoretical approach in science of postulating objects with real-value quantities—habits with strengths in Hull's theory (e.g., Hull, 1952), units with activations and link strengths in connectionism, or electrons with energy levels.

The symbolic–subsymbolic distinction has been developed extensively for two modules in ACT-R, the declarative and procedural modules.

The Symbolic–Subsymbolic Distinction
in the Declarative Module

With respect to the declarative module at the symbolic level, ACT-R has networks of knowledge encoded in what we call *chunks*. Figure 1.9 illustrates a declarative chunk encoding a fact from the Berry and Broadbent (1984) sugar factory task. This structure connects the elements of an event in that task: a factory had produced 10,000 tons of sugar in the previous month, 800 workers were assigned to the factory in the current month, and 7,000 tons of sugar was produced in the current month. Figure 1.9 illustrates the connections that provide Newell's distal access. Thus, a query such as, "If the past production was 10,000 tons and I use

---

24. However, be aware that this ACT-R use of "subsymbolic" to designate the quantities under the symbols is not the same as the more standard use of "subsymbolic" to refer to the connectionist elements, which are at a finer grain size than symbolic units. The "sub" in the more common usage can be read as "pieces of symbols," whereas in our usage it is the quantities "under the symbols."

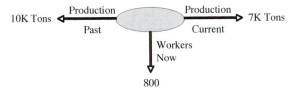

Figure 1.9. Representation of a declarative chunk
encoding a fact from the Berry and Broadbent (1984)
sugar factory task.

800 workers, how many tons will I get now?" can make contact with the
answer of 7,000 tons.

What if multiple chunks were stored with different current output
associated with 10,000 tons in the past and 800 workers? What if there
was no chunk with the answer for this exact query? One needs to specify
the neural processes by which an appropriate chunk is selected as an answer. Chunks have *activations* at the subsymbolic level. The most active
chunk will be the one retrieved, and its activation value will determine
how it is retrieved. The activation values of chunks are determined by
computations that attempt to abstract the impact of neural Hebbian-like
learning and spread of activation among neurons.[25] Chapter 3 will elaborate on these subsymbolic activations and review some of the successes
of this mechanism in capturing many aspects of human cognition, including performance in the Berry and Broadbent sugar factory task.

The Symbolic–Subsymbolic Distinction
in the Procedural Module

As noted above, the procedural module consists of production rules.[26]
Figure 1.10 illustrates a production rule that might apply in solving the
equation $3 + x = 8$. Figure 1.10a is an instantiation of the rule for this

25. Hebbian learning is a neural learning by contiguity first described by Hebb (1949)
and which is related to many current connectionist learning algorithms.

26. While there is a widely felt discontent with "symbols" and their connotations,
there is an evenly more widely felt discontent with "rules" and their connotations. I have
encountered it not only from connectionists, but also from many mathematics educators. I have been advised that ACT-R would have greater appeal if I just did not use the
phrase "production rule" but instead something like "action selection." Perhaps such a
name switch would more accurately reflect what the rules (or the mappings) do, but
I fear such a name switch now would engender new confusions even greater than the
ones it might eliminate.

specific equation. The rule responds to a pattern that appears in a set of modules—in this case, to the encoding of the equation in the visual module and the setting of the control state to solve that equation in the goal module. An action is selected that requests the retrieval from declarative memory of the difference between 8 and 3 and sets the control state to note a subtraction is occurring. As I discuss throughout the book, it is generally thought that the basal ganglia play a critical role in achieving this pattern recognition, action selection, and action execution.

Figure 1.10b illustrates the general rule that is behind the instance in figure 1.10a. The rule is not specific to the numbers 3 and 8. Whatever number appears in the arg1 slot of the visual buffer is copied to the arg2 slot on the declarative retrieval request. Similarly, whatever number appears in the value slot of the visual buffer is copied to the arg1 slot of the retrieval request. Thus, this production is a pattern that specifies how information is to be moved from one location to a distal location. This is symbolic exactly in the distal access sense Newell used in the quote above.

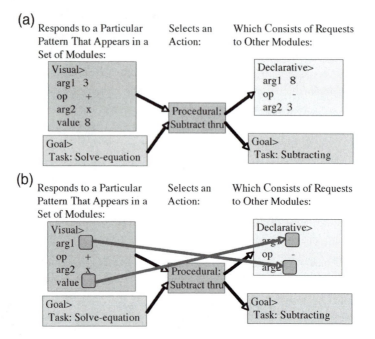

Figure 1.10. Illustration of a production rule in ACT-R: (a) the buffer contents might operate upon in a specific case; (b) the general pattern encoded in the rule that would apply to this case.

There are situations (developed in chapter 4) where multiple production rules might apply. In such situations the decisions about which rule to apply are determined at the subsymbolic level, where production rules have *utilities* and the production with the highest utility is chosen. The utilities of productions are determined by computations that are designed to abstract the essential aspects of the neural reinforcement learning that determines action selection.

Final Reflections on the Symbolic–Subsymbolic Distinction

While the structures in figures 1.9 and 1.10 are symbolic in the Newell sense, it is hard to see how anything in them is symbolic in the sense of "meaningless squiggles" or "ungrounded meaningless symbols" or in the sense of "denoting something." Nothing in the production rule in figure 1.10 is fundamentally different from the pattern-matching capabilities of standard connectionist networks, and indeed, we created a connectionist implementation of an early version of ACT-R (Lebiere and Anderson, 1993). The links in figures 1.9 and 1.10 simply represent the kinds of connections seen in any neural model, albeit at a higher level of abstraction.

It is true that when one looks at the actual code that specifies a model for purposes of simulating it, one will see things that look like the cognitive science stereotype of a symbol as a piece of text. However, this is true of computer simulations of any theory. Compare the specification of a set of chunks for the ACT-R simulation program in table 1.1 with the specification of a connectionist network. There is the tendency to confuse the notation of either specification with "symbols." They are perhaps symbols for the simulation program, but they are not the symbols of the ACT-R architecture or the connectionist network.[27] The ACT-R specification uses the word "workers" and the connectionist specification uses the word "digits," but in both cases these are just mnemonic labels to help the person read the code. Neither model's behavior would change if some random sequence of letters were substituted instead. Much of the debate about symbols reflects confusion between notation and theory. Of course, the graphic representations in figures 1.9 and 1.10 are just notations, too.

---

27. Actually, they are largely not manipulated by the simulation program either, but are notations about how to compile the simulation into code that "just does it."

Table 1.1.   Comparison of Specification for ACT-R Chunks and a
             Connectionist Network

Specifying ACT-R Chunks	Specifying a Connectionist Network
(add-dm	set hiddenSize 20
(Fact1	addNet digits.$hiddenSize
isa addition-fact	addGroup input 20 INPUT
past 10K	addGroup hidden $hiddenSize
workers 800	addGroup "hidden 2" $hiddenSize OUT_NOISE
present 7K)	COSINE_COST
(Fact2	addGroup output 3 OUTPUT
isa addition-fact	connectGroups input hidden -p RANDOM -s 0.5
past 9K	connectGroups hidden {"hidden 2"} output
workers 900	loadExamples digits.ex -s "clean set"
present 9K)	loadExamples digits2.ex -s "noisy set"
(Fact3	setObj learningRate 0.1
isa addition-fact	setObj input.numColumns 4
past 8K	viewUnits
workers 1000	autoPlot
present 11K))	graphObject

However, in this book I tend to use such graphic notations because they tend to better convey the theoretical claims.

The reader may still feel there is some significant difference between the ACT-R specification and the connectionist specification in table 1.1. There is, and it is a difference in the level of abstraction at which the theory is specified. In science, choosing the best level of abstraction for developing a theory is a strategic decision. In the case of connectionist elements or symbolic structures in ACT-R, the question is which level will provide the best bridge between brain and mind and thus answer Newell's question. In both cases, the units are a significant abstraction from neurons and real brain processes, but the gap is probably smaller from the connectionist units to the brain. Similarly, in both cases the units are a significant distance from functions of the mind, but probably the gap is smaller in the case of ACT-R units. In both cases, the units are being proposed to provide a useful island to support a bridge from brain to mind. The same level of description might not be best for all applications. Connectionist models have enjoyed their greatest success in describing perceptual processing, while ACT-R models have enjoyed their greatest success in describing higher level processes such as equation solving.

To return to the title of this chapter and the book, the function of a cognitive architecture is to find a specification of the structure of the brain at a level of abstraction that explains how it achieves the function of the mind. I believe ACT-R has found the best level of abstraction for understanding those aspects of the human mind that separate it from the minds of other species. In the rest of the book, I try to use this architecture to develop key insights about the human mind. Chapter 5, in particular, addresses the question of how the human mind is unique.

Appendix 1.1: A Short History of ACT-R

Figure 1.11 provides the history of the ideas that are part of the current ACT-R. The origins of ACT-R can be traced back to two books published in 1973. The first was *Human Associative Memory*, which I wrote with Gordon Bower, describing the HAM theory of memory. HAM was one of several then-new efforts to create a rigorous theory of complex human cognition by specifying the theory with sufficient precision that it could be simulated on a computer. Another aspect of this effort that has carried

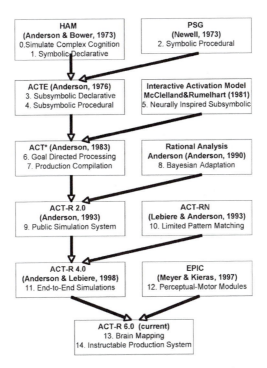

Figure 1.11. An illustration of the source of the ideas and practices in current ACT-R.

over to modern ACT-R is the idea of a symbolic representation for declarative memory. The proposal in HAM was for a specific propositional representation that was similar to the proposals of Norman and Rumelhart (1975) and Kintsch (1974). Propositional representations did not generalize well in many applications, so over time the declarative representation has devolved into a more general relational representation.

The second 1973 book was the Carnegie Symposium volume edited in 1973 by Bill Chase that contained two landmark papers by Newell. The first was his famous "You can't play 20 questions with nature and win" essay, in which he lamented the tendency of cognitive psychology to divide the world into little paradigms, each with its own set of questions and logic. In his second paper, Newell (1973a) introduced his answer to this dilemma by describing his first production system theory of human cognition. This single system performed the diverse set of tasks that occupied cognitive psychology. The idea of a production system provided the missing ingredient to convert the inert declarative representation of HAM into a functional theory of human cognition.

I combined HAM's declarative system and Newell's procedural system into the first version of the ACT theory (Anderson, 1976), which went beyond either earlier proposal in assuming that there were subsymbolic quantities that controlled access to the declarative and procedural elements. For declarative memory, activation-based quantities were used, inspired by the spreading activation model of Collins and Quillian (1972). For the procedural system, a strength quantity was used, based on ideas in psychology that have their origins in behaviorist theories. Both of these concepts evolved as I considered neural realizations of these quantities and their role in enabling adaptation to the environment.

In 1983 I published a book describing the ACT* system. In it, the subsymbolic computations were changed to be more consistent with the emerging ideas of connectionism. The source I most often referenced was the McClelland and Rumelhart (1981) interactive activation model. There were two other things that ACT* contained that are part of the modern ACT-R theory. One was goal-directed processing—a top-down control to cognition currently served by ACT-R's goal module. The other was a set of ideas for production learning, among which were proceduralization and composition that form the basis for the modern production compilation mechanism (see chapter 4).

I had called the 1983 theory ACT* (pronounced "act star") in a very loose analogy to the Kleene star to reflect my belief that it was "the final major reformulation within the ACT framework" (Anderson, 1983, p. 18). I said, "My plan for future research is to try to apply this theory wide and far, to eventually gather enough evidence to permanently break the theory and develop a better one" (p. 19). As it turned out, I spent much of the period from 1983 to 1993 engaged in two activities. One of these was the development of a version of intelligent tutoring systems called cognitive tutors (for a review of those years, see Anderson, Corbett et al., 1995). This work, while initially motivated to test the ACT* theory and successful in many ways, actually ended up having little direct influence on the theory. The main outcome for ACT-R of that effort was a better technical understanding of how to build production systems. The other activity was the already-mentioned work on rational analysis of cognition (Anderson, 1990). While it was started with the intention of abandoning the architectural approach to human cognition, it actually wound up establishing an additional theoretical foundation for the subsymbolic level in ACT-R.

ACT-R came into being in 1993 with the publication of a new book that was an effort to summarize the theoretical progress made on skill acquisition in the intervening 10 years (e.g., Singley and Anderson, 1989) and tune the subsymbolic level of ACT-R with the insights of the rational analysis of cognition. The "R" in ACT-R was to denote the influence of rational analysis. Accompanying that book was a computer disk containing the first comprehensive implementation of the theory. The fact that we could produce this implementation reflected both our growing understanding (derived from all the production system implementations we had produced) and the fact that LISP, the implementation language of these theories, had become standardized.

The appearance of generally available, fully functioning code set off a series of events that was hardly planned. The catalyst for these events was the emergence of a user community. Starting in 1994 on the suggestion of Werner Tack and the insistence of Christian Lebiere, we began holding summer schools and workshops. The creation of that user community resulted in a whole new dynamic to the theory. One dimension of change was to the language of the theory. It became a language spoken among all members of the community, rather than a language spoken by authors of the theory to readers of the theory. Sharing the language among so many forced a greater standardization and consistency which in turn made it possible for a wide range of researchers to contribute to development of the theory.

The last book in the ACT series, until this one, was published in 1998 (Anderson and Lebiere). The 1998 book described ACT-R 4.0, which was a much more mature system than the 1993 ACT-R 2.0. Past books in the series had been planned as writing exercises concurrent with the development of the theory and intended to stimulate and discipline that development, whereas ACT-R 4.0 was already basically in place when the 1998 book was being written. It was written to display a number of running models built by different researchers, all working in this architecture. By this time there were two notable changes in the architecture. First, reflecting the effort of Lebiere and Anderson (1993) to create a connectionist simulation of ACT-R, we became aware of the need for a pattern matcher that was both more flexible and also more limited in its assumptions about the power of the processes that went into matching a single production. The resulting pattern matcher implemented in ACT-R 4.0 represented a serious claim about what could be recognized in 50 ms of cognition, which in turn meant that we could take our production rules more seriously. Second, we began producing what I have come to call "end-to-end" simulations that interact with the same (typically computer-based) environment that human participants do, and that actually do the task. This prevented us from making hidden assumptions about linkage to the external world that can protect a theory from disconfirmation.

To enable such end-to-end simulations, we had already begun to create perceptual and motor interfaces. As one of these efforts, Mike Byrne had implemented many of the perceptual and motor modules from Meyer and Kieras's (1997) EPIC system (see chapter 2 for a discussion of EPIC) into a system called ACT-R/PM—the "PM" standing for perceptual-motor. It grounded ACT-R in serious models of human perception and action, enabling the creation of "embodied" ACT-R models. It became apparent that understanding the perceptual-motor aspects of even abstract tasks such as algebra was essential. We decided that these perceptual-motor aspects should be fully integrated into the theory rather than mere add-ons. EPIC's modular organization also strongly influenced our movement to a modular structure.

Another development pushing ACT-R to a modular organization was our entry into fMRI brain imaging research. Slowly, the mapping between brain regions and modules emerged that is shown in this chapter and throughout the book. This work has influenced many aspects of ACT-R. For instance, as described in Anderson (2005a), it led to the separation of the imaginal and goal modules, which had previously been combined in a single goal module.

Another important event since 1998 was the development of a successful theory of production compilation (described in detail in chapter 4) with Niels Taatgen, which brought ideas from the 1983 ACT* into the modern ACT-R world. With the theory of production compilation, ACT-R now has a theory of procedural learning to match the successful theory of declarative learning. We also began developing a theory of how such productions could be learned from instruction. Learning from instruction plays a significant role in the model in figure 1.7 and is expanded upon in chapter 5. An important feature of this is that ACT-R now has a mechanistic explanation of how subjects go from the instruction for a task to performance of the task. (Previously, we just programmed in task-specific productions.) One of the last remnants of magic had been eliminated from the theory.

This history brings us pretty much up-to-date. The current simulation version of ACT-R is 6.0, written and maintained by Dan Bothell. In part, its creation was motivated by the desire to better represent the modular structure in the software and to facilitate the development of new modules. That is the history. I speculate on the future of ACT-R in appendix 6.1.

2

The Modular Organization of the Mind

The human mind is what emerges from the actions of a number of largely independent cognitive modules integrated by a central control system. Figure 1.5 showed the organization of some of these information-processing modules. The basic purpose of this chapter is to elaborate on this modular organization and the reasons for it. The first section gives a brief overview of the functional needs of the human mind and physical constraints of the human brain that force a modular solution. The second section describes the modular structure in ACT-R and how that relates to issues about modularity more generally in cognitive science. The final three sections illustrate this modular organization in three empirical studies: a study of driving behavior, a study of perfect time sharing, and an fMRI study.

Function and Structure

Humans and other creatures live in a complex world where multiple simultaneous demands are placed on them. They have multiple resources to meet these demands, but there are also severe limitations on how these resources can be deployed. Roughly, these demands and resources can be divided into perceptual, motor, and central:

1. *Perceptual:* We need to be capable of detecting important information coming in via multiple sensory media. For instance, when driving we need to be able to process a car changing into our lane and to respond to a horn warning us of danger.

2. *Motor:* We need to be able to take appropriate actions, and we often have to perform multiple actions simultaneously, such as using our feet to locomote while we use our hands to manipulate.

3. *Central:* Our actions and our thoughts must be coordinated to achieve our needs. Many activities are more than just a sum of their parts—preparing a successful meal, delivering a successful lecture, and so on. Success depends on not only what actions are taken, but also on the order in which they are performed.

With respect to perceptual and motor abilities, we are not much different than other primates, but we are quite different when it comes to central control. Our ability to organize novel combinations of behavior has given our species its unique ability to acquire high proficiency at a wide range of skills for which we were not specifically prepared by evolution. Examples of such skills include driving a car in modern society, ocean navigating in traditional Polynesian society, doing mathematics in our scientific practice, and serving tea in the Japanese ritual. Each of these competencies requires that we exercise an internal control over our behavior. The ability for such inner control is much more advanced in our species, a point considered at length in chapter 5.

Driving a car is probably an example that most readers of this book can relate to. Indeed, driving a car while holding a conversation is probably the paradigm case of multitasking in the modern world. Consider the demands being placed on a driver:

Perceptual: The visual system is being presented with a complex array of rapidly changing information that needs to be monitored for important events while still processing the visual cues that guide basic driving. The auditory system has to process the speech and also respond to critical sounds (e.g., a horn honking) from the outside.

Motor: The hands are occupied with steering and shifting; the feet with using the accelerator, break, and clutch; the vocal system with speech.

Central: Driving requires integrating low-level steering adjustments with high-level decisions such as how fast to progress and when to change lanes. In addition, the driver has to worry about avoiding traffic tickets and getting off the highway at the right exit. If the driver is engaged in a conversation, this task also has to be coordinated with the rest.[1]

Ignoring the demands of speech, the basic perceptual and motor demands of driving are something other primates are capable of. However, while chimpanzees might drive vehicles as part of a circus act, we would never let them on the road, because they are incapable of the central control that real driving requires.

Structural Constraints of the Brain

These functional demands would not be nearly as interesting if there were no limitations on the brain's ability to achieve them. What is really interesting is not the mere fact of limitations, but the nature of these limitations. The standard contrasts between brain and computer are instructive here: the computer is fast and serial, and the brain is slow and parallel.[2] Feldman and Ballard (1982) proposed a "100-step" constraint on action—many things that we do (e.g., decisions made while driving) take place in far less than a second, during which our neural system can progress through no more than 100 states. In that same time, modern computers can execute trillions of instructions. On the other hand, we have tens of billions of neurons performing these computations.

There are two basic forms of limitation on parallelism. One is a matter of number: while we have perhaps 100 billion neurons, we do not have 100 trillion. Each neuron comes with a cost in space and metabolic support, and evolution has found fit to pack only so many into the human brain. Thus, some computations are just not feasible, and it does not take long to discover these limitations as a driver of a car. The second limitation is one of communication: only so many neurons can be packed into any small space, and the farther apart these neurons are, the longer it takes them to communicate and the more structure has to be used to string the "wires" between the locations. Cherniak (1990) argues that

1. Modern cars with their radios, cell phones, temperature controls, GPS systems, and other devices give us many other things to engage our perceptual, motor, and central systems.

2. This contrast can be overstated. Modern computers do many things in parallel and strive to achieve capacity increases by parallelism. Similarly, the brain is not above trying to achieve speed to increase processing power, as witnessed by the major investment it makes in myelination to increase the speed of critical information transfer.

simple calculations of space imply that most connections must be local. Therefore, the brain has opted for the sensible design of placing neurons performing related computations close together.

The visual system nicely illustrates the power and limitations of neural information processing. A large portion of the primate brain is given over to processing the visual array; more than 30 such separate regions have been identified (Van Essen and DeYoe, 1995). At any point in time, the input is being processed in the brain from our entire visual field. However, there is also a strategic allocation of resources by our visual system. Our eyes have foveae; the information coming in from each fovea gets a disproportionate investment throughout the nervous system. We do not give the same investment to achieving high acuity throughout the visual field because it would be just too expensive—our brains would have to be an order of magnitude larger if they devoted as equal processing to all sections of the visual field. Every time we move our foveae to a new location, we are choosing to dedicate our most powerful processing resources to what we deem most important. The eyes of drivers are normally a dead giveaway as to what they are concerned with at any instant. For many purposes, it almost seems that the only thing we are aware of is what is close to our foveae. However, we only have to have an object fly at us from our periphery (we will duck) to be assured that some parts of our nervous system are still processing the rest of the visual field.

The visual system also illustrates the push to have related information processing close together. While visual information processing is occurring in many areas of the brain, each of the 30 or more visual areas is specialized to process a different sort of information about the visual signal. Some regions do basic extraction of visual information, some are involved in object recognition (the ventral stream), and others are involved in extracting action affordances (the dorsal stream). Also, many of the early visual areas are topographically organized; cells that process similar areas of the visual field are placed close together.

The need for local, parallel computing in the brain is the fundamental structural fact driving the modular organization of the human mind. Essentially, parts of the brain are given over to performing related computations so that it is easier for the necessary neurons to interact. The extreme of localization is the cortical minicolumn—the parcellation of the brain into small units of about 100 neurons that have a very restricted mission. For instance, cortical columns in the primary visual cortex are specialized to process information about one orientation, from one location, in one eye.

The need to do as much computing locally as possible is not enough by itself to require a modular organization. One could imagine a brain organization where function gradually shifted over the brain without any discrete clumping into modules. In part, this is the organization of the brain. It manifests at a smaller scale in the topological organization of columns within areas such as primary visual cortex—nearby columns process nearby regions of the visual field. At a larger scale, different cortical areas that do similar processing are often adjacent, such as primary visual cortex and secondary visual cortex. However, there is also a clear clumping of areas in the cortex such that there are discrete changes in cytoarchitectural features defining distinct regions that seem to correspond to distinct functions. These regional differences are reinforced by the fact that different fiber tracts project to these regions. Maybe the emergence of modules in the mind is just a consequence of accidental variations in cortical anatomy. However, at the end of this section I note Herb Simon's argument that such hierarchical organizations, including those in the brain, are not accidents, but rather are requirements for functioning systems.

This claim that neural computation is localized goes against a longstanding tradition to regard information about a particular function as spread out over the entire brain. Lesion data going back to Lashley (1950) have been cited in favor of this conclusion—in one of his studies he found that he could remove any part of a rat's cortex and it could still run a maze that it had learned. Lashley concluded that "the memory trace is located in all parts of the functional area; that various parts are equipotential for its maintenance and activation" (p. 469). Brain imaging data have also been cited in favor of this equipotential viewpoint—in performing any task, numerous disparate regions of the brain show activity. However, interpreting such results as evidence for equipotentiality fails to appreciate the fact that different regions can perform different functions, all required for successful execution of the task. For instance, in the model for the algebra task (figure 1.7), there were visual, procedural, declarative, goal, imaginal, and manual modules simultaneously active in different brain regions. Also, the modern interpretation of Lashley's results is that the rat had multiple representations of the maze (e.g., spatial and motor[3]) and that damage to any area of the cortex affected only one representation.

An excellent example of the complexity of brain representation concerns the phenomenon of blindsight (Weiskrantz, 1986). Damage to the primary visual cortex leaves patients in a state where they cannot identify an object that is presented to them and they claim not to know it is there. However, they can still point to the object when asked. Thus, damage to a specific area results in a specific deficit, but similar information processing is occurring elsewhere and can serve for certain tasks.

Coordination: The Basal Ganglia

While different regions of the brain do their own processing, they have to coordinate at least occasionally to achieve a functional system. Consider working out a solution to an algebra problem. At the mechanical level, the eyes must move appropriately to guide the hand. Memory must be interrogated for arithmetic facts relevant to the numbers that are seen in the problem. If one tries a particular type of solution rather than another (e.g., factoring rather than the quadratic formula), control must be exercised to keep the actions moving toward that solution rather than the other. To achieve this coordination, tracks of brain fibers connect multiple cortical regions. Particularly important are paths of communication that connect cortical regions via subcortical regions. The connections through the basal ganglia have attracted a lot of attention from various researchers (see figure 2.1).

The basal ganglia are a connected set of subcortical structures. Most of the cortex sends projections to the caudate and putamen, which are collectively referred to as the striatum. Various researchers (e.g., Amos, 2000; Frank et al. 2001; Houk and Wise, 1995; Wise et al., 1996) have proposed that the striatum performs a pattern-recognition function—essentially recognizing patterns of activation distributed over the cortex. This portion of the basal ganglia projects to a number of small regions known collectively as the pallidum.[4] The projections to the pallidum are substantially inhibitory, and these regions in turn inhibit cells in the thalamus, which project to

3. See discussion of place and response learning in chapter 4.
4. See areas labeled GPe and GPi in figure 2.1. Loosely, one can also include areas labeled SNr and STN in figure 2.1. STN participates in a more complex loop than the one described here. Note the great reduction in the number of cells in going from the striatum to the pallidum (numbers in figure 2.1).

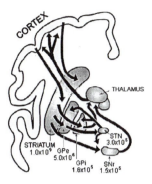

Figure 2.1. Schematic diagram of the major structures of the basal ganglia and their interconnections. Abbreviations: GP, globus pallidus; GPi, internal segment of globus pallidus; GPe, external segment of globus pallidus; EP, entopeduncular nucleus; STN, subthalamic nucleus; SNr substantia nigra, pars reticulata. Numbers indicate the total number of neurons within each structure. From Wickens, J. Basal ganglia: Structure and computations. *Network: Computation in Neural Systems, 8*, R77–R109. Reprinted by permission of the publisher. Copyright 1997 by Taylor & Francis Ltd., www.tandf.co.uk/journals.

select actions in the frontal cortex. Graybiel and Kimura (1995) have suggested that this arrangement creates a "winner-lose-all" system such that active striatal projections strongly inhibit only the pallidum neurons representing the selected action, which then no longer inhibit the thalamus from producing the action. This is a mechanism by which the winning procedure (in ACT-R, a production) is determined. According to Middleton and Strick (2000), at least five nonmotor regions of the frontal cortex receive projections from the thalamus and are controlled by this basal ganglia loop.[5] These regions play a major role in controlling behavior.

There are three key features in this characterization of the basal ganglia loop:

1. It allows information from disparate regions of the brain to converge in making a decision.
2. It requires a great compression of information from what is happening in these individual regions because the number of receiving neurons is so much smaller.

5. These regions in turn have projections to posterior cortex and can influence processing there. There is also evidence of projections directly from the basal ganglia to the temporal lobe (Middleton and Strick, 1996).

3. Processing that involves this multisynaptic loop is necessarily much slower than processing that can occur in a single brain region.

The existence of structures, such as the basal ganglia, that have these properties is almost a necessity given the need for coordination of information and the limitations on the human nervous system. While the basal ganglia have been targeted as a promising site to be performing this coordination function, there is no reason to suppose this is the only such system. Also, while the basal ganglia are a paradigm case of a brain region that coordinates communication among multiple cortical regions, one cortical region can communicate directly with another without any coordination with other sites. A good example is the frontal eye fields, which play an important role in voluntary eye movements. They are a portion of the dorsolateral frontal cortex directly connected to posterior visual areas.

Summary

To achieve the rapid processing required for functionality of the mind, different information-processing functions are computed as much as possible by different independent modules associated with different brain regions. However, the need for coordination requires communication among these modules. A particularly prominent sort of coordination is where multiple modules communicate with a single coordinating module, such as the procedural module associated with the basal ganglia.

While this section is about the brain and how structural and functional considerations force it to a modular organization, it is worth stopping for a moment to recognize that this is an instance of a much more general phenomenon. Simon (1962) noted that nearly all complex systems whose design is driven to achieve a function have a hierarchical organization of nearly decomposable subsystems. In this he included such artifacts as books and computers, biological entities, social organizations, and cognitive activities including problem solving and language. He argues that a hierarchical structure facilitates the evolution and reproduction of such systems. Specifically, it is possible to tinker with one subsystem without disrupting another subsystem. In such hierarchies, the parts (modules) tend to occupy a small portion of contiguous space or time. This physical compactness promotes high interaction within a unit of the hierarchy, and the distances between the units result in much lower bandwidth interactions among the units.

Modular Architecture

ACT-R's Modules

The overall structure of ACT-R is illustrated in figure 2.2, which is an elaboration of figure 1.5 and illustrates the eight modules that are standard as part of the ACT-R 6.0 simulation system.[6] There are two perceptual modules: a visual module and an aural module. There are two response modules: a manual module and a vocal module. The other four modules are responsible for different aspects of central processing. The imaginal module holds a current mental representation of the problem. For instance, in the context of solving an equation such as $3x - 7 = 5$, it might hold a representation of an intermediate equation such as $3x = 12$. The declarative module retrieves critical information from memory such as that $7 + 5 = 12$. The goal module keeps track of one's current intentions in solving the problem—for instance, one might intend to factor a quadratic equation. Finally, the procedural module embodies various rules for behavior, such as the rules for solving equations. A later section of this chapter reviews the current proposal for associating these modules with specific brain regions.

Each of these modules is capable of massively parallel computation to achieve its objectives. For instance, the visual module can process the entire visual field, and the declarative module can search through the large database of memories. However, when it comes to communication among the modules, there are serial bottlenecks. The only way these modules can communicate is through buffers associated with each module. Only a little information can be put into a buffer associated with the module—a single object perceived, a single problem state represented, a single control state maintained, a single fact retrieved, or a single program for hand movement. Each buffer can hold only a chunk (a structured unit bundling a small amount of information; see figure 1.9 for an example of a chunk).

Communication among these modules is achieved via a procedural module (associated with the basal ganglia). The procedural module can

---

6. There is no implication that these are the only modules of the mind; these are just the ones currently implemented in ACT-R.

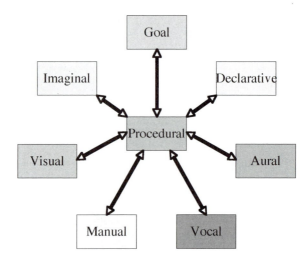

Figure 2.2. The modules implemented in ACT-R 6.0.

respond to information in the buffers of other modules and put information into these buffers. The response tendencies of the central procedural module are represented by production rules such as the one
illustrated in figure 1.10. A significant architectural constraint in ACT-R
is that only a single production rule can execute at a time. Moreover, it
takes 50 ms for a production rule to fire—which I think of as the time
needed to complete the multisynaptic loop through the basal ganglia.
Since communication among the modules must progress through the
procedural module, it becomes the overall central bottleneck in information processing.

While we have extended the term "module" to the procedural system, it is worth noting that there are ways in which it is not like
the other modules. In particular, it does not have a buffer associated
with it in which it can deposit structures. It really is just a system of
mapping cortical buffers to other cortical buffers and is not really an
object in itself. Related to this difference is that we have associated
the procedural module with the basal ganglia, which are not cortical
structures.

It is interesting to consider what about the architecture in figure 2.2
might be uniquely human. Elsewhere (Anderson, 2005a) I have argued
that the goal module has unique properties in the human that enable humans to achieve a distance from their immediate circumstances that other
primates cannot. This enables human means–ends analysis, as described

by Newell and Simon (1972), motivating their early general problem solver (GPS) theory:

> I want to take my son to nursery school. What's the difference between what I have and what I want? One of distance. What changes distance? My automobile. My automobile won't work. What is needed to make it work? A new battery. What has new batteries? An auto repair shop. I want the repair shop to put in a new battery; but the shop doesn't know I need one. What is the difficulty? One of communication. What allows communication? A telephone...and so on. This kind of analysis—classifying things in terms of the functions they serve and oscillating among ends, functions required, and means that perform them—forms the basic system of GPS. (p. 416)

The key to means–ends problem solving is the ability to disengage from what one wants (the end) to focus on something else (the means). Papineau (2001) has argued that means–ends analysis is a unique human capability. Means–ends reasoning underlies human tool making. Benjamin Franklin claimed that tool making was the distinguishing human trait. While there have been modest demonstrations of tool making in other primates, Franklin was right that this is a capacity qualitatively different in the human species. The goal module is what enables this capacity. Chapter 5 delves more into what underlies the remarkable cognitive plasticity of the human species.

Before progressing to examples that illustrate the module system, it is useful to consider the relationship of this proposal to other ideas in cognitive science. The ACT-R architecture can be viewed as a summary of an emerging consensus in the field. However, there still are significant controversies entangled in the consensus; these tend to obscure that consensus. I consider two issues of controversy that are particularly relevant to the module system. One concerns the ideas set forth by the philosopher Jerry Fodor (1983) and the lively discussion that has followed. The other concerns long-standing and evolving issues in experimental psychology regarding capacity limits on cognitive processing.

Fodor Modules

Fodor proposed that a fragment of human cognition was achieved by what he called modules. He thought a modular structure best characterized certain input systems such as vision. He listed no less than nine properties he associated with input modules, six of which are reviewed below:

1. *Domain specificity*   Fodor argued that a module processes only a restricted set of stimuli. This is transparently true for ACT-R's visual and aural modules, but formally it is equally true for all the modules. Just as the visual module processes only visual input, the declarative module process only memories and the goal module process only control states.

2. *Mandatory operation*   Fodor thought that when certain input arrived, the modules had to act, and how they acted could not be modified. Thus, we cannot help seeing and hearing the world in a certain way. This is equally true of all modules: memory cannot help how it responds to a retrieval request, nor can the goal module help how it responds to re-quest for a control change, nor can the procedural module help how it responds to a certain pattern in the buffers of other modules, and so forth. All this comes down to saying that these are mechanical systems that function according to specific laws (chapters 3 and 4 elaborate on the laws describing the declarative and procedural systems). However, as part of Fodor's claim, he held that these modules were not affected by the system's beliefs. Thus, for instance, we see a visual illusion even if we know that it is an illusion. The degree to which there is top-down influence on perception is hotly debated, and there are many demonstrations of con-textual effects on perception. However, it should be noted that nothing in the ACT-R architecture prohibits such influence. The input to a module can include higher level beliefs as well as sensory information.

3. *Information encapsulation*   Fodor emphasized that the information that modules process is internal and that they do not need to make requests of other systems for information. This is again something largely true about ACT-R modules. Almost all information processing occurs within individual modules, although modules do offer a narrow band (their buf-fers) for trading information with other modules. Thus, we have "near-encapsulation" reflecting the predominance of short- over long-distance connections in the brain.

4. *Fast operation*   Fodor argued that, as a consequence of information encapsulation, modular processes are the fastest cognitive processes. This is again true of ACT-R modules. However, it does take some time for

the modules to do their thing, and the overall speed of cognition will be determined by these module times (e.g., see figure 2.8).

5. *Shallow outputs* Fodor described the outputs of modules as "shallow." Here he was very much influenced by his focus on input systems. He viewed these systems as just reporting the "facts"—for example, "there is a red square" rather than "there is a position on a checkerboard." While not all of the ACT-R modules report simple perceptual results, the restriction of buffer contents to single chunks makes the output of the modules very limited.

6. *Fixed neural architecture* Fodor argued that dedicated neural structures are associated with these modules, again an attribute of ACT-R modules. This tends to come with strong nativist claims, such as that the basic functioning of the architecture is prespecified and not something that can be learned. At some level, ACT-R agrees that the functioning of a module is not learned, but certainly the contents of modules—such as what is in the declarative module—are influenced by experience. The principles for encoding and retrieving experiences, not the experiences themselves, are prespecified in the declarative module. Given evidence about widespread neural plasticity, all modules are similarly capable of adjusting their behavior with experience, even if they cannot change their basic principles of processing. However, this book considers learning processes only in the procedural and declarative modules. Learning in other modules, such as perceptual learning in the visual system, tends to be a much slower process and has not yet been modeled within ACT-R.[7]

Each of the claims by Fodor could be questioned, even with respect to input modules. However, as they are stated above, they do not seem much like the stuff of controversy. They come close to summarizing emerging consensus. Nonetheless, Fodor's claims have been associated with substantial controversy because of further claims that he and others have made about modules. It is worth reviewing three of these extensions:

1. *Language* Fodor proposed that a dedicated input module processes the syntax of language. This proposal, combined with claims about information

---

7. However, we have begun some promising interactions with the Leabra research group (O'Reilly and Munakata, 2000) to enhance the ACT-R visual module with the kinds of slow learning that characterize their visual modules (e.g., Taatgen et al., 2006).

encapsulation and the innate basis of syntax, has generated considerable debate in cognitive science. While there is not a linguistic module among the eight modules in figure 2.2, ACT-R is quite agnostic on the issue of whether there are special language modules, or what they might do.[8] The modules in figure 2.2 are by no means a complete account of the human mind, and it remains to be determined what is missing.

2. *Content-specialized modules*   Others have proposed modules with rather specialized content, such as for primitive numeric judgment (Dehaene et al., 1999), recognition of faces (Kanwisher et al., 1997), and detection of cheaters in social situations (Cosmides and Tooby, 2000). This is sometimes called the "Swiss Army Knife" model of cognition, in which there is a blade (module) for every purpose (Duchaine et al., 2001). Fodor does not particularly endorse these sorts of modules, and he is especially dismissive of the proposal for a cheater detection module (Fodor, 2000). In any case, ACT-R is agnostic about such proposals, just as it is about proposals for language modules.

3. *Central cognition*   Fodor seems to want to restrict such modules to input (and perhaps output) systems. He does not think there are central modules. For instance, he says there appears to be no brain center that performs the logical operation of modus ponens (Fodor, 2000, pp. 60–62). Fodor's claims about central cognition extend beyond just denying that there are central modules; he argues that central cognition cannot be understood computationally. It is here that ACT-R and Fodor part ways. Evidence for central modules and a computational explanation of higher level cognition comes from the whole body of work that has been done by the ACT-R community.

Consider Fodor's remark about no central module for modus ponens. This reflects his predisposition to see central cognition as logical processing. This is not the conception of cognition in ACT-R or, indeed, in any of the cognitive science tradition emanating from Newell and Simon (1972). In that work they treated reasoning as a special case of problem solving and were already beginning to treat problem solving as

8. I have not always been so agnostic. I argued in Anderson (1983) that language processing did not involve special modules and depended instead on modules used in general cognitive processes. I was also dismissive of evidence involving localization of language.

handled within a production system. Interestingly, while Fodor is right about there being no brain center for modus ponens, the basal ganglia do appear to implement something like a production system, and production rules provide much of the power of modus ponens.

Fodor's reason for doubting that cognition can be modeled computationally comes from his concern with the frame problem. The frame problem was started in artificial intelligence as a technical concern with how to update knowledge in logical systems (McCarthy and Hayes, 1969), and workable solutions have been developed. However, philosophers such as Fodor have focused on bigger epistemological issues that are only somewhat related. In Fodor's mind, the real issue is information encapsulation, and he argues that the knowledge that humans bring to bear on a task cannot be bounded. The most important intellectual discoveries require bringing together disparate pieces of knowledge. He thinks that this exceeds the capacity of any computational system, but he does not really specify any specific case of knowledge integration that is beyond a computational system. Fodor talks about analogy generally as being beyond the bounds of computational systems, and yet there are successful computational models of analogy making (e.g., Gentner et al., 2001; Hummel & Holyoak, 2003; Salvucci and Anderson, 2001). The last task described in chapter 5 was deliberately selected because it required people to put knowledge together in novel ways. I hoped this would bring ACT-R face to face with Fodor's problem. While it did pose some challenges to the architecture, it turned out to be quite amenable to computational modeling that was faithful to human behavior. Moreover, it was quite capable of being modeled within a modular architecture. In summary, Fodor's worries seem not to have been realized in a documented instance of human cognition.

Modules and Capacity Limits

The basic motivation for a modular structure is to get the best performance possible given the limitations of brain processing. Experimental psychology has long been concerned with sorting out the behavioral manifestations of the limitations on human information processing. In experimental psychology, this often takes the form of trying to identify which processes occur in parallel and which processes occur serially. While it is not logically necessary (Townsend and Wenger, 2004), the assumption typically is that parallel processes are not capacity limited and serial processes are. This is approximately the way it works out in ACT-R. Because different modules can function autonomously and in parallel, they allow the system to process multiple things in parallel. Because the computations within a module can also progress in parallel, they often can avoid capacity limitations, although within a module there is potential for interference among different simultaneous processes (chapter 3 discusses interference in memory). The hardest limitations occur in the communication between modules. Because so little can be placed in a buffer, it is hard to communicate information rapidly from one module to another. For instance, the visual system can hold up processing as it attends to different objects, one at a time, serially putting them in its buffer until the desired object is found.

Another serial limitation arises from the necessity for all modules to communicate through the production system. Since the production system can execute only a single rule at a time, it becomes the central bottleneck (Pashler, 1998) in the overall processing. Therefore, cognition can be slowed when there are simultaneous, different demands for processing the information in the buffers of the modules. The idea that such a central bottleneck exists reflects another emerging near-consensus in cognitive psychology; ACT-R gives an architectural expression to this consensus.[9]

However, the idea of a central bottleneck in information processing does come in for repeated challenges. Curiously, one of the prominent recent challenges comes from the Meyer and Kieras (1997) EPIC architecture—curious, because EPIC is a production-system architecture that has been influenced by the ACT architecture and in turn has strongly influenced the current ACT-R architecture in its modular design. Indeed, substantial aspects of the simulations of the ACT-R perceptual and motor modules are taken directly from EPIC. Meyer and Kieras also made clear to us that models of human cognition would never be adequate if they continued to focus solely on the ethereal intellect and did not acknowledge cognition's perceptual-motor grounding. The limitations of the perceptual-motor components have substantial impact on many higher level cognitive processes.

One category of limitation that ACT-R takes from EPIC is that each of these peripheral modules suffers its own serial-like bottleneck. Different perceptual modules can attend to one thing at a time, and

---

9. Interestingly, if we accept that this central bottleneck resides in the loop through the basal ganglia, we can even see in figure 2.1 where this bottleneck becomes most narrow: the cells that make up the pallidum, which we associate with production rule selection, are really quite few.

motor modules can program one thing at a time. This limitation is realized in ACT-R through the existence of limited-capacity buffers associated with the modules. These buffers are the means of communication among modules. The only thing that the central production system can detect is what is put into the buffers. Thus, while the visual system may be processing many things at once, the rest of the system can only respond to that little bit put into the visual buffer. Similarly, the non-peripheral modules can only communicate through small buffers: only a single thing can be retrieved from memory, a single situation imagined, and so on.

The major point of disagreement with EPIC is whether the central production system also has a central bottleneck limitation. ACT-R's production system is limited in that only one production rule can fire at a time. In contrast, unbounded, many production rules can fire simultaneously in EPIC. Curiously, while the theories differ in terms of the number of rules that can fire at once, both theories agree that it takes 50 ms for a production rule to fire. Indeed, this seems an emerging point of consensus among many production-system architectures (Anderson, John et al., 1995).

There are functional reasons for limiting production rule firing to a single rule at a time. This avoids the problem of multiple rules making contradictory demands on the same module. Thus, for instance, ACT-R does not have to worry that different production rules will fire that ask for contradictory changes to an imagined problem representation. In EPIC, where such contradictory rules can fire in parallel, explicit coordinating production rules are needed to avoid such conflicts or deal with them when they arise. While EPIC models come with special hand-crafted control rules that seem to work, these rules are task specific and would need to be learned for each new task. It is unclear what can guide the system to form the right control rules; certainly people do not get explicit instruction at this level of detail. No learning mechanism has been proposed in the EPIC framework. In contrast, as discussed in chapter 4, production learning has been a recent success story in ACT-R. Production learning in ACT-R involves learning new productions from old; this is easier to do if the learning mechanisms do not have to deal with simultaneous productions firing.

While such functional issues are critical, most of the attention of the field has been on empirical evidence for a central bottleneck. This involves dual-task experiments where participants are asked to carry out two tasks in parallel. The second example in this chapter involves such an experimental task. The first example, which comes next, also involves dual tasking, but it is a task where the real emphasis is on functionality rather than the experimental details that separate parallel from serial production rule firing.

Driving: Modules in Action

Before getting into examples that involve detailed experimental analyses of the behavior of specific modules, it is important to start with an example that illustrates the functionality of the overall architecture. Driving is such an example; as noted above, it requires a driver to do many things at once. The most critical task is controlling the vehicle—exercising lateral control (steering) to keep the vehicle correctly in the lane and longitudinal control (acceleration and braking) to maintain a safe speed and distance from the car ahead. While it is most critical to monitor the vehicle immediately in front, a good driver should also monitor for other vehicles and objects, such as cars in an adjacent lane. Dario Salvucci (e.g., Salvucci, 2005, 2006; Salvucci et al., 2001) has developed a driving model in ACT-R that incorporates the two subtasks of control and monitoring:

> *Control:* The basic ideas for the vehicle control in Salvucci's
> model can be found in many mathematical models of driving
> (e.g., Donges, 1978). The input for control involves keeping
> track of two points—a near point directly in front of the vehicle
> that indicates where one is in the lane, and a far point (e.g., the
> vanishing point of the road, the car ahead, or the tangent point
> of the road). The output is an adjustment to the lateral and
> longitudinal control parameters. The control model runs in a
> tight loop in which each of these points is noted and the control
> parameters of the driving are updated. At a minimum, this loop
> consists of three productions (each 50 ms long)—one produc-
> tion to note the near point, one to note the far point, and one to
> update the control parameters. This system requires the visual
> system to update the locations of these points and the motor
> system to translate the control information into motor com-
> mands. Once given the control parameters, motor modules can
> make their adjustments autonomously of the central production

system, and therefore the loop does not have to wait upon the completion of these motor actions. In summary, the control model calls upon the visual module, the procedural module, the manual module, and an implicit pedal module.

Monitoring: The monitoring model selects which lane to encode and whether to encode information in front or behind (in the rear mirror). Whenever it identifies a new vehicle, it notes its lane and position. This information is held internally and used to help guide such decisions as whether to change lanes. The minimum loop for this is a production cycle of two rules: one chooses where to monitor, and the second determines whether there is an object in that position. Thus, the monitoring model calls upon the visual module, the procedural module, and the declarative module.

One of Salvucci's contributions, over and above the driving model itself, is the proposal of a scheme for interleaving the two subtasks. After each iteration of the control cycle, the model determines how stable the driving situation is. If it is not stable, the control cycle repeats; if it is stable, the control cycle times out for roughly 500 ms (there is a noisy timing process) and monitoring takes over. Salvucci's model cannot wait much longer than 500 ms without suffering serious control problems. Such a system naturally devotes more attention to control in difficult driving situations (e.g., a lane change) and more attention to monitoring in easy situations (staying in a lane on a straight highway).

Salvucci is able to use distribution of eye movements to track this shift between the two tasks. His eye movement theory (EMMA [Eye Movements and Movements of Attention]; Salvucci, 2001) assumes that the eyes follow shifts of attention in order to achieve higher resolution. However, eye movements are slow and stochastic and do not provide total tracking—for instance, there are no 50 ms saccades from near to far point for each control cycle. Still, the overall correspondence between eye movements predicted by his driving model and the data is quite impressive—figure 2.3 shows the match between human and model proportions of gazes to different parts of the visual array.

The more telling analysis by Salvucci concerned the switch between control regions and monitoring regions. For this purpose, forward gazes to the same lane were classified as control gazes, and all other gazes where classified as monitoring gazes. Figure 2.4 shows the probability of switching from monitoring to control (part a) and from control to

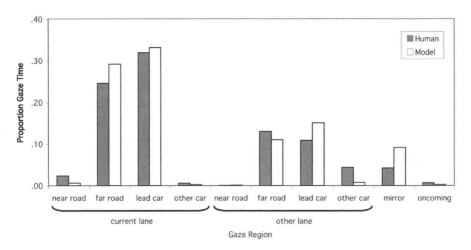

Figure 2.3. Aggregate portion of gaze time for visual regions in a multilane highway experiment. From Salvucci, D. D. (2005). Reprinted by permission of the publisher. Copyright 2005 by Cognitive Science Society, Inc.

monitoring (part b) as a function of time performing that activity (monitoring or control). As the model predicts, these two distributions are quite different. The switching from monitoring shows a peak at about 0.5 s, while the probability of switch from control is concentrated at short intervals. This difference is a consequence of the need to switch back to control after half a second. The length of time spent on control depends on road conditions and the stability of the vehicle.

One of the interesting features of driving is that we interleave it with many activities. When Salvucci's model turns to such interleaved activities as tuning a radio or dialing a cell phone, the demands of the secondary task largely push out situational monitoring, resulting in an alternation between the secondary task and the critical control task that guarantees the car stays on the road and avoids accidents. However, the switch of control between the two tasks is basically the same, driven by the same need to return to control at approximately half-second intervals to maintain safe driving. One obtains distributions of fixations between control and one of these secondary tasks much like the distribution in figure 2.4 between control and monitoring.

Figure 2.5 comes from a study of cell phone use. It compares the time to key each digit in a 10-digit number when not driving (baseline) versus when driving. There are longer breaks before the beginning and before each group in the American 3–3–4 grouping of the telephone digits. In

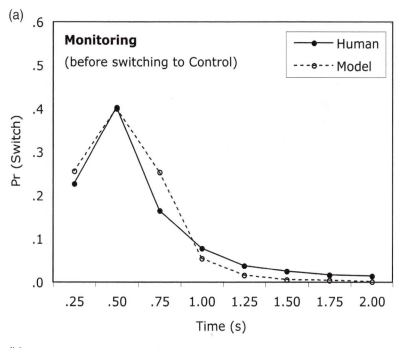

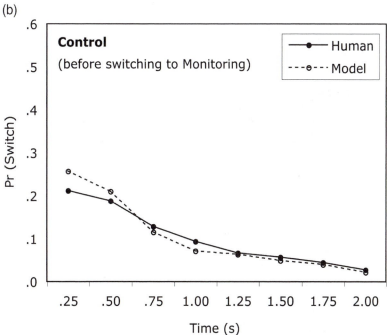

Figure 2.4. Time before switching for monitoring (a) and control (b). From Salvucci, D. D. (2005). Reprinted by permission of the publisher. Copyright 2005 by Cognitive Science Society, Inc.

(a)

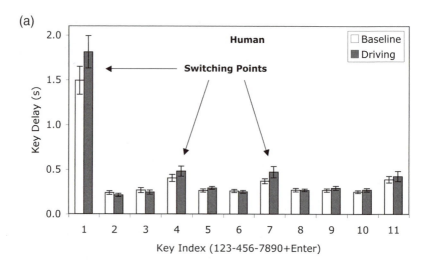

(b)

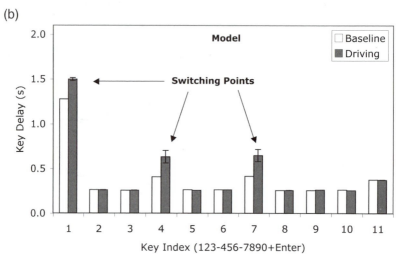

Figure 2.5. Task-switching points as illustrated by key delay times for human drivers (a) and model simulations (b). Errors bars represent standard errors. From Salvucci, D. D. (2005). Reprinted by permission of the publisher. Copyright 2005 by Cognitive Science Society, Inc.

Salvucci's model, these are the points where the system is retrieving the groups of numbers. Salvucci's model will switch back to control while these retrievals are progressing. The retrievals may complete while the model still is in the control subtask, and then the model cannot get back immediately to keying. Thus, the effect of driving is to slow down the keying of digits at these points. The times to key the other digits are not affected.

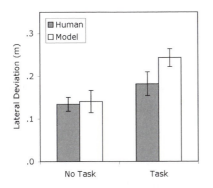
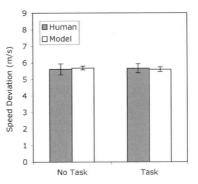

Figure 2.6. Aggregate effects of dialing on driving as measured by lateral deviation and speed deviation. Errors bars represent standard errors. From Salvucci, D. D. (2005). Reprinted by permission of the publisher. Copyright 2005 by Cognitive Science Society, Inc.

Figure 2.6 shows the effect of dialing a cell phone number on two measures of safe driving, lateral deviation and speed deviation. The model correctly predicts that dialing a phone number has an effect on lateral deviation and that there is not an effect on speed deviation. Apparently, only lateral deviation is affected by the relatively minor increase in delay in returning to control. The effects are quite modest. While the model overpredicts the effect of dialing on lateral deviation, all lateral deviation measures in figure 2.6 are well within the safe zone. Examples such as that in figure 2.6 illustrate the relatively small cost that can occur when we insert a new task into the performance of a skill. This is possible because of the autonomous processing of the modules—for instance, the keying of a chunk from the telephone number can continue while the participant has returned to monitoring and control.

In conclusion, Salvucci's driving model illustrates that real-world interleaving of task demands can be achieved within a modular structure such as that in ACT-R. The goal module handles the switches among the tasks. Salvucci has been concerned with extending the goal module so that it can handle arbitrary combinations of tasks.

The purpose of this driving example was to get the big picture across. There are lots of important details to driving, for which the reader is encouraged to go to the Salvucci sources. The next example bores down into some of the details of how individual steps of cognition interleave in a dual task, but in a much simpler task where these details will not be too many.

Dual Tasking: Modular Parallelism and Seriality

The second example goes to the psychology laboratory to look in more detail at the kinds of temporal organization of the modules that underlie the driving example. There are two types of parallelism and two types of seriality associated with all of the ACT-R modules:

Within-Module Parallelism: Within each module, massively parallel computation is happening. For instance, the whole visual field is being simultaneously processed; a retrieval request involves a simultaneous search through multiple memories; the procedural component must simultaneously test all production rules looking for a match; motor programming requires the simultaneous execution and monitoring of multiple muscles, and so forth.

Within-Module Seriality: The need for communication and coordination poses serial bottlenecks within each module. For instance, a single visual object is attended, a single memory is retrieved, a single production rule is selected to fire, a single molar action is chosen to be performed. In the case of perceptual modules (and declarative memory is like a perceptual module that perceives the past) and the procedural module, all the parallel computation must settle in a choice.

Between-Module Parallelism: Computation in one module can proceed in parallel with computation in another module. Thus, there is the potential for the parallel threads. In driving, for instance, vision is progressing in parallel with motor, which is progressing in parallel with central activities such as retrieval of a phone number.

Between-Module Seriality: However, in many cases one module must wait on another because it depends on the information from that module. Thus, for instance, we cannot dial a phone number before we retrieve it.

The ACT-R and EPIC conceptions of this situation are identical except for the central bottleneck. Because only one production can fire at a time (within-module seriality), communication among other modules can be held up (between-module seriality). ACT-R's position is more uniform in that it claims every module has a bottleneck. EPIC, on the other hand, claims no central bottleneck. This has put EPIC in opposition to central bottleneck theories such as that of Pashler and has created a fair amount of controversy and interest in the literature.

Much of the evidence for a central bottleneck involves studies of what is called the psychological refractory period (PRP; for a review, see Pashler, 1994), where one is asked to do two tasks. In the typical PRP experiment, a first task is presented, and then, after a short delay but usually before the first task is finished, a second task is presented. The fact that the first task is still ongoing produces some delay in the performance of the second task. This has been taken as evidence for the existence of a central bottleneck. Meyer and Kieras (1997) argued that these effects arise because participants are asked to give the output of the two tasks in the order they occur and they thus have to put tests in the execution of the second task to assure that it comes out second. From this perspective, a better paradigm would be one where participants are asked to perform two simultaneous tasks as fast as they can with no constraint on order of response. Usually, the result in such experiments is considerable interference between the two tasks, but combinations of tasks can be found where, with enough practice, near-perfect time sharing occurs and the two tasks are performed together nearly as fast as alone. One such example of near-perfect time sharing was demonstrated in a series of experiments that began with Schumacher et al. (2001) and were continued by Hazeltine et al. (2002). Meyer et al. (2001) argued that these experiments provide evidence of an EPIC-like theory with unlimited central processing rather than an ACT-R-like theory with a central bottleneck.

In the basic experiment used in these studies, participants responded to the presentation of a circle and a tone. The circle appeared in one of three horizontal locations, and participants made a spatially compatible response with their right hand, pressing index, middle, or ring finger to left, middle, or right locations. The 150-ms tones were 220 Hz, 880 Hz, or 3,520 Hz, and participants responded "one," "two," or "three." In the single-task condition, participants did just the visual-manual task or just the aural-vocal task. In the dual-task condition, both stimuli were presented simultaneously and participants were asked to do both tasks simultaneously. Over many days of practice, participants come to respond virtually as quickly to each task in the dual-task condition as in the single-task conditions. Thus, participants were able to perform two tasks at once with virtually no cost.

Anderson, Taatgen, and Byrne (2005) did an extensive analysis of the version of this paradigm that was reported by Hazeltine et al. (2002).

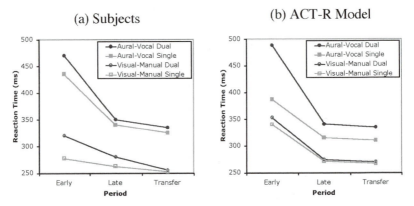

Figure 2.7. Learning to time share: (a) experiment 1 from Hazeltine et al. (2002); (b) ACT-R simulation.

Figure 2.7 displays the performance of the participants and the perform-ance of an ACT-R model for the task. The figure shows the time to perform the aural-vocal task and the time to perform the visual-manual task, sepa-rately plots the time to do each task in isolation and in conjunction with the other task, and plots data from three points in the task performance: the first two sessions, two sessions late in the experiment, and two later sessions where some additional transfer tasks were inserted. Even in the first two sessions, there is a relatively modest dual cost of about 50 ms, but this reduces to about 10 ms by the end of the experiment. The model reproduces the overall speed increase and the reduction in the dual-task cost from about 50 ms to about 10 ms. Compared to the data, it produces a somewhat larger dual cost in the aural-vocal task and a smaller dual-task cost in the visual-manual task. However, for present purposes, the important observation is that the model, despite its serial production-rule firing, can produce small dual-task effects that are of the same order of magnitude as seen with human participants. Hazeltine et al. (2002) ran these same participants through a series of additional experiments and eventually got the average dual-cost effect down to 3 ms (by my calcula-tions from their data). Anderson et al. (2005) ran their model to the limit and got its dual cost down to 4 ms.

The details of the model are described in Anderson, Taatgen, and Byrne (2005); figure 2.8 illustrates the behavior of the model early in the experiment (part a) and late (part b). That figure tracks the activity of five modules: the vocal module generating speech, the aural module processing sound, the procedural module interpreting production rules,

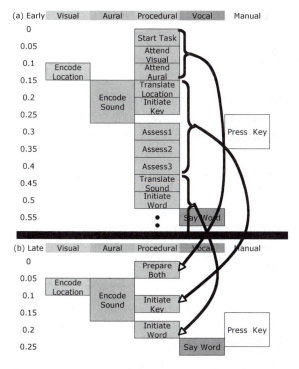

Figure 2.8. ACT-R module activities early in the experiment (but not as early as illustrated in figure 2 of Anderson, Taatgen, and Byrne, 2005) and relatively late in the experiment.

the visual module processing vision, and the motor module controlling hand movements. In both parts a and b, the visual and aural modules are evoked once to encode information and the vocal and manual modules are evoked once to generate output. The big difference between early and late is the number of rules that have to fire—three productions that initiate processing are collapsed into one; five rules that generate the finger press and assess the outcome are collapsed into one; two productions (plus some later assessment rules not shown) are collapsed into a single rule that generates the word.[10] The learning process that allows ACT-R to compress the initial productions into just three are discussed in chapter 4.

10. Actually, one production rule needs to be learned for each separate stimulus–response mapping. This means three visual-manual rules and three aural-vocal rules must be learned, but only one of each will apply on a particular trial.

For present purposes, what is of interest is the mixture of parallelism and seriality. Let us review the four types of categories described above:

Within-Module Parallelism: Each box in these figures reflects a lot of parallel activity happening within the module.

Within-Module Seriality: However, each box reflects the conclusion of this parallelism in a single action. The within-module combination of parallelism and seriality also applies to the procedural system: all the productions are tested in parallel, but only one gets to fire, creating the central bottleneck in figure 2.8a.

Between-Module Parallelism: Different modules can operate in parallel. So, for instance, in figure 2.8b the execution of the finger press overlaps at different times with the encoding of the tone, the production that selects the word to say, and the generation of the word.

Between-Module Seriality: What is determining the ultimate timing of the response, particularly in figure 2.8b, is the communication of information between modules. For instance, the finger cannot be pressed until the rule selects which finger to press, and this rule cannot fire until the location is encoded.

Figure 2.8 illustrates why near-perfect time sharing does not occur initially but is achieved ultimately. Initially, the demand on the central production system is high, and firing of productions for one task must wait on the firing of productions for the other task. In the illustration in figure 2.8, the execution of the aural-vocal task waits on the execution of the visual-manual task, but it could have been the other way around. After extensive practice, however, there are very few productions, and the rules for each task can "fit in" while noncentral aspects of other tasks are performed. In figure 2.8b, the rule that chooses the finger can fire during the encoding of the sound and the rule that maps the sound onto the word can fire while the key is being pressed.

In the example in figure 2.8, it is particularly convenient that it takes longer to identify the tone than to identify a location, as this creates a gap for the visual-manual production rule to fire. Note in figure 2.7 that the aural-vocal task takes substantially longer than the visual-manual task. Much of the research in the later Hazeltine et al. (2002) report was aimed at eliminating this difference, either by making the visual-manual task more difficult or by changing the onsets of the two tasks, and near-perfect time sharing was still observed. Also, even in the original task, while the aural-vocal task was longer on average, on some trials participants did complete it before the visual-manual task. The model predicts this because of variability in the length of the steps. The length of the boxes in figure 2.8 just represents their average length; the variability of stages can result in a partial overlap of times when productions could fire. This is why the model predicts some small dual-task cost even when the model achieves its ultimate compact form in figure 2.8b. This residual dual cost reflects the average amount that one production in figure 2.8b will delay another.

With highly practiced participants, Hazeltine et al. (2002) never found dual costs greater than about 10 ms even when they tried to manipulate the length of the visual-manual task or the relative onset of the two tasks. Somewhat surprisingly, the model does not predict dual costs greater than an average of 10 ms. One would have thought these manipulations would have created a greater degree of overlap with the central bottleneck. However, the variability in timing that produces some overlap when the average times for the stages are completely nonoverlapping in figure 2.8b creates nonoverlap when the average times are maximally overlapping. Also, the maximum delay that one task can produce in another is the 50 ms for the one production rule that must fire for that task. Since only one task can be delayed on a single trial, the maximum average delay in the performance of the two tasks is only 25 ms. Thus, it is not that hard to imagine how, with variability in timing and the slack time in figure 2.8b, one can get a stubborn small delay (less than 10 ms) that does not seem to change much.

Delays can get much more substantial in situations such as that for the beginning of the experiment in figure 2.8, where more central processing is going on. Byrne and Anderson (2001) studied a number of complex tasks (including doing addition and multiplication simultaneously) where the time to do two tasks at once was sometimes even greater than the sum of the times to do each singly. Such tasks provide strong evidence for the ACT-R conception of matters rather than the EPIC conception. Tests of a central bottleneck are much more telling when the amount of central processing becomes substantial.

However, it would be a mistake to leave this discussion focusing on the residual differences between the ACT-R and EPIC conceptions. In fact, the views are identical on most scores, and the ACT-R conception has been strongly influenced by the EPIC position. Moreover, the EPIC and the ACT-R positions at a general level have substantial overlap with many other conceptions in the field, such as that of Pashler (1998) or Card et al. (1983). It is also worth noting that while productions can fire in parallel in EPIC, in many of the Meyer and Kieras PRP models they enforce seriality on production firing. Thus, there is an increasing consensus on how parallel processing and serial processing combine both within modules and between modules, even though we are still working out details such as the role of a central bottleneck.

Mapping Modules Onto the Brain

Localizing Eight Modules

As discussed above, modular organization is the solution to a set of structural and functional constraints. The mind needs to achieve certain functions, and the brain must devote local regions to achieving these functions. This implies that if these modules reflect the correct division of the functions of the mind, it should be possible to find brain regions that reflect their activity. Our lab has developed a mapping of the eight modules in figure 2.2 onto specific brain regions, illustrated in figure 2.9,[11] which we have used in an extensive series of fMRI experiments. The eight regions can be organized into four peripheral modules and four central modules. The four peripheral modules are as follows:

1. *Visual module:* While large portions of the brain are devoted to processing the visual signal, we have found one region, the fusiform gyrus in the temporal lobe, that seems to best reflect the focused visual processing of attended information. Other research (Grill-Spector et al., 2004; McCandliss et al., 2003) has shown that this plays a critical role in perceptual recognition.

2. *Aural module:* This is associated with secondary auditory cortex but not the primary auditory cortex. As in the case of the

11. The regions appear on the surface in figure 2.9a but are below the actual surface of the cortex to varying degrees. Figure 2.9b is a midline illustration of the two structures buried truly deep in figure 2.9b. The coordinates given for the brain regions in this figure are slightly different than those in figure 1.8. This reflects a correction that has been made to deal with the fact that our reference brain was acquired very slightly misaligned with the central line of the brain (the line between the anterior and posterior commissure).

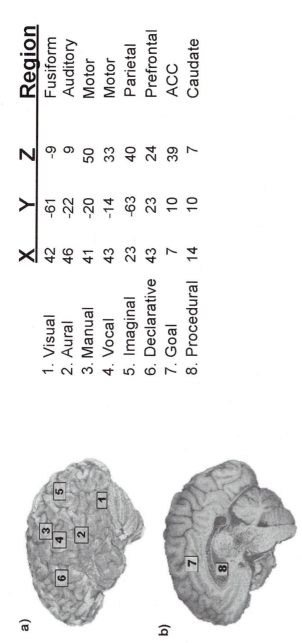

	X	Y	Z	Region
1. Visual	42	-61	-9	Fusiform
2. Aural	46	-22	9	Auditory
3. Manual	41	-20	50	Motor
4. Vocal	43	-14	33	Motor
5. Imaginal	23	-63	40	Parietal
6. Declarative	43	23	24	Prefrontal
7. Goal	7	10	39	ACC
8. Procedural	14	10	7	Caudate

Figure 2.9. An illustration of the locations of the eight regions of interest: (a) regions close to the surface of the cortex; (b) regions deeper in the brain. The Tailarach coordinates are given for the right-side regions (left homologue can be obtained by switching the sign of the x-coordinate). Most of the regions are cubes 5 voxels long, 5 voxels wide, and 4 voxels high (a voxel in our research is 3.125 mm long and wide and 3.2 mm high). The exceptions are the procedural (caudate), which is 4 × 4 × 4 voxels, and the goal (anterior cingulate cortex, ACC), which is 5 × 3 × 4 voxels.

visual module, we are tapping a region that reflects relatively advanced processing of the auditory signal rather than early processing.

3. *Manual module:* This is reflected in the activity of the region along the central sulcus that is devoted to representation of the hand. This includes parts of both the motor and sensory cortex.

4. *Vocal module:* Further down the motor strip is a region that represents the face and tongue. It also includes parts of both the motor and sensory cortex.

The four central regions are widely distributed throughout the brain:

5. *Imaginal module:* We have associated the imaginal module with a posterior region of the parietal cortex. This association is roughly consistent with the research of others who have found that this area is involved in spatial processing (Dehaene et al., 2002; Reichle et al., 2000). However, the exact functions of different parietal regions remain a matter for study. We have found this region to be sensitive to representational changes in tasks as varied as equation solving (Anderson, 2005a) and the Tower of Hanoi problem (Anderson, Albert, and Fincham, 2005). Its response seems largely insensitive to the input modality; it seems to instead reflect the effort made in transforming a mental representation.

6. *Declarative module:* We have found a region of prefrontal cortex to be sensitive to both retrieval and storage operations. Focus on this area is again consistent with a great deal of memory research (Buckner et al., 1999; Cabeza et al., 2002; Fletcher and Henson, 2001; Lepage et al., 2000; Wagner, Maril et al., 2001; Wagner, Paré-Blagoev et al., 2001). However, the exact memory function of different prefrontal regions again seems a matter for continuing study.

7. *Goal module:* We have associated the goal module that directs the internal course of cognition with a region of the anterior cingulate cortex. There is consensus that this region plays a major role in control (Botvinick et al., 2001; D'Esposito et al., 1995; Posner and Dehaene, 1994), but again, there is hardly consensus on how to characterize this role and chapter 4 will provide some discussion of these contrasting views.

8. *Procedural module:* As noted above, there is a general belief that the basal ganglia play a role like that of production rules in terms of pattern recognition and selection of cognitive actions. The region of basal ganglia that we have selected is the head of the caudate, although in some studies this region has not been particularly responsive.

As the citations above indicate, there is nothing particularly novel about the association of these brain regions with these functions. What is novel is the association of these regions with parts of an integrated architecture and their use to trace out the components of that architecture. It is important to recognize that we have used the same predefined regions across a number of studies, including the ones described in this book. This has a number of advantages over using exploratory regions. For instance, it avoids the problem of trying to correct for the danger of getting a spurious result in all the tests that go into exploratory studies. Furthermore, the estimate of the response produced in these regions is not biased by the selection process.

Two points need to be made to qualify any simple conclusion of a one-to-one mapping of function onto structure. First, as noted above, the brain tends to distribute similar but distinguishable processes to different regions. For instance, more than 30 regions perform visual processing. Again, multiple regions in the frontal and temporal cortices serve memory functions. Thus, there is no claim that the one region we have identified is the only region associated with a function. Second, there is no necessary reason why these brain regions should perform only a single architectural function. Nonetheless, in the range of studies that we have used in our laboratory, we have been fortunate to be able to associate the activities of these regions with just the assigned functions.

The Experiment

Having postulated eight modules and their associated brain regions, it would be nice to be able to describe a single study that exercised all of these modules. We performed such an fMRI study, the details of which are reported in Anderson et al. (2007). The experiment manipulated the input module by presenting material either visually or aurally. Similarly, it manipulated the output module by having the participants respond either vocally or manually.

A rather peculiar cognitive task was chosen in order to separate the behavior of the imaginal module (parietal) from the declarative module (prefrontal). Much imaging research finds that these two regions, although widely separated, often give similar responses. This happens because memory retrieval and representational changes are naturally correlated. In order to make a retrieval request, one needs to create a representation to hold the elements of the retrieval request. Following that, the consequence of a successful retrieval is often to change the underlying representation. Consider the task of solving the equation $7x + 3 = 38$, described in chapter 1 (regarding figure 1.7). Representation of this equation may lead to the request for the difference between 8 and 3. Successful retrieval of $8 - 3 = 5$ enables the re-representation of the equation as $7x = 35$, which in turn enables another retrieval request to determine the value of 35 divided by 7. Thus, retrieval and representation operations tend to occur together, and we get similar behavior in prefrontal and parietal regions, as can be seen by comparing figures 1.8, b and d. To break this natural correlation, one needs an artificial task where successful retrievals will not necessarily result in re-representations so that re-presentations can take place without retrieving any information to guide them.

Table 2.1 illustrates how the experiment attempted to manipulate retrieval and representation demands orthogonally. In the first phase, outside the fMRI scanner, participants memorized information that they would use in the second phase of the experiment that took place in the scanner. The material to be memorized involved associations between two-letter words and two-digit numbers, such as

AT → 23 and BE → 24

In the second phase of the experiment, participants either heard or saw permutations of the words "Dick," "Fred," and "Tom" paired with visual presentation of the two-letter words or two-digit numbers. Table 2.1 illustrates the various conditions of the experiment. Participants were told that the two-digit codes that they had learned were instructions for transforming the three-word sequences. Thus, 23 meant that the second and third words should be switched. Applied to "Tom, Dick, Fred," it would produce "Tom, Fred, Dick." Some two-digit codes were "no-ops" such as 24 because one of the digits is greater than three and thus, in this case, does not require a transformation. The difference between

Table 2.1.   Illustration of the Four Conditions of the Experiment
(associations: AT → 23, BE → 24)

	No Transformation	Yes Transformation
No Substitution	**Stimulus:** Tom Dick Fred **Probe:** 24 **Response:** Tom-Dick-Fred	**Stimulus:** Tom Dick Fred **Probe:** 23 **Response:** Tom-Fred-Dick
Yes Substitution	**Stimulus:** Tom Dick Fred **Probe:** BE **Response:** Tom-Dick-Fred	**Stimulus:** Tom Dick Fred **Probe:** AT **Response:** Tom-Fred-Dick

no-op digit pairs and ones that require an operation is referred to as the *transformation* factor in table 2.1. Participants can be given either the digit pair directly, in which case no retrieval is required, or a word from which they have to retrieve the digit pair. The requirement to perform this retrieval is referred to as the *substitution* factor in table 2.1 because it required the participant to substitute the digit for the word. The expectation was that the transformation factor would draw more upon the parietal region for manipulating problem representation and that the substitution factor would draw more upon the prefrontal region for retrieving information.

In addition to the factors represented in table 2.1, participants could either hear the words or see them—a manipulation of an input factor. Finally, participants could either say the words or key them out (they had learned to associate Dick with the index finger, Fred with the middle finger, and Tom with the ring finger), a manipulation of an output factor.

Figure 2.10 is an attempt to display the effects of the four factors (input modality, output modality, transformation, and substitution) on the eight regions associated with the modules. It displays for each of the eight regions the *F*-values that come from a statistical test of the significance of each of the four factors—input modality, output modality, transformation, and substitution. Stars indicate which statistical tests are significant. The results are largely as expected: the input modality has the strongest effects on perceptual regions, the output modality has the strongest effect on motor regions, transformation has the largest effect on the parietal region, and substitution has the largest effect on

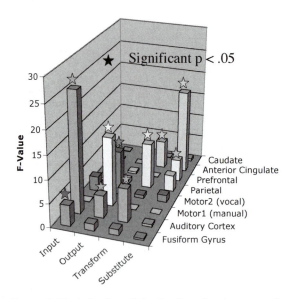

Figure 2.10. A display of the *F*-values for the main effects of input modality, output modality, transformation, and substitution for the eight predefined brain regions. Stars indicate significant effects ($p < .05$). Reprinted from Anderson, Qin, Jung, & Carter (2007) with permission from Elsevier.

the prefrontal region. As expected, both cognitive factors, transformation and substitution, have affects on the cingulate, but neither the input or output modality affects this region. The caudate is a disappointment, not responding significantly to any of the factors (it was expected to respond like the cingulate and show effects of both the substitution and transformation factors). Two of results for the auditory cortex require a little comment. Output modality has an effect on this region because participants hear themselves giving the response. The effect of transformation here is not expected and anomalous; the transformation condition has the weaker response.[12]

12. Perhaps this effect is just a spurious significant result among all the tests. However, in a number of studies we have seen a tendency for decreased BOLD (blood oxygen level–dependent) response in the auditory region when there is increased cognitive engagement. Perhaps it reflects the fact that subjects are distracted from the rather aversive sound of the scanner.

In summary, the general pattern of results is largely consistent with the proposed associations. The failure to get the expected effects in the caudate is the most distressing. Across the experiments run in our lab, we have only sometimes found the caudate to respond to manipulations (e.g., it did in figure 1.8e). This may be related in part to the relatively weak magnitude of response in this region.

Predicting the BOLD Response

As illustrated in chapter 1, ACT-R does more than just specify what regions will be affected by what factors. It predicts the exact time course of the BOLD (blood oxygen level–dependent) response in each of these regions. To illustrate these predictions, figure 2.11 shows the detailed procedure of the experiment as it was administered in the fMRI scanner. Each trial involved 28.5 s in which there were 19 scans of the brain lasting 1.5 s each. Participants either heard or read words at the rate of one each half-second. Then they either had a 4-s delay or not. The purpose of the delay was to manipulate the shape of the BOLD response for purposes of testing the model.[13] Then they saw the digit or word command. They were instructed to perform the transformation mentally and to press the right thumb key when they were ready to give the answer. The time to press the thumb key is the most important behavioral measure, reflecting the time to comprehend the instruction and plan the response. When the thumb key was pressed, subjects had to key out their letters quickly (if the output modality was manual) or say them quickly (if the output modality was vocal). Then they were given feedback in the form of the correct sequence, presented at the rate of one word per half-second. There were large effects of about 1.5 s for either substitution or transformation on time for the thumb press. Thus, the cognitive factors were having large effects on the task; this helped in separating out representation and retrieval effects. Interestingly, neither input nor output modality had an effect on time to do the task, despite the large effects these factors had on the brain regions associated with the perceptual and motor modules.

13. The delay allows the BOLD response from the initial encoding to begin to return to baseline.

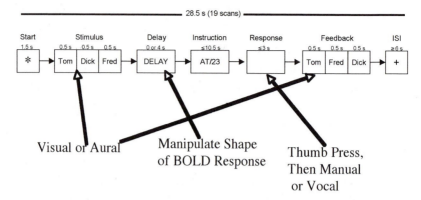

Figure 2.11. The 28.5-sec structure of an fMRI trial. ISI, interstimulus interval.

Anderson et al. (2007) report an effort to fit a detailed ACT-R model to each of the regions. These fits are reproduced in figure 2.12. The following are the key concepts for understanding the predictions of the model:

1. The x-axis gives the time from the beginning of a trial (see figure 2.11).
2. The y-axis gives the change in the BOLD signal from baseline at the beginning of the trial.
3. When a module is engaged, it will make a metabolic demand.
4. This metabolic demand will show up in the BOLD response as an effect smeared over time. The BOLD response reaches a peak approximately 4-5 seconds after the demand.

The methodology behind producing such fits is discussed in appendix 2.1. The discussion here focuses on the three largest effects from figure 2.10: input modality on the auditory region, output modality on the manual region, and substitution on the anterior cingulate. This provides a representative of an input module, an output module, and a central module.

Figure 2.12b illustrates the time course of the BOLD response in the auditory region and the fit of the model. For purposes of this display, it plots separately the data for the visual and auditory presentation. To better test the time course of the BOLD response, it also plots separately the results for the delay and no-delay conditions. The differences among the conditions are quite striking. Particularly compelling is the aural delay condition where there are separate rises for the initial presentation of the words and for the feedback. It might seem odd that the model predicts the small rises in the visual condition. However, these occur only

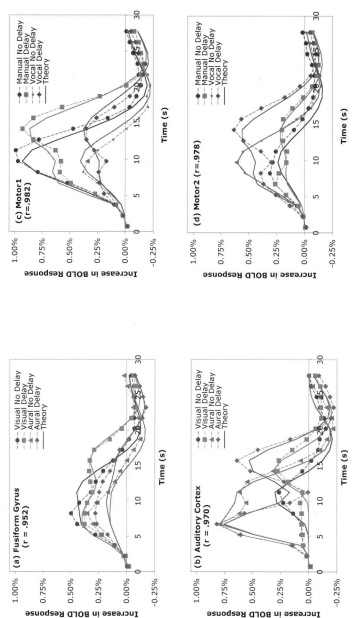

Figure 2.12. Observed (dashed lines connecting points) BOLD responses and predictions (solid lines) for the eight predefined regions. The data and predictions are plotted as a function of the mean time of each scan. (a) Effects of input modality and delay of the left fusiform gyrus. (b) Effects of input modality and delay on the left and right auditory cortex. (c) Effects of output modality and delay on the left motor area that is associated with the right hand. (d) Effects of output modality and delay on the left and right motor areas that are associated with the face and tongue.

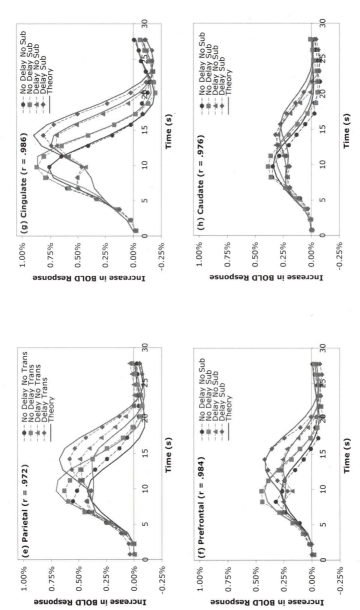

Figure 2.12. (*continued*) (e) Effects of transformation and delay on the left parietal region. (f) Effects of substitution and delay on the left prefrontal region. (g) Effects of substitution and delay on the left anterior cingulate. (h) Effects of substitution and delay on the right caudate. Reprinted from Anderson, Qin, Jung, & Carter (2007) with permission from Elsevier.

for the participants who are seeing the material but saying the answers. The rises reflect their processing of their own speech. Another interesting feature of this region is that delay has no effect on area under the curves. Essentially, the same amount of auditory processing is being differently distributed for the delay and no-delay conditions.

Figure 2.12c shows the data for the region of the motor cortex that corresponds to the hand. This figure breaks out the data according to whether the response was manual or vocal. Again, the BOLD responses for the different conditions are strikingly different. There is some response even in the vocal condition. In part this reflects the fact that all participants, including those in the vocal condition, issued their timed response as a thumb press. However, it also reflects a failure to totally separate the motor region devoted to the hand from the nearby region devoted to the face.[14] Note in this figure that the motor region begins to respond in the delay condition before the actual response. This reflects motor rehearsal by the participants to bridge the delay. In contrast to the aural region, this area shows greater area under the curves in the delay condition, reflecting the rehearsal of the responses in the delay period.[15]

Figure 2.12g shows the data for the anterior cingulate broken down according to whether a substitution was required. Whenever there are multiple rules that can apply to a situation but only one or a few are appropriate, a special control state needs to be set to select the appropriate rule, and the anterior cingulate will show an increased response reflecting the setting of this control state. Thus, the model predicts the effect of substitution because it must set a special control state to wait for the result of the retrieval. Also, the BOLD response is greater (measured by area under the curve) in the delay condition because a control state must be set to bridge that delay. The model also predicts the effect of transformation on this region (not shown in figure 2.12g) because a control state must be set to bridge the interval while the representation is being transformed. While the anterior cingulate responds to these three factors, it does not respond to either input or output modality, as figure 2.10 illustrates. As

14. The face area (figure 2.12d) also shows some response in all conditions, but it does respond much more strongly in the vocal condition.

15. This is not the first experiment to find motor rehearsal, but it was a surprise when it occurred in the first such study (Anderson, Qin et al., 2004). It led to a change in our models to include such motor rehearsal. As such, it is an example of how imaging can inform the development of a model.

emphasized in Anderson et al. (2007), it is a region that responds to the abstract information-processing demands of the task.

The general pattern of effects in the experiment (figure 2.10) and the ability to explain the exact shape of the BOLD response (figure 2.12)[16] provide strong support for an association of these regions with these modules. The associations displayed in this experiment have been replicated in many experiments in our lab and are roughly consistent with other results in the literature. They give strong reason for believing that brain regions can be mapped onto function despite the doubts expressed by researchers such as Uttal (2001).

Overall Conclusions

With respect to Allen Newell's question of how the human mind can occur in the physical universe, this chapter offers a general answer and some specific details. The general answer is that the mind partitions itself into specific information-processing functions, and these functions are achieved in relatively localized brain regions where the processing can be done effectively. There are paths of connections among these regions that assure the coordination of these functions into a coherent sequence of activities. The specific answers are the eight modules, their associated regions, and their coordination by the central production system.

The general answer of a modular partition seems the only way to achieve the multipurpose functionality that humans need to meet the demands of their world given the structures of their brains. However, the specific answers offered here are far from final. Certainly, these eight modules do not exhaust the functions of the mind or the regions of the brain. However, beyond the issue of completeness, one can wonder whether the proposed partitioning of function and paths of communication are correct. One movement in recent research has been to partition the brain and its functions much more finely than is done here. Such efforts include the memory functions of the prefrontal cortex (e.g., Badre et al., 2005), the control functions of the

---

16. It should also be noted that much poorer fits are obtained when one tries to fit the wrong module to one of these regions. For measures of goodness of fit, see Anderson et al. (2007).

anterior cingulate (e.g., van Veen and Carter, 2005), and the representational functions of the parietal cortex (e.g., Dehaene et al., 2002). Also as noted, the loop through the basal ganglia does not begin to exhaust the paths of communication in the brain. In the hindsight of a decade or two, the partitioning offered here in this book might seem rather crude. As Newell warned we would be, we are just a little ways into an answer. Nonetheless, the structure–function associations proposed in this chapter are sufficiently similar to many other ideas in the field that it seems unlikely that further refinements will completely overturn these associations.

The successes reviewed in this chapter and elsewhere in the book strongly suggest that Fodor was wrong in his pessimism about central modules and the impossibility of a computational theory of central cognition. Figure 2.2 illustrates declarative, imaginal, goal, and procedural modules that are all central modules. There has been considerable success in associating these modules with specific brain areas. They seem to meet Fodor's criteria for being called a module. Moreover, they play effective computational roles in models of a wide variety of cognitive tasks.

Chapters 3 and 4 look at two of the modules about which the ACT-R architecture has the most to say, the declarative and the procedural modules. Chapter 5 concerns what in this architecture might be uniquely human.

Appendix 2.1: Predicting the BOLD Response

Our laboratory has developed a methodology for relating the profile of activity in modules like those in figure 2.2 to blood oxygen level–dependent (BOLD) responses from the brain regions that correspond to these modules. The fundamental idea is to use a timeline of module activity like that in figure 1.7. Anderson et al. (2007) provide specification of the timelines behind all the predictions in figure 2.12, but for present purposes let us just look at predictions from the timeline for the auditory cortex (figure 2.12b) and just for the delay condition with auditory input. Figure 2.13a presents this timeline as a demand function for this condition giving the proportion of time the module is active in each 1.5-s scan. There is a peak of 100% activity when the words are presented during the second scan. The time at which the feedback is presented varies a bit, and so there is a distribution of times at which module is active later to process this feedback.[17]

The basic theory we have developed of the BOLD response claims that the while a module is engaged there is an increased metabolic demand in the corresponding region producing a hemodynamic response. We have adopted the standard gamma function that other researchers have used for the hemodynamic response (e.g., Boyton et al., 1996; M. S. Cohen, 1997; Dale and Buckner, 1997; Glover, 1999). If the module is engaged, it will produce a BOLD response t time units later according to the function

$$H(t) = m\left(\frac{t}{s}\right)^a e^{-(t/s)}$$

where m governs the magnitude, s scales the time, and the exponent a determines the shape of the BOLD response such that with larger a the function rises and falls more steeply. Figure 2.13b illustrates the function assumed for the auditory region. As is typical of such functions, it shows a slow response that peaks about 4–5 s after the actual activity. The peak of the function is at $a*s$. The parameter a is 7 for this function, and s is 0.63 s; $a*s$ is 4.41 s, which is where the function in figure 2.12b peaks.

The BOLD response accumulates whenever the region is engaged. Thus, if $D(t)$ is a demand function giving the probability that the region is engaged at time t, then the cumulative BOLD response can be obtained by convolving this function with the hemodynamic function

$$B(t) = \int_0^t D(x)H(t-x)dx$$

This is the prediction for the BOLD response that we will observe in the region associated with that demand function. Figure 2.13c shows the predicted BOLD response in this case. The observed response preserves some of the structure of the demand function in figure 2.13a, but the convolving with the BOLD response blurs some of the temporal structure and delays the peaks.

In summary, a model for the time course of this task yields demand functions $D(t)$ like that in figure 2.13a. By convolving the demand functions with the hemodynamic function, one can obtain predictions for the

---

17. See Anderson et al. (2007) for a discussion of the slight negativity at the end.

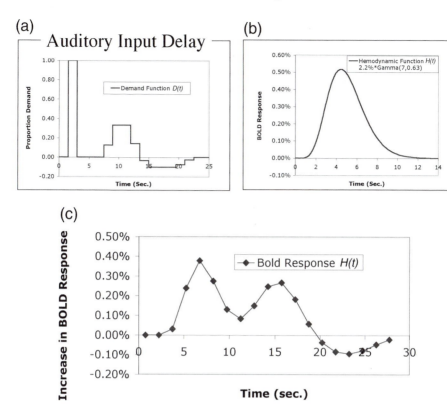

Figure 2.13. (a) An illustration of the methodology behind the predictions for the aural demand function for the auditory-delay condition in figure 2.12b. (b) The hemodynamic function assumed. (c) The resulting prediction of the BOLD response for the auditory region.

BOLD response in the regions associated with the modules. Anderson (2005a) can be consulted for ways of assessing the match between the predictions and the data. A similar convolution methodology is frequently used in analysis programs for fMRI data where one takes the condition structure of trials in an experiment and convolves it with a hemodynamic response to produce a condition-sensitive pattern of activity. This pattern is regressed against brain activity to find which regions are sensitive to these conditions (e.g., Friston, 2003). The methodology we used is finer grained conceptually (using model behavior within a single trial) and is used for confirmatory purposes rather than exploratory purposes.

3

Human Associative Memory

Declarative memory is the module by which we are able to perceive our past. Like the visual system, it can be judged as a glass half full or as a glass half empty. It can be judged as high capacity: just as the visual system processes the rich array in the visual field, so memory maintains and processes what seems a vast warehouse of knowledge. It is capable of powerful parallel processing in which a single memory prompt (e.g., What was the name of your high school?) can zoom in on the appropriate memory to retrieve. On the other hand, we often find that there are more things missing from our past than are still contained in that vast warehouse. We find ourselves struggling to retrieve a memory that may still be there but somehow is not available (e.g., What was the name of that teacher in ninth grade?). Just as the visual system chooses to devote most of its resources to a small fraction of the visual field around the fovea, so it seems our declarative memory has concentrated its resources on a fragment of our past. Much of this chapter is about how memory makes that resource allocation. The fundamental claim of this chapter is that a declarative memory tries to give us, moment by moment, the most appropriate possible window into our past.[1]

This window into our past gives us our identities. Many thinkers, going back as far as John Locke (and apparently St. Augustine before him), have argued that memory is critical to our sense of self-identity. How could

---

1. The title of this chapter refers to the HAM theory (Anderson and Bower, 1973) that attempted to address the memory literature of the early 1970s. HAM was a theory of declarative memory and was the starting point in the development of the ACT-R theory of declarative memory (see appendix 1.1).

you have an identity if you could not recall any experiences from your past? HM is a famous amnesiac patient who, at the age of 27, lost the ability to form new memories after an operation in 1953. He has been studied for decades since. HM has normal memories of his life up to the age of 16 but suffers retrograde amnesia for the 11 years before the surgery. He appears in many ways to be a normal person with a clear self-identity, but his identity largely consists of the person he was when he was 16, where his memories stopped (although he realizes he is older, and he has learned some general facts about the world). He thinks his mother is still alive, and he grieves over her death every time he learns about it. In many ways, it seems we are what we can remember about our past.

Varieties of Learning

Although HM cannot acquire new conscious memories he is capable of showing learning in other ways. He was able to learn how to solve new puzzles such as the Tower of Hanoi (Cohen, Eichenbaum et al., 1985)[2] and to traverse mazes (Milner, 1970), although he will claim not to recognize such problems. Somehow, he came to learn about people, including John F. Kennedy, Lee Harvey Oswald, and John Glenn, although they all became famous after his operation (O'Kane et al., 2004). He is also capable of being primed in his recognition of visual patterns (Gabrieli et al., 1990). Such results make the point that there are multiple kinds of learning. Four different kinds of learning can be defined by whether the learning involves declarative memory or procedural memory, and by whether the learning involves the creation of new symbolic structures or just subsymbolic tuning of existing structures. Table 3.1 provides a 2 × 2 classification of these different types of learning. While this chapter is concerned only with the declarative side of this table, it would be useful to start with an illustration of each kind of learning to set a larger context for the discussion in this chapter:

1. *Fact learning*　We can form new memories in declarative memory. This is what many people mean when they talk about "memory." While

---

2. The conclusion of this study was that HM was able to learn the recursive strategy in the Tower of Hanoi. This conclusion has come in for reexamination (e.g., Xu and Corkin, 2001). While it seems that amnesiacs can get better at the Tower of Hanoi (perhaps by other strategies), the evidence seems pretty conclusive that HM is no longer able to learn the recursive strategy for Tower of Hanoi.

Table 3.1. ACT-R's Taxonomy of Learning

	Declarative	Procedural
Symbolic	Fact learning	Skill acquisition
Subsymbolic	Strengthening	Conditioning

one can extend "memory" to refer to the products of the other sorts of learning in table 3.1, this is the only kind of learning that results in new conscious memories. Since Tulving (1972), it has been common to distinguish between episodic memories such as what one ate for dinner last night or the paired associate "vanilla-7," and semantic memories such as "Lincoln was president of the United States" or "a canary is an animal." The former can be distinguished from the latter because we can retrieve the specific context in which they were learned. However, it is not a homogeneous set of things that get sorted into the semantic category by this distinction. Items such as the Lincoln fact are probably not really any different than the paired-associate fact. The Lincoln fact is just a three-term association between Lincoln, president, and the United States, while the vanilla-7 "fact" is also a three-term association between vanilla, 7, and an experimental context. Both were explicitly learned, one in a classroom and one in a laboratory. The difference is that the Lincoln fact has been encountered in so many contexts that we no longer have access to the context in which it was specifically learned. They both belong in declarative memory. However, other items, such as the canary fact, may not reflect any declarative memory we have ever formed but rather perceptual, categorical, and inferential abilities to recognize and reason about objects.

2. *Strengthening*   In addition to acquiring new declarative memories, one can make them more available by mere exposure. My favorite example is the study of insight performed by Kaplan (1989). I recounted one of my own experiences in this experiment in my textbook (Anderson, 2005b, p. 187). Here I tell the story of another member of our department at Carnegie Mellon University. We all were given a set of riddles and were able to solve some but not others. One of the riddles my colleague was stuck on was the following: "What can go up a chimney down but can't go down a chimney up?" We were then given a couple of weeks to try to solve these. During that time, this participant

received a mistaken phone call from a woman[3] who asked him to bring home the umbrella she had left in his office. After establishing that she had the wrong number and they did not know each other, they hung up and that was that. Shortly afterward, he went back to the riddle and came up with the answer: an umbrella. He was quite unaware of the role of the telephone call in his solution. However, the statistics in Kaplan's thesis, based on a number of faculty members and a number of incidents, established a causal relationship. None of the faculty members was aware of the manipulation; rather, we credited our solutions to our own cleverness.

3. *Skill acquisition*   A different kind of learning involves the acquisition of new procedures (production rules in ACT-R). A good example in my case is typing. I am a fairly skilled touch typist who can hit the keys without looking (I have to, because the letters on the keys of my keyboard have been erased by repeated striking). Consciously, I have no idea where the keys are on the keyboard. I do remember reproducing a keyboard as an exercise in high school, but I have long since forgotten where the keys are. Thus, I have acquired typing procedures that allow me to display this knowledge without any conscious access. Indeed, if I try to think of where the keys are or what keys I am striking, my typing falls apart. I have to take a deep breath, think about the message I want to convey, and get going again. This intrusion of conscious access on performance is reported by players of many sports (e.g., don't think about your golf swing). However, it is not just true for motor skills—try thinking about the syntactic rules you are using while speaking.

4. *Conditioning*   With experience, we can come to learn that certain actions are more effective in certain situations. Conditioning is generally regarded as the most ubiquitous version of learning.[4] Research on it goes all the way back to Pavlov's conditioning experiments, where dogs learned to salivate to a bell that signaled food (for a review, see Anderson, 2000). Humans are certainly capable of conditioning, and in many cases they exhibit conditioning behavior that is indistinguishable from that of

---

3. Who was actually an accomplice of Kaplan.
4. I would not want to suggest that everything that is called conditioning involves production rules or cognitive procedures in any sense. This is particularly apparent when we look at nonmammalian conditioning, as in the sea slug *Aplysia*.

other mammals. Indeed, conditioning has been established in many non-vertebrates. For instance, the *Aplysia* (a sea slug) can learn to withdraw its gill in response to touch if that touch has been associated with shock (Carew et al., 1983). Conditioning can be found so widely throughout the animal kingdom because it does not require any capacity to form new declarative or procedural memories; it requires only that there already be a response tendency that can be strengthened. In the case of the *Aplysia*, it already has a weak tendency to withdraw its gill in response to touch; conditioning just strengthens this tendency. Conditioning can take much more refined forms in humans thanks to their acquired skills. For instance, Best et al. (1998; see also Reder & Schunn, 1999) showed how such unconscious learning helped participants make better choices about where to land planes in an air traffic controller task.

This chapter is about the declarative column in table 3.1 (chapter 4 is about the procedural column). I review the structural and functional constraints that shape the nature of declarative memory, and then explain how declarative memory works in response to these constraints. This chapter ends with a discussion of a set of empirical examples that illustrate how declarative memory works.

The Structure and Function of Declarative Memory

Like all aspects of cognitive architecture, declarative memory arises as the result of trying to achieve certain functions within the constraints of the brain. In the case of declarative memory, the constraint is that memories usually have to pass through a set of structures located in the medial temporal cortex.

The Medial-Temporal Structures

The hippocampus is a subcortical structure located in the medial temporal cortex. As figure 3.1 illustrates, it receives input from essentially the entire cortex and is connected bidirectionally back to most of the cortex, making it ideally situated to store snapshots of the cortex and reinstate them as needed. The surgery that resulted in HM's amnesia involved extensive removal of these structures to treat severe epilepsy. Other people who suffer damage to their hippocampus similarly have serious memory loss, Alzheimer's patients, for instance. Despite the importance of the general region, there is considerable uncertainty about the roles of the different parts of this region. For instance, some have argued that recognition memory is not supported by the hippocampus per se but rather by adjacent structures (e.g., Aggleton and Brown, 1999; Eichenbaum et al., 1994; Vargha-Khadem et al., 1997), while Zola and Squire (2000) argue that lesions restricted to the hippocampal region can result in recognition memory deficit.[5]

The general temporal-hippocampal region is a critical bottleneck in forming permanent declarative memories. In HM, information is unaffected before that bottleneck: he is capable of keeping track of the immediate facts that he is dealing with and appears relatively normal on first encounter. However, they do not get past that bottleneck: if his attention turns away from these facts and he comes back later (even a few minutes later), he has forgotten them. He can form almost no new declarative memories, and moreover, the 11 years of memories before his surgery were wiped away by the surgery.

The relevant hippocampal structures are not huge (and perhaps only a subset are involved in declarative memory).[6] Therefore, one might speculate that there is a nontrivial limit on what can be held in declarative memory. There have been a number of attempts to estimate the storage capacity of declarative memory (e.g., Treves and Rolls, 1994; Moll and Miikkulainen, 1997). While these attempts do not exactly agree on how the hippocampus works or what the exact limit is, they agree that it is limited in its ability to store information.

There are a number of reasons for the limit on the size of human declarative memory. One class of factors concerns the physical limits of

5. Despite all the evidence for the importance of the hippocampal and medial temporal structures, prefrontal structures are often more sensitive to memory manipulations in imaging studies. There were early speculations that the brain imaging was not able to detect hippocampal contributions (Buckner and Koutstaal, 1998; Fletcher et al., 1997), but there now have been a number of successful studies (Schacter and Wagner, 1999). Still, it appears that prefrontal regions are often more sensitive indicators of memory storage and retrieval, and we have focused on a left prefrontal region that seems to be quite sensitive (as in figures 1.8b and 2.12f). A general view is that prefrontal regions are involved in encoding and retrieval (Buckner, 2000) but that they are not the permanent repositories of declarative memories. Patients with hippocampal damage will show substantial activation in prefrontal areas, just like normal patients when they are trying to memorize material. However, this fails to result in permanent memory.

6. And there are suggestions that it increases in size for those who face high memories demands, such as taxi drivers who must remember a great many routes (Maguire et al., 2003).

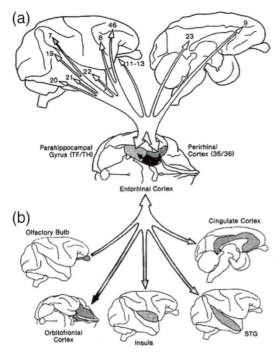

Figure 3.1. Bidirectional connections between the hippocampal system and other cortical areas. All areas go through the entorhinal cortex, which is an interface to the hippocampus. (a) Regions (frontal, temporal, and parietal) that connect with the parahippocampal gyrus and the perirhinal cortex, which in turn connect with the entorhinal cortex. (b) Areas that have direct connections with the entorhinal cortex. Reprinted from *Neural Models of Plasticity: Experimental and Theoretical Approaches*, Squire, L. R., Shimamura, A. P., & Amaral, D. G., Memory and the Hippocampus, pages 208–239. Copyright 1989 with permission from Elsevier.

size and metabolic costs, analogous to the factors that limit the size of memory on your computer. However, another class of factors arises from the nature of declarative memory itself. Because of its flexibility, the conditions for retrieving a particular declarative fact are not prespecified. The flip side of this is that when we make a query of our memory, the number of potentially relevant memories can be nearly unbounded. The cost of sorting through these could be considerable, so it makes sense to throw away those memories that are unlikely to be needed. Consider how overwhelmed we would be if we gave a typical query to Google and had to actually search through the thousands (or millions) of hits it can report. Google in this case is only useful if the first few dozen hits are relevant. For all intents and purposes, the millionth hit in this list has been forgotten (and my attempts to get Google to list those distant hits suggests Google doesn't have them).

Additional memories can interfere with one another. Catastrophic interference was one of the early landmark discoveries in the history of connectionism. McCloskey and Cohen (1989; see also Ratcliff, 1990) attempted to train a connectionist network to learn two successive lists of paired associates in what is called the A–B, A–C paradigm. In the first list, one might learn to respond to a stimulus such as vanilla (the A term) with 7 (the B term) and in the second list to vanilla (A again—the stimuli are the same in the two lists) with 4 (the C term). Humans have difficulty with these competing associations, and it takes more trials to learn both lists to criterion than if the lists do not share stimuli. The connectionist network McCloskey and Cohen were working with had much greater difficulty than humans, however, and the first list was completely overwritten by the second list. If these lists are intermixed and slowly learned, then conventional connectionist networks can eventually be brought to maintain the two sets of associations, but people learn quickly and without such intermixing of the two lists. This demonstration became a major reference point and stimulated a round of thinking about more complex connectionist systems. A class of theories arose (e.g., McClelland et al., 1995; Norman and O'Reilly, 2003; O'Reilly and Rudy, 2001) postulating two different learning systems. One performed the typical connectionist slow learning and had high generalization and interference; the other displayed fast learning but showed little generalization and interference. The former was associated with the cortex and the latter with the hippocampus and related structures.[7]

The fact that HM and other amnesiacs retain memories from earlier in their lives despite loss of the hippocampus region is evidence that it is not the only structure supporting declarative memory. According to McClelland et al. (1995), the hippocampus is special in that it can

---

7. However, this is not the only view. For instance, Gluck and Myers (1997) have argued that different hippocampal structures are responsible for both gradual pattern extraction and one-shot distinct learning.

learn quickly and accurately without interference. However, other brain structures can slowly acquire such memories through repeated training. Memories can slowly be transferred from the hippocampus to neocortical regions by rehearsal. Every time we recall a memory, this is another encoding opportunity for the slow learning mechanisms of the neocortex. However, the cortex can also be slowly trained by repeated exposure, without going through the hippocampus. Presumably, such direct neocortical learning is how HM was able to learn about people such as John F. Kennedy, who became famous after his surgery. Nonetheless, the nearly total anterograde amnesia (inability to form new memories) of such patients indicates that the hippocampus is the main path for acquisition of new declarative memories. In addition, their extensive retrograde amnesia (loss of memories before the event that produced the amnesia) indicates that it plays the primary role in supporting declarative memories for a long time after their initial acquisition.

While the hippocampus places serious limits on the capacity of declarative memory, it does not limit all learning, because much of what we learn is not stored in the hippocampus. According to the class of connectionist theories just noted, much of our knowledge is stored as general patterns rather than as specific facts in the neocortex. Another kind of knowledge is procedural knowledge, considered in chapter 4, which is associated with another subcortical structure, the basal ganglia.

There has been a debate about the involvement of the hippocampus in semantic memory. Vargha-Khadem et al. (1997) reported the cases of three children who suffered bilateral hippocampal damage early in their childhood and yet attained reasonable levels of language and factual knowledge. Despite their poor memory for day-to-day events, they still managed to attend mainstream schools. Eichenbaum (1997) suggested that this reflected the difference between the hippocampus and the parahippocampus,[8] which was not damaged in these patients. He suggested that the parahippocampus was sufficient for the encoding of semantic memories but that the hippocampus was required for the binding of episodic information. Squire and Zola (1998) argued that the acquisition of semantic memory might have been achieved through the residual episodic memory that these children had (they were not totally unable to

---

8. A cortical structure on the input path from many cortical regions to the hippocampus—see parahippocampal gyrus in figure 3.1.

recall episodic information). They also argued that, since we do not know how well these children would have done had they not suffered their injuries, it is impossible to judge how normal their semantic memory development is. As noted above, the category of semantic memory is a mixed bag of things. Certain things attributed to semantic memory (e.g., our ability to recognize a bird) may not depend on the hippocampus at all. Others (e.g., who is the mayor of New York City) probably do have at least some of their origins in episodic memory and would be more difficult to acquire in the presence of hippocampal damage.

Why Do We Have Declarative Memories?

In principle, the information we have in declarative memory could be stored procedurally. Consider the memory that Lincoln was the president of the United States. One might imagine a production rule to deliver this fact when needed, something like

> If the goal is to retrieve a president of the United States,
> Then return Lincoln as an answer.

As chapter 4 discusses, this is more efficient than retrieving a declarative memory. Rather than having to go through the steps of searching declarative memory, representing the results, and extracting an answer, this production rule just produces the answer.

Probably the reader has a sense of unease with the production rule for the Lincoln answer. It does not enable us to answer other questions about Lincoln's presidency, such as when he was president, and so provides no basis for answering questions such as "When was Lincoln president?" or "What was the famous proclamation that Lincoln signed?" However, one can propose other rules to retrieve information for these kinds of questions, as well. In the case of the Lincoln fact and the typical American's knowledge about Lincoln, it perhaps does not stretch credibility completely beyond belief that all such information could be stored in separate rules that produce answers to specific probes. This is basically the idea that the behaviorist John B. Watson (1930) had when he claimed memories were just habits (see box 3.1).

However, this kind of account of memory has fundamental problems, despite Watson's efforts to put a sensible face on this. To illustrate, consider the following memory that I once formed from my daily routine (I explain in the next subsection more of the context of forming this memory): I went

---

BOX 3.1 Memories Are Just Habits
Watson (1930)

What the man on the street ordinarily means by an exhibition of memory is what occurs in some such situation as this: An old friend comes to see him, after many years' absence. The moment he sees this friend, he says: "Upon my life! Addison Sims of Seattle! I haven't seen you since the World's Fair in Chicago. Do you remember the gay parties we used to have in the old Windmere Hotel? Do you remember the Midway? Do you remember," ad infinitum. The psychology of this process is so simple that it seems almost an insult to your intelligence to discuss it, and yet a good many of the behaviorists' kindly critics have said that behaviorism cannot adequately explain memory. Let us see if this is a fact.

When the man on the street originally made the acquaintance of Mr. Sims, he saw him and was told his name at the same time. Possibly he did not see him again until a week or two later. He had to be re-introduced. Again, when he saw Mr. Sims he heard his name. Then, shortly afterwards, the two men became friends and saw one another every day and became really acquainted—that is, formed verbal and manual habits towards one another and towards the same or similar situations. In other words, the man on the street became completely organized to react in many habit ways to Mr. Addison Sims. Finally, just the sight of the man, even after months of absence, would call out not only the old verbal habits, but many other types of bodily and visceral responses.

. . . .

By "memory," then, we mean nothing except the fact that when we meet a stimulus again after an absence, we do the old habitual thing (say the old words and show the old visceral—emotional—behavior) that we learned to do when we were in the presence of that stimulus in the first place (pp. 235–237).

---

to Starbucks on the way to work and ordered a coffee and summer cobbler. I remembered this event 24 hours later after not thinking about it in the interim, which confirms that it was a successful example of one-shot learning. Consider some of the different memory probes that I might have encountered that would have resulted in retrieving this memory:

I get food poisoning and have to identify what I ate.
The doctor asks me how much caffeine I had that day.
I wonder why I am gaining weight.
Someone asks me where I got that terrific cobbler.

My wife asks me why I took so long to get to work.
I can't find my wallet and need to remember where I might
    have lost it.

And so on—you get the picture. Each of these probes would require a different rule because they represent a different condition under which I would need to retrieve the memory. There is no way I could have established production rules or habits to reproduce the memory to all of these probes. Rather, what I acquired was a memory that was lying in wait, ready to jump in should any associated prompt appear. This flexibility of access to our own past is a critical feature of our overall intellectual flexibility as humans. Essentially, given a wide variety of prompts, we can retrieve the memory without having to preprogram ourselves to retrieve the memory to any specific prompt. This flexibility of access is why these memories are available for declarative report and conscious reflection: because we can access the memories for any purpose, we can access them for reporting and reflecting. In essence, flexibility of access is what makes a memory declarative.

The Triage of Memories

This Starbuck's memory was part of an exercise that I performed one day when I was curious about my memory. I challenged myself to write down 25 things that I could distinctly remember (they were not just part of my daily routine) from the previous day between getting up and arriving at work. I wrote down these 25 events and stored them away in a file on my computer that I did not go back to for more than a year. With respect to the Starbuck's memory above, I can report that I had completely forgotten it when I found it on this list a year later. The only thing on that list that I think I remember is a report on the impact of the Swiftboat ads on Kerry's poll numbers that had been on the morning newscast.[9] Looking over the 24 other memories I wrote down, I can report that they were all forgotten at no loss to me. While those memories were still lying in wait a day later on the off chance that they should prove critical, they eventually lost their relevance and were lost from my memory—who would want to remember that exact Starbuck's event a year later? Declarative memory,

9. A significant episode in the 2004 American presidential election.

faced with limited capacity, is in effect constantly discarding memories that have outlived their usefulness.[10]

As discussed in chapter 1, Lael Schooler and I studied the likelihood that a memory would be needed again and treated this as a measure of the memory's usefulness.[11] This research served as a guide for the design of the subsymbolic level of ACT-R's declarative memory. As illustrated in figure 1.4a, if a memory has not been needed for a while, it becomes very unlikely that it will be needed in the future. In particular, we showed that there was a power-function relationship between how likely a memory would be needed on a particular day and how long it had been (t) since it was last used:

Odds needed = At^{-d}

where A is a scaling constant and d is the decay rate. This power relationship implies a linear relationship between the dependent variable (odds of use on current day) and the independent variable (time since last use) after the measures have been log transformed:

Log(odds) = $\log(A) - d\log(t)$

This function just deals with the time since an item has been last used. Anderson and Schooler (1991) found that each time an item appeared, it added an increment to the odds that the item would appear again and that these increments all decayed away according to a power function. Thus, if an item has occurred n times, its odds of appearing again is

$$\text{Odds} = \sum_{k=1}^{n} At_k^{-d},$$

where t_k is the time since the kth occurrence. This equation turns out to predict a wide variety of effects in human memory.[12] So, for instance, it

10. Actually, as described further below, ACT-R adopts a more continuous solution to this, just as the brain must. Memories are not suddenly deleted but rather are gradually weakened. A weak memory that cannot be retrieved in a neutral context might be retrieved if given the appropriate associative prompt. Eventually the memory cannot be recalled at all and is effectively deleted.

11. The discussion that follows ignores the inherent importance of the memory, and perhaps this is why the Swiftboat memory stuck with me.

12. Its most notable failing is that it does not predict the spacing effect that closely presented items are forgotten more rapidly than widely spaced items. Interestingly, this function also fails to describe the environment, which also shows a spacing effect (Anderson and Schooler, 1991). Pavlik and Anderson (2005) followed up a suggestion in Anderson and Schooler with a successful model of spacing effects in the environment and in memory.

predicts that both the retention function (memory performance as a function of delay) and the learning function (memory performance as a function of practice) have the shape of power functions.[13] It thus seems that memory makes information available in proportion to how likely it is to be useful.

Combining Context and Past History

The equations above are examples of how the past history of use of a memory predicts the odds that the memory will be needed. However, they ignore the context of the current situation. My favorite example of this involves the distinction between my wife's name and my locker combination. My wife's name is probably the declarative memory I most often need to recall, while my locker combination is used with relatively low frequency. That fact notwithstanding, when I am in the locker room, my locker combination is more likely to be needed than my wife's name. It would be nice if my cognitive architecture adjusted the availability of my memories as a function of context and made it easier to retrieve my locker combination in that context.

Schooler and Anderson (1997) explored how context and past history of use combine. Schooler (1993) found that, in some contexts, one word strongly predicted the likelihood that another word would occur. For instance, in the period of time he investigated, the word "AIDS" occurred in the *New York Times* headlines on only about 2% of the days. However, during that time, if the word "virus" also appeared in the headlines, the probability of "AIDS" appearing jumped to 75%. As another example, in caregiver speech to children, the word "play" only occurred in about 1% of the utterances. However, if the word "game" also occurred in that sentence, the probability jumped to 41%. These examples illustrate the fact that the appearance of certain items in the environment make it much more likely we will be asked to remember other items.

Schooler was interested in how this factor of environmental context interacted with the factor of time since the word last occurred. Figure 3.2 shows the relationship for the *New York Times* database and the caregiver

13. There is considerable discussion in the literature as to whether the memory functions are exactly power functions or whether they correspond better to some other function (e.g., Delaney et al., 1998; Heathcote et al., 2000; Myung et al., 2000; Rickard, 1997; Rubin et al., 1999). The argument Schooler and I developed was not that the memory or the environment functions were exactly power functions. Rather, our argument was that whatever the environmental function was, it would be mirrored in memory.

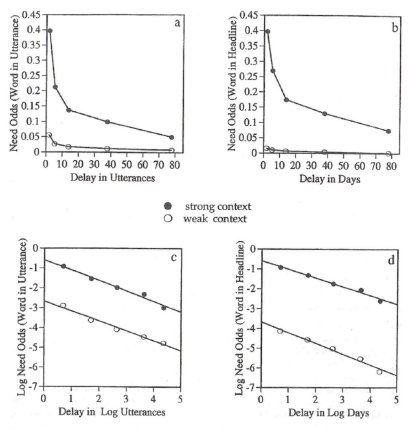

Figure 3.2. Environmental recency curves from the analysis of the CHILDES (a database of children language) and *New York Times* databases. The left column shows the odds of a word being mentioned in an utterance as a function of the number of intervening utterances since it was last mentioned and whether the utterance included a strong associate (strong context) or did not (weak context). The right column shows the odds of a word being included in a particular headline as a function of the number of days since the word was last included and whether the headline included a strong associate. Reprinted from Schooler & Anderson (1997) with permission from Elsevier.

speech database. Parts (a) and (b) plot odds against delay for cases where there is a high associate (odds of "AIDS" given "virus") and cases where there is not a high associate. They show standard negatively accelerated retention curves for the high associate case and what appears to be a much weaker retention effect for the low associate case. However, parts (c) and (d) show what these relationships are like after a log transforma-

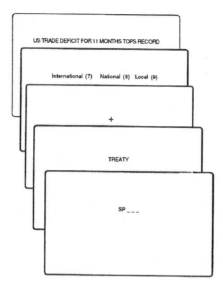

Figure 3.3. The structure of the experiment in Schooler and Anderson (1997). Reprinted from Schooler & Anderson (1997) with permission from Elsevier.

tion of both axes. This reveals a linear relationship that is a sign of a power function. Also, the lines are basically parallel, and the effect of a high associate is just to raise the intercept of the function.

Schooler explored the issue of whether this relationship was also true of human memory. Figure 3.3 illustrates one of his experiments. Participants saw a series of headlines and had to classify them as international, national, or local (this task was just to guarantee their attention). After each headline they performed the task of interest: a primed completion task in which first a prime word ("treaty" in figure 3.3) would appear and then a word fragment that they had to complete with a word from a past headline. In the case in figure 3.3, the fragment is "SP – – –," and it should be completed as "Spain." (During the period of time Schooler investigated, there was a statistical association between treaty and Spain in *New York Times* headlines.)

Schooler manipulated both the delay from that past headline and whether the prime and the word were associated. Figure 3.4 shows the results of one of his experiments in terms of odds that the participant could successfully complete the prime, and the mean time to complete if successful. Both quantities yielded linear parallel functions on log-log scales just like the environmental statistics. This was a particularly signifi-

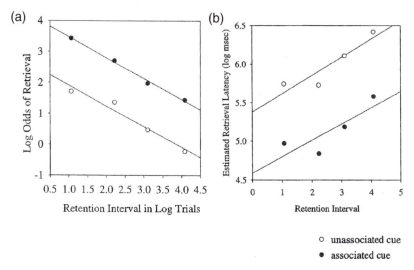

Figure 3.4. Results from Schooler and Anderson (1997): (a) log odds of completing a word fragment as a function of log retention interval; (b) log latency to complete a word fragment as a function of log retention interval.

cant test of the rational analysis of memory because a relationship in the environment was used to make a prediction about human memory that had not yet been tested in the experimental literature. It indicates once again that human memory reflects the statistics of the environment.

In summary, the function of declarative memory is to make knowledge available in a form that can be used for a wide variety of purposes. There are limits on the amount of information that can be maintained in this form and usefully retrieved. Therefore, the declarative system performs a triage on the memories, devoting its limited resources to those that are most likely to be needed. The next section considers how the declarative memory system achieves this triage and how it functions in the overall cognitive architecture.

Declarative Memory in a Cognitive Architecture

The human memory system operates in a fully functioning cognitive architecture that actually does tasks. Many theories of memory treat memory as though the end goal of the system were to retrieve memories. However, that is rarely the case outside of the memory laboratory. Almost every task involves declarative memory, and in almost all of these tasks the declarative memory module has to interact in complex ways with other modules. Chapter 1 demonstrated this with the algebra model (involving retrieving memories of instructions and arithmetic facts) and chapter 2 with the driving model (involving retrieval of information about where other cars were in various lanes). A serious constraint on the declarative system is that it has to function correctly in these tasks as well as match the data from "pure memory" experiments. Newell (1992) complained that the current theories of memory did not worry about whether the theories would work in a full system: "Why don't psychologists address it or recognize that there might be a genuine scientific conundrum here, on which the conclusion could be that the existing models are not right..." (p. 473).

Figure 2.2 illustrated the modular structure of the mind, in which the declarative module essentially allows the system to perceive its past just as the visual module allows the system to perceive its current environment. The system's past is basically the chunks that existed in the buffers associated with the various modules; these chunks represent the only part of its information-processing of which it was ever aware. These chunks are all deposited in declarative memory (figure 3.1 illustrates the mapping of cortical regions to the hippocampus). Of course, just because a chunk is deposited in declarative memory does not mean that it will be retrieved. This section focuses on the subsymbolic level in the declarative system that determines the availability of individual memories.

The Subsymbolic Level: Activations and Associative Strengths

Chunks in declarative memory have activation values that determine the speed and success of their retrieval. The activation of a chunk both reflects its inherent strength, called base-level activation, and its strengths of association to elements in the current context. Formally, this is expressed by what is called the activation equation:

$$A_i = B_i + \sum_{j \in C} W_j S_{ji}$$

where A_i is the activation of chunk i; C is the context, which is defined as the set of the elements j currently in the buffers; B_i is the base-level activation of chunk i; W_j is an attentional weighting given to element j in the context; and S_{ji} is the strength of association between element j and chunk i.

This is a standard neural activation equation where the activation of some neural element i is determined by its base-level activation and the activation it receives from input elements j. Figure 3.5 shows a network

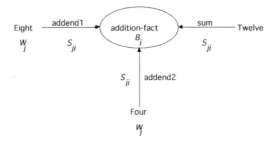

Figure 3.5. A representation of a chunk with its subsymbolic quantities.

interpretation of this equation. It represents the memory for 8 + 4 = 12 by a central node connected to its elements. That node has some relatively stable base-level activation B_i. It also receives activation from the context elements j according the strengths of association S_{ji} between these elements and the memory.[14]

The Anderson and Schooler (1991) analysis described above explains what the memory system accomplishes by performing this neural computation: it makes most available those memories most likely to be needed. The log odds of needing a memory can be considered a sum of a quantity that reflected the past history of that memory and context (e.g., figure 3.2, c and d). In Bayesian terms, this can be rendered by the following formula:

$$\text{Log}[\text{posterior}(i|C)] = \log[\text{prior}(i)] + \sum_{j \in C} \log[\text{likelihood}(j|i)],$$

where *posterior*(i|C) is the posterior odds that memory i will be needed in context C, *prior*(i) is the prior odds that memory i will be needed based on factors such as recency and frequency (in figure 3.2, it reflects

14. Those who work with the ACT-R theory will note that this formulation does not include a random noise component or a partial matching component. With respect to the random noise component, I have deleted it merely for simplicity of exposition, and its influence will be partly reflected in the retrieval probability equation in table 3.2. With respect to partial matching, I have come to the conclusion that the current ACT-R simulation errs in treating associative spread and partial matching as independent sources of information. When an element just appears in a buffer, it serves as a general bottom-up associative prime to memory. When it appears as part of a memory probe, it is a top-down constraint on recall, as in the fan experiments to be described. This top-down role should supersede the evidence associated with its appearance in a buffer, not be treated as additional information. Thus, for purposes of the activation equation, the definition of S_{ji} depends on whether the j is a bottom-up cue or a top-down constraint. In actual running models, this is essentially how it is treated, in that the models typically use either the bottom-up information or top-down information and do not try to add them together.

how long it was since the memory was used), and *likelihood(j|i)* is the likelihood ratio that element j would be part of the context given that i is needed (in figure 3.2 it reflects the strength of association to the current context). The activation equation basically performs this calculation where the activation A_i is *log[posterior(i|C)]*, the base-level activation B_i is *log[prior(i)]*, and the product $W_j S_{ji}$ corresponds to *log[likelihood(j|i)]*.

Table 3.2 gives the activation equation and the other basic ACT-R equations for the subsymbolic level of declarative memory. The base-level learning equation specifies how the activation varies with the past history of usage of the chunk. It is based directly on the work in Anderson and Schooler (1991) studying how the pattern of past occurrences of an item predicts the need to retrieve it. In this equation, t_k is the time since the *k*th practice of an item. Each presentation has an impact that decays as a power function (producing the power law of forgetting), and different presentations add up (producing the power law of practice; see Anderson et al., 1999). In the ACT-R community, 0.5 has emerged as the default value for the decay parameter d over a large range of applications, although slightly lower values have appeared in some attempts to model very long-term memory (e.g., Pavlik and Anderson, 2005). This base-level learning equation has been the most successfully and frequently used part of the ACT-R subsymbolic level. Pavlik and Anderson (2005) describe how this equation and elaborations on it reflect the changes produced by long-term potentiation, which is thought of as the major mechanism of learning in the hippocampus.

Table 3.2.   ACT-R Equations Involving Activation

Name	Equation
Activation equation	$A_i = B_i + \sum_{j \in C} W_j S_{ji}$
Base-level learning equation	$B_i = \ln\left(\sum_{k=1}^{n} t_k^{-d}\right)$
Attentional weighting equation	$W_j = W / n$
Associative strength equation	$S_{ji} \approx \ln(prob(i \mid j) / prob(i))$
Retrieval time equation	$Time = Fe^{-A_i}$
Retrieval probability equation	$Prob = 1/(1 + e^{-(A_i - \tau)/s})$

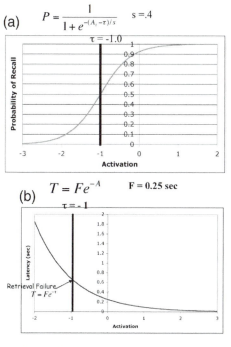

Figure 3.6. (a) The relationship between activation and probability of recall;
(b) the relationship between activation and latency of recall.

As for the associative components (the W_j S_{ji} values), the attentional
weighting equation sets the W_j to W/n, where n is the number of sources
of activation.[15] W is a parameter that is thought to reflect individual differences in the ability to make memory retrieval context sensitive (e.g.,
Daily et al., 2001). As specified in the associative strength equation, the S_{ji}
values reflect how much the presence of j makes i more probable. There
have been a number of ideas about how experience sets these quantities
(e.g., Anderson and Lebiere, 1998; Anderson, Bothell et al., 2004; Pirolli,
2005). In ACT-R they are currently set by default to reflect the fan (the
number of links coming out of each term) of the j, as explained in the
next section.

Figure 3.6 illustrates the retrieval probability equation (part a) and
the retrieval time equation (part b) for typical parameters for the ACT-R

15. The division by n is similar in character to such constraints as setting the sum of
the attentional weights in the generalized context model (Nosofsky, 1986) to 1.

theory.[16] These behave sensibly, with increasing activation resulting in increased probability of recall and decreased latency. As illustrated in figure 3.6a, there is a threshold activation, τ, below which memories will not be retrieved. Because there is random noise in activation values (related to the parameter s), sometimes chunks will fall above the threshold and other times they will fall below. Figure 3.6b illustrates the exponential relationship between the activation values and the time it takes to retrieve a memory. Appendix 3.1 describes the neural mechanisms that might be producing this relationship. Basically, we imagine a parallel process by which the various chunks compete according to their activation values, and one is selected and put in the declarative buffer.

The equations in table 3.2 provide a formalization of a mechanism that produces the relationships that Anderson and Schooler (1991) noted; the probability and speed of retrieval vary with the likelihood a memory will be needed (e.g., figure 3.4). The next four sections describe examples of how these equations play out in various tasks.

A Model for a Fan Experiment: Demonstrating
the Activation Processes

The first experiment in Pirolli and Anderson (1985) illustrates the contributions of both base-level activations (B_i) and associative strengths (S_{ji}) to the retrieval process.[17] This is one example of the many fan experiments (for a review, see Anderson and Reder, 1999) performed to create situations where cues to memory vary in their associative strength (the S_{ji}). Participants in the Pirolli and Anderson experiment memorized two types of sentences. One type involved eight sentences such as

The lawyer liked the doctor
The soldier kicked the sailor

where each term ("lawyer," "liked," "sailor," etc.) occurred in just a single sentence. The other type involved eight sentences such as

16. If the reader interprets activation as something like the rate of firing of neurons, it would be puzzling to see negative activation values in figure 3.6. However, these activation quantities are more abstract. As in appendix 3.1, they might be conceived of as the input that drives the actual neural firing rates (in which case negative values just mean the firing rate goes below base line).

17. See Anderson, Bothell et al. (2004) for a similar fit to the second experiment in this report.

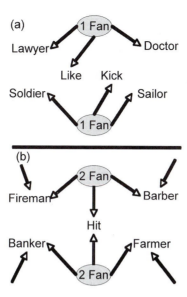

Figure 3.7. A graphical representation of two sentences in the
one-fan condition (a) and the
two-fan condition (b).

The fireman hit the barber
The fireman thanked the chef
The banker hit the farmer
The sailor touched the barber

where each term ("fireman," "hit," "barber") occurred in two sentences.[18] The first set defined the one-fan condition, and the second the two-fan condition. Figure 3.7 illustrates the basic structure being created in memory. The term "fan" refers to the number of links coming out of each term; increasing fan will decrease the strength of association, S_{ji}, between the term and the fact. This is because when a term is associated with more facts, its appearance becomes a poorer predictor of any particular fact.

After memorizing the material, the participants were asked to recognize sentences they had studied and reject foils that they had not studied but were recombinations of the same words (e.g., "The lawyer liked the

18. This is not the complete set of eight: only the first sentence has all of its items repeated in four sentences shown; the other sentences would have their items repeated in the four sentences not shown.

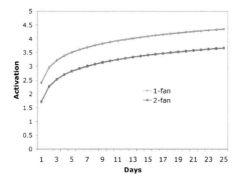

Figure 3.8. Activation of the chunks in Pirolli and Anderson (1985) as a function of fan and practice.

sailor" or "The banker hit the chef"). Interest focused on how quickly they could make these judgments, providing a measure of how available the individual facts were. Participants practiced recognizing the same set of sentences for 25 days. This practice should increase the base-level activation, B_i, of the particular facts.

The ACT-R theory allows one to determine the activations on each day of the experiment for both conditions.[19] Figure 3.8 illustrates the growth in activation.[20] The prediction is for two parallel activation functions that increase with practice. The curves in figure 3.8 reflect parameter-free

19. According to the associative strength equation (table 3.2), the strength of association, S_{ji}, from a term j to a fact i is determined by the ratio of the base probability of the fact to the conditional probability of the fact given the term. There were 16 target facts in all. In addition, 16 foils were mixed in with each testing of 16 targets, so any fact occurred with base probability 1/32. If a concept such as doctor was presented, the conditional probability of a fact associated with that concept was 0.50 in the one-fan case (because half the time it was a foil) and 0.25 in the two-fan case (two targets and two foils per block). Thus, according to the associative strength equation, the strengths of associations were $\ln[(1/2)/(1/32)] = \ln(16)$ for one-fan facts and $\ln[(1/4)/(1/32)] = \ln(8)$ for the two-fan facts. Because each of the sources has the same fan and the attentional weighting equation with $W = 1$ implies a 1/3 weighting for the activations from the subject, verb, and object, this means that the total associative activation is either $\ln(16)$ or $\ln(8)$. The base-level learning equation can be shown to imply that the base-level activation, B_i, increases as a function $(1 - d)*\ln(\text{days})$. The typical value of the decay rate d is 0.5. Therefore, the equations in table 3.2 imply that activation will be $0.5[\ln(\text{days})] + \ln(16)$ in the one-fan condition and $0.5[\ln(\text{days})] + \ln(8)$ in the two-fan condition.

20. Constants can be added to these activation values, but these complications do not change the basic predictions to follow. With respect to a different detail, days are represented as half-days since we are interested in the average (halfway) performance during the day. Thus, for day n the value $n - 0.5$ is used in the calculation of the predicted activation.

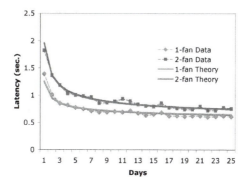

Figure 3.9. Time to recognize sentences in Pirolli and Anderson (1985) as a function of fan and practice. Solid curves reflect predictions of the ACT-R model.

predictions of the theory. Thus, for instance, the theory predicts that the average activation in the last five days of the two-fan condition will be close to the average activation in days 4–8 of the one-fan condition.

One cannot observe activations, but this experiment collected latencies that reflect the activations (figure 3.6b); these latencies are displayed in figure 3.9. Indeed, the average latencies are the same (0.76 sec) between the last five days of the two-fan condition and days 4–8 of the one-fan condition. This figure also shows the predicted latencies for this experiment. Obtaining predictions from the activation functions in figure 3.8 requires the estimation of an intercept, to reflect encoding and response times, and a latency scale parameter (F in the retrieval time equation). The intercept parameter was estimated at 0.55 s and the scale at 8.00 s. Because of the nonlinear mapping of activation onto latency (figure 3.6b), practice also reduces the absolute size of the fan effect, but the effect remains quite significant even after 25 days of practice. The predictions of the absolute times depend on the intercept and latency scale parameters, but the theory predicts, without parameter estimation, the basic pattern of results in this experiment. This means that the correlation between theory and data tests the parameter-free predictions of the theory; that correlation is 0.983.

The theory is that the results in figure 3.9 occur because memory is responding to two statistical effects in the environment:

1. The more often a memory is retrieved, the more likely it is to be retrieved in the future. This produces the practice effect and is reflected in the base-level activations of the ACT-R theory.

Table 3.3.   Materials from Peterson and Potts (1982)

Examples of Learned Facts	
1 fact studied	Julius Caesar was left-handed.
4 facts studied	Beethoven never married.
	Beethoven suffered from syphilis.
	Beethoven was a very poor student.
	Beethoven died of pneumonia.
Examples of Test Items	
Known Facts	
0 facts studied	Thomas Edison was an inventor.
1 fact studied	Julius Caesar was murdered.
4 facts studied	Beethoven was a musician.
Learned Facts	
1 fact studied	Julius Caesar was left-handed.
4 facts studied	Beethoven never married.
False Facts	
0 facts studied	Thomas Edison was a congressman.
1 fact studied	Julius Caesar was a printer.
4 facts studied	Beethoven was an exceptional athlete.

2. The more memories associated with a particular cue, the worse a predictor it is of any particular memory. This produces the fan effect and is reflected in the strengths of association in the ACT-R theory.

If this analysis is correct, these results should not be restricted to artificial laboratory material such as those in this experiment but should pervade all of our memories.

Practice and fan effects do extend to memories created outside of the laboratory. Table 3.3 shows examples of material from Peterson and Potts (1982). Participants studied one or four facts that they did not previously know about famous historical figures (but that were true[21]), such as that Julius Caesar was left-handed. They were then tested on memory for three kinds of facts illustrated in table 3.3:

21. Or, in the case of the Beethoven syphilis fact, believed to be true at the time.

1. *Known facts* that they knew before the experiment
2. *Learned facts* that they had learned as part of the experiment
3. *False facts* that they had not learned and that should be recognizable as very unlikely.

Participants had to recognize as true the first two categories of facts and reject as false the third category of facts. Participants were tested two weeks later about historical figures for whom they had not learned any experimental facts, about figures for whom they had learned one fact, and about figures for whom they had learned four facts. The speed with which they could judge the known facts and the studied facts is shown in figure 3.10. This figure shows the results separately for facts that they knew before the experiment and facts learned in the experiment. The prior facts are recognized much faster, reflecting the greater practice and base-level activation of the prior facts. The number of facts that had been learned in the experiment affects both new and prior facts, reflecting the fan effect on strengths of association.

From the perspective of the task facing declarative memory—making most available those facts that are most likely to be useful—these results make perfect sense. The already known facts have been used many times in the past, and at delay of two weeks they are likely the ones needed, so

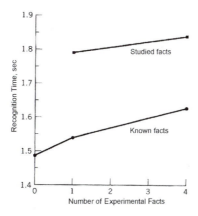

Figure 3.10. Data from Peterson and Potts (1982): time to recognize newly learned facts and facts already known as a function of the number of facts learned about a person in the experiment.

the base-level activation works to make them most active. On the other hand, the more things one knows about an individual, the less likely any one fact will be, so they cannot be all made as active. The activation equations in table 3.2 capture these relationships.

Fan Effects in the Prefrontal Cortex

As noted in chapters 1 and 2, our laboratory has used a predefined prefrontal region to track retrieval from declarative memory. This region is close to areas that other researchers have also found strongly implicated in memory encoding. For instance, areas close to our prefrontal regions were found in a pair of landmark experiments that appeared back to back in the same issue of *Science* magazine: Wagner et al. (1998) investigated memory for words, and Brewer et al. (1998) studied memory for pictures. In both cases, participants remembered some of the items and forgot others. Using fMRI (functional magnet resonance imagery) measures of the hemodynamic response, these researchers contrasted the BOLD (blood oxygen level–dependent) response at the time of study for those items that were subsequently remembered and those that were subsequently forgotten. Wagner et al. found that a left prefrontal region was predictive of memory for words, whereas Brewer et al. found that a right prefrontal region was predictive of memory for pictures. Figure 3.11a shows the results for words; figure 3.11b, the results for pictures. In both cases, the rise in the hemodynamic response is plotted as a function of time from stimulus presentation. In both cases, remembered items produced a greater BOLD response in the prefrontal regions, supporting the conclusion that the prefrontal region is indeed involved in storing a memory successfully. A striking feature of these two studies is that the left and right prefrontal regions are almost exact homologues of one another and are within a centimeter of the predefined prefrontal regions used in our laboratory.

As developed in chapters 1 and 2 (especially appendix 2.1), the basic assumption underlying our fMRI work is that the longer a module is active, the more metabolic energy is spent and the stronger the fMRI signal is. Thus, the interpretation of the Wagner et al. and Brewer et al. results is that participants remembered more on those trials where they worked longer at encoding the memory. While this might be a fairly obvious interpretation of the Wagner and Brewer encoding results, when it comes to retrieval the consequences of this interpretation might be a little surprising. The greater the activation of a memory, the less time

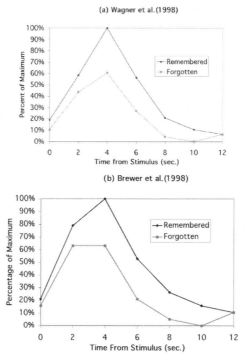

Figure 3.11. The results of two experiments using a subsequent memory manipulation: (a) Wagner et al. (1998) show difference between remembered and forgotten words in the left prefrontal cortex; (b) Brewer et al. (1998) show difference between remembered and forgotten pictures in the right prefrontal cortex.

it will take to retrieve it. Therefore, the prediction is that greater activation will map onto *weaker* fMRI response, in contrast to the naive assumption that more activation would mean a stronger response. This naive assumption is based on the idea that greater metabolic expenditure would be required to support the greater activation of the target memory. However, even if this were true, the cells corresponding to the target memory are only a tiny fraction of the total cells in the region. If the BOLD signal reflected summed responding of all cells, there is no reason to expect it would be greater just because a few cells are more active. What is important is how long that region must work before it produces the target memory.

The fan paradigm is an excellent choice to test out this analysis of the BOLD response. Since greater fan results in decreased activation, the prediction is that higher fan will result in a stronger fMRI response. Sohn et al. (2003, 2005) confirmed this prediction. These researchers used a variant of the fan paradigm used by Pirolli and Anderson (1985) that involved person-location sentences such as "The lawyer is in the park." They contrasted cases where the fans of the person and location were low (resulting in high activation) with cases where the fans were high (resulting in low activation).

Figure 3.12 illustrates the relevant module activity in the case of high fan versus low fan. That figure indicates that the average response time was 1,200 ms in the case of low fan and 1,350 ms in the case of high fan. In both cases, the system goes through the following sequence of stages:

1. Encoding the person and location, which involves developing a representation in the imaginal module (parietal region)
2. Retrieving the memory trace (prefrontal region)
3. Updating of the representation to note if it matches the trace (parietal region)
4. Programming a manual finger press to indicate the decision (motor region)

The only thing that differs is the length of the retrieval step. This leads to the prediction that the BOLD response should vary with fan in the prefrontal region, but not in parietal or motor regions that reflect the other modules. This prediction is particularly interesting for the parietal region because our parietal region is close to (but not identical with) regions that have been implicated in episodic memory (Wagner et al., 2005). Nonetheless, we assume that our region is involved in problem representation and will not show fan effects.

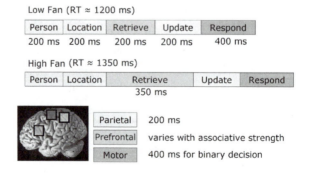

Figure 3.12. Activity of the imaginal, declarative, and manual modules during the retrieval of low and high fan facts in Sohn et al. (2004).

Given the verbal nature of the material and the fact that the participants were responding with their right hands, it made sense to look at left regions. Figure 3.13 shows the results obtained in the left parietal, prefrontal, and motor regions. The response first rises from baseline in the parietal (part a), then in the prefrontal (part b), and finally in the motor (part c). This corresponds to the order in which they should be active (figure 3.12). As predicted, there is an effect of fan only in the

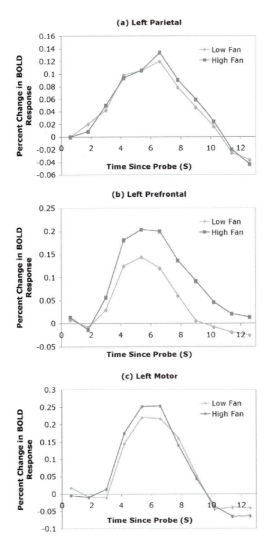

Figure 3.13. BOLD response to low- and high-fan facts in left parietal (a), left prefrontal (b), and left motor (c) regions.

prefrontal region. Moreover, the size of the effect is basically what would be predicted from the latency analysis in figure 3.12. The retrieval time for the high fan items is 350 ms, while it is 200 ms for the low-fan items. The ratio of high times to low is 1.75. The area under the high-fan curve in figure 3.13b is 0.87%, while it is 0.49% for the low-fan curve. This ratio of high to low is 1.78. Our basic theory of the BOLD response implies that it should be proportional to the time a module is active.

It is worth emphasizing that the fMRI BOLD signal during retrieval gives an inverse measure of memory activation: a greater BOLD response reflects an item with lower activation. Basically, when the BOLD signal is greater at retrieval, memory has lost the bet that its activation levels have placed, and it is having to pay a higher metabolic cost to retrieve an unexpected memory.[22]

Instance-Based Decisions and Actions

The two previous examples are typical laboratory tasks that focus directly on memory. While they are the sorts of experiments one wants to perform to test specific assumptions of a theory, psychology's focus on such tasks produces a rather distorted picture of what memory is about. Memory is involved in almost everything we do, but most of the time we think of ourselves not as remembering but rather as doing something else. If one goes to the ACT-R website (act-r.psy.cmu.edu), one will find that the majority of the models are not overtly about memory. Nonetheless, these models make use of declarative memory because declarative memory both carries the general knowledge required to do a task and also maintains some of the information needed locally in the performance of the task.

This section is concerned with a particular kind of situation in which memory plays a role both important and easy to understand. When we have to make a decision, we often call on our memory for similar situations in the past. For instance, when I go downtown in Pittsburgh to park for a Steelers game, I call on memories about where I have parked for past Steelers games or perhaps other events in the area. Upon recalling a particular situation, I decide if I was happy with the outcome (e.g., whether I got caught in a huge line coming out of the garage). If it passes that

22. Of course, the concepts of "losing the bet" and "unexpected" are relative. Within the experiment, the system is probably betting highly on all experimental memories relative to others and expects that these are the memories that are likely to be needed.

threshold, I ask whether there is any reason to suppose the same outcome won't hold again. If the remembered action passes muster, I act on it; if it does not, I go back and retrieve another memory and see if it is better. If I act on a memory, I might use the memory to adjust my behavior a little— for instance, choosing a different location to park closer to the exit.

Note that I am relying on memories rather than reasoning on the basis of general principles. In some cases this is because I have no principles to reason from. In other cases, it is just easier to recall and act. In still other cases, I trust past experiences more than the principles. A number of people have noted this instance-based reasoning and raised it to a theoretical proposal. Logan (1988) proposed his instance theory of automatization and argued that learning ubiquitously moved from an algorithmic (principles) process to a simple instance-based process wherein people repeated the action they retrieved a memory of. Medin and Schaffer (1978), Nosofsky (1984), and others have proposed that we classify objects by retrieving instances they are similar to. Nosofsky and Palmeri (1997) elaborated this with their exemplar-based random walk (EBRW) model, wherein they proposed that people retrieve a number of instances similar to the current example and classify the example according to the category most often retrieved. In various guises, instance-based decision making has been proposed as prescriptive models—for instance, case-based decision theory in decision making (Gilboa and Schmeidler, 2000), case-based reasoning in artificial intelligence (Reisbeck and Schank, 1989; I. Watson, 1997), and instance-based learning (Aha et al., 1991).

Probably the most common type of ACT-R model involves some sort of instance-based retrieval. The behavior of these models is strongly colored by the activation processes that determine what will get retrieved. The success of these models in such a wide range of domains is one of the strongest sorts of evidence for both the general correctness and the general functionality of the theory of declarative memory reviewed in this chapter. Box 3.2 provides brief descriptions of eight such models: the first four are models for the typical psychology laboratory tasks, and the next four are models that venture into the real world in various ways.

The models are described in a box to avoid having the text descend into too much low-level detail. However, as Newell noted, the answer to his question has to have the details. If readers go to the original sources for those details, they will find the declarative memory equations playing out over and over again in widely different domains. In each case, these equations are basically achieving the goal identified by the rational

BOX 3.2 Eight Instances of Instance-Based Models

1. *Alpha-arithmetic:* Logan (1988) introduced an alpha-arithmetic task to illustrate his theory. Participants were presented with such problems as C + 3 = ? where the answer is gotten by counting three letters forward in the alphabet to F. Initially, participants solved these problems by going through the alphabet (Logan's algorithmic stage), but eventually they came to retrieve the answers. Their time to perform the task sped up according to a power function. Anderson and Lebiere (1998) showed that this task can be easily modeled in ACT-R, and indeed, it has become a standard task in the ACT-R tutorial.[23]

2. *Categorization:* Anderson and Betz (2001) show that the ACT-R implementation of Nosofsky and Palmeri's EBRW model yields essentially identical predictions about categorization as do the original models. This turns out to depend on the base-level learning equation interacting correctly with similarity-based retrieval.[24] The Anderson and Betz model also shows how instance-based classification can coexist with rule-based classification (basically like using principles). Which process gets selected depends on their relative success.

3. *Psychophysical judgments:* Petrov and Anderson (2005) showed that the ACT-R retrieval model can explain the nature of psychophysical judgments. It applies most directly to situations where a participant might have to assign a numerical value (e.g., "5") to a stimulus to indicate its magnitude. Given a particular physical stimulus to label, such as a line length, the model retrieves the numerical value associated with a similar line length in a past rating. Either it gives that value or, if the length associated with the memory is too high or low, it will adjust the value up or down. This model matches up well with participants in terms of both explaining how well they do and explaining effects that occur in such data because of the sequence of stimuli presented. The sequential effects depend on the changes in the base-level activations of past memories.

4. *Berry and Broadbent sugar factory:* Lebiere et al. (1998) present an ACT-R instance model of participant performance in the Berry and

continued

---

23. Logan's (1988) model is one where each experience leaves its own trace and these traces race against each other for retrieval, whereas in ACT-R multiple encounters with a fact such as C + 3 = F are merged into a single trace that gets strengthened. However, the timing predictions of the two models match up (see Anderson et al., 1999). Also ACT-R predicts the reduction in variance noted by Logan.

24. For purposes of keeping the mathematical development limited, this chapter has not gone into effects of similarity in ACT-R, but see Anderson and Lebiere (1998, their chapter 3).

Broadbent (1984) sugar factory task. This is a task where the participant tries to control the output of a sugar factory in a month by assigning a number of workers to that task. It is one example of many ACT-R models that control a dynamic system (e.g., Wallach and Lebiere, 1998; Gonzalez et al., 2003; Schoppek, 2002). The sugar factory task has attracted a lot of attention because, while it is simple, it has an obscure rule that people seem unable to be able to articulate and yet they get increasingly good at controlling the factory. Thus, it is a well-known instance of the distinction between explicit and implicit knowledge. The Lebiere et al. (1998) model retrieves similar past instances to the current situation and bases its actions on the memories retrieved. It is similar in many ways to the Dienes and Fahey (1995) model. In these models, successful behavior is possible by storing cases of what works, and the model does not have to extract any principles.

5. *Rock, paper, scissors:* West et al. (2005) describe an ACT-R model for rock-paper-scissors. When presented with a decision about what to action to choose in the current situation, the model tries to retrieve information about what its opponent has done given a similar local history. It then chooses the move to beat that prediction. Rock, paper, scissors is a game where one can win by taking advantage of sequential regularities in a weak opponent but one does not want to become predictable in trying to do so. The ACT-R model is able to capture the behavior of strong players. It can pick up on statistical regularities because the frequencies of various sequences of opponent moves will be reflected in the base-level activations of the chunks representing them. Thus, one is most likely to retrieve the most probable sequence. On the other hand, because retrieval in ACT-R is probabilistic it can largely hide any regularities in its behavior.

6. *Backgammon:* Sanner et al. (2000) developed a backgammon-playing program based on ACT-R memory principles. This program learned from the games it played, storing associations between game features, moves, and eventual outcomes. It was able to learn to become a respectable player in a 1,000 games, which is the typical learning investment of a human. It did not achieve the performance level of the best backgammon programs such as the world champion TD-Gammon (Tesauro, 1992) but that program required hand tuning and millions of training trials.

7. *Past tense:* Taatgen and Anderson (2002) describe a model of children's learning of past tense. Initially, when faced with the task of generating the past tense of a verb, it would try to retrieve a previous example of a past tense for that verb or another verb. If it retrieved a different verb, it would have to adapt the inflection to the current verb. Eventually, the model learned the general past-tense rule for English but had to rely on memory for the irregular verbs. This model gave a good account of many aspects of the learning of English past tense, as described in more detail in chapter 4.

continued

Box 3.2 *continued*

8. *Sentence interpretation:* Budiu and Anderson (2004) produced a model that tried to interpret sentences by retrieving a memory of a something similar to the current sentence and then adapting it. This allowed the model to comprehend such metaphors as "The night sky was filled with drops of molten silver" by retrieving the most overall similar memory (presumably of a night sky filled with stars) and adapting that. This same interpretation process turns out to explain the Moses illusion (Park and Reder, 2004; Reder & Kusbit, 1991)—given the question "How many animals of each kind did Moses take on the ark" many people say 2, not noticing that it was Noah, not Moses, who took the animals on the ark. In this case they retrieve the similar instance and miss the difference.

analysis of declarative memory: to make most available that information which is most likely to be useful.

The Role of Memory in Heuristic Judgments

All the examples in box 3.2 show the declarative system behaving adaptively and successfully by counting on retrieval of past experiences for purposes of making successful judgments. However, there is also a countertradition in psychology that sees reliance on memory for specific experiences as a source of error in judgment. For instance, in their classic paper, Kahneman and Tversky (1973) argued that people used availability in memory to make judgments and that these judgments are often bad. For instance, they asked participants to estimate the proportion of English words that begin with the letter k versus words with a k in the third position. How might participants perform this task? One obvious heuristic is to retrieve instances of words that begin with k or words that have k in the third position and to then base one's judgment on how many can be retrieved. The problem is that it is much easier to retrieve words that begin with a particular letter than ones having that letter in the third position. Thus, participants estimated that more words begin with letter k than have k in the third position. In fact, three times as many words have k in the third position than begin with k. Generally, participants overestimated the frequency with which words begin with various letters.[25] Based on such results, Kahneman and Tversky argued that reliance on memory tends to lead to errors in judgment.

More recently, Goldstein and Gigerenzer (1999, 2002) have argued that availability in memory typically improves the quality of judgments. In one study they looked at the ability of students at the University of Chicago to judge the relative sizes of various German cities. For instance, which city is larger—Bamberg or Heidelberg? Most American students know that Heidelberg is a German city, whereas most do not recognize Bamberg: one city is available in memory, and the other is not. Goldstein and Gigerenzer showed that when faced with such pairs, students almost always pick the city they can recognize. One might think this shows another fallacy in memory. However, Goldstein and Gigerenzer show that the students are more accurate when they make their judgment for pairs of cities like this (where they recognize one and not the other) than when they are given two cities they can recognize and must use other bases for judgment. Thus, far from a fallacy, this proves to be an effective basis for making judgments. Also, American students do better at judging the relative size of German cities using this heuristic than either American students judging American cities or German students judging German cities, where this heuristic cannot be used because almost all the cities are recognized.[26]

Schooler and Hertwig (2005) report a detailed analysis of why this works in terms of the ACT-R theory of memory. They used the data collected by Goldstein and Gigerenzer on the frequency with which various German cities were mentioned in the Chicago *Tribune* between January 1, 1985, and July 31, 1997. They exposed an ACT-R model to a history of mention based on these frequencies, assuming that each mention of the city affected the base-level activation of the memory for that city according to the base-level learning equation. Figure 3.14 shows the relationship between the resulting activation levels and the probability that the students at the University of Chicago would recognize the cities. It

---

25. The generality of this result has been challenged (Sedlmeier et al., 1998).

26. My German informant (Angela Brunstein) tells me that almost all Germans would recognize Bamberg and Heidelberg but many would be puzzled by which is larger. Interestingly, Google search on English texts reports on 37 million hits on Heidelberg and 3.5 million on Bamberg. Google search on German texts reports 30 million hits on Heidelberg and 12 million on Bamberg—a much closer ratio and many more hits on Bamberg.

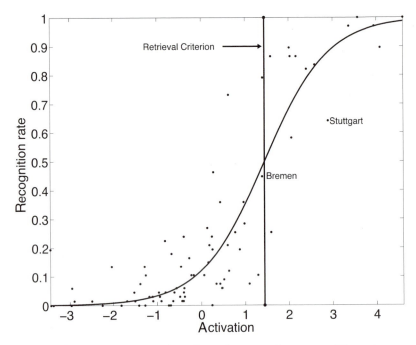

Figure 3.14. Recognition rate plotted as a function of activation. The points indicate the observed recognition rates of the 83 German cities. The S-shaped curve relates the activation of a city's record to its estimated recognition rate. For instance, Bremen has an observed recognition rate of 0.45, an activation of 1.39, and an estimated recognition rate of 0.48. Stuttgart has an observed recognition rate of 0.64, an activation of 2.89, and an estimated recognition rate of 0.88. From Schooler & Hertwig (2005). Copyright American Psychological Association. Reprinted with permission.

also shows the predicted probability of recognition according to the retrieval probability equation with the threshold, τ, set to be 1.44 units and the activation noise factor, s, set to be 0.73. This recognition behavior leads to success in the judgment task because it turns out that the size of German cities correlates well (0.82) with their frequency of mention in the Chicago *Tribune*.

In an interesting exploration, they consider what would happen to the usefulness of this recognition heuristic if the decay rate parameter (d in the base-level learning equation in table 3.2) was varied. They show that at values around 0.5 (the current default value in ACT-R) the recognition heuristic performs quite well, getting 61% of the cities correct.

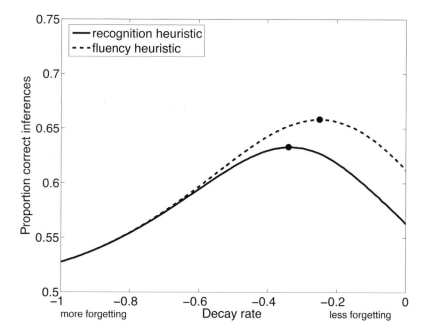

Figure 3.15. Proportion of correct inferences made by the recognition and fluency heuristics on all comparisons of the 83 largest cities in Germany. The amount of forgetting in the system was varied from 0, corresponding to no forgetting, to –1, a high forgetting rate. The peaks of each curve are marked with dots.

The best setting of this parameter is 0.34, which produces 63% correct.[27] However, as the decay rate goes to 0 (no forgetting) or to 1 (rapid forgetting), the recognition accuracy falls toward chance levels of 0.5. Figure 3.15 illustrates this for the recognition heuristic and a variant that they call the fluency heuristic. At high forgetting rates, most cities could not be recognized and there would be no basis for judgment. At low forgetting rates, most cities are recognized and there is again no basis for judgment. Thus, more knowledge is not always better, reinforcing the general adaptiveness of forgetting that Schooler and Anderson argued for.[28]

27. Pavlik and Anderson (2005) argue that to model long-term retention it is useful to have a decay rate that is lower than the default of 0.5.
28. Lebiere (1998) in his lifetime simulation of cognitive arithmetic did a similar parameter analysis and came to similar conclusions.

Thus, the forgetting process is serving a critical role in making the recognition heuristic as accurate as it can be. However, it is not operating alone. When people can recognize both of the two cities, they can call on other knowledge and improve their performance. This did not help the students at the University of Chicago that much because they knew little about the relative size of German cities. Nonetheless, such knowledge can be helpful in some domains. The recognition heuristic works best when it is embedded in a fully functioning architecture that can integrate different sources of knowledge to come to the best possible decision given its knowledge.

The Role of Declarative Memory in the Cognitive System: A Reprise

Because of its flexibility, declarative memory is a valuable resource in our intellectual arsenal. The last two sections of this chapter discuss how memory can be recruited to solve a wide range of problems. However, memory plays out in everyday life in other ways, as well. As noted at the beginning of this chapter, our declarative memories with their rich autobiographical detail are critical to our sense of being distinct individuals. Another important use of declarative knowledge in the human case involves processing the instructions that we receive from others (as discussed in chapters 4 and 5). Perhaps the most common use of memory is recalling where things are. While occasionally we cannot find our car in the parking lot, usually memory works so well for such tasks that we are not even aware of how often we are going back to where we last saw or put something. Much of the evidence for a connection between memory and the hippocampus in lower animals involves spatial memories.

As noted above, Newell (1992) expressed considerable frustration with the failure of memory researchers to consider the functionality of the memory systems they were proposing. Annoyed with the carping at the Soar system, he said

> Psychologists and linguistics almost never ask themselves about function. In their own work they act as if such questions are irrelevant. That would be OK—there needs to be division of labor in science—except that they are suspicious of those who do ask questions about functions. They call it "AI bias." To pick an example from the reviews, no psychologist has ever asked whether

the plethora of STM [short-term memory] models that have been generated since the 1960s could actually be functionally adequate for a system to be intelligent. It is absolutely not the case that because one has, say, the classic data about digit span, Brown-Peterson decay, and so on, plus an STM model of these that explains that data, that one can infer that the STM is the model of the memory apparatus that humans have. An additional data point to be explained by such models is how, with whatever limitation the particular STM theory posits, it is possible for the human to function intelligently. (p. 473)

This chapter has provided something of an answer to Allen Newell's question of how humans can behave intelligently within the limits of their memories. Their success depends critically on the fact than human memory is embedded in an overall cognitive system, and Newell would be pleased with this cognitive architecture aspect of the answer. However, it is also the case that these limits can enable the human to behave more intelligently. Newell might be surprised by that part of the answer.

Appendix 3.1: Analysis of Retrieval Time Process

To repeat the equation from table 3.2, the time to retrieve a chunk is related to the activation of the chunk by the retrieval time equation:

$$\text{Time} = Fe^{-A}$$

The activation A in this equation is the momentary activation of the chunk and is subject to random fluctuations. Anderson and Lebiere (1998; see their appendix) have already shown how the random variation in activation, combined with this latency function, results in a Weibull distribution of response times, which has the shape of typical latency distributions with the extended tail of long latencies.

In the appendix of that book, we also considered what neural processes might lead to such a latency function. The goal of this appendix is to update that analysis in light of new information about the neural basis of decision making. This information is largely drawn from studies of eye movements in simple visual tasks. For instance, a monkey might see a visual field of moving dots. Some proportion of the dots is moving randomly, but some proportion is moving left or right, and the monkeys

have to move their eyes in a direction to indicate the direction of systematic movement. Recordings can be obtained from many brain regions that
are involved in the control of saccadic eye movements—the middle temporal area, the lateral intraparietal area in extrastriate cortex (Roitman
and Shadlen, 2002), the frontal eye field (Schall, 2001; Thompson et al.,
1997), and the superior colliculus (Basso and Wurtz, 1998). The typical
result is an initial increase in the activity of cells that code for movement
in the target direction and in distractor directions. However, the distractor
activity will lag or decrease, while the target activity reaches a threshold
rate of firing, at which point the saccadic movement is initiated. These
cells appear to behave as accumulators for decisions: when they have
accumulated sufficient evidence (as indicated by their firing rate), they
drive a response. For more difficult judgments (a harder discrimination of
direction), the firing rate grows more slowly, as if the evidence is growing
more slowly, but builds up to the same threshold before the saccade is
initiated. On trials where an error is made, the buildup to threshold will
be seen in the cell coding for the saccade in the wrong direction. It is as
if the wrong cell had won the race to reach the threshold on that trial.
There have now been a number of attempts to model these data relating
the neural firing to the distribution of response times (for a review, see
P. L. Smith and Ratcliff, 2004). The proposal below is particularly influenced by a recent paper by Ratcliff et al. (2007).

One of the reasons why this research is generating excitement is that
it is seen as illustrating a possible neural basis for decision making in general. The task of memory retrieval can be conceived of in these terms.
The activation of each memory provides evidence that this memory is
the one to be retrieved, and one can think of its activation as driving some
evidence accumulator. All the possible memories are competing, similarly
driving their evidence accumulators. The memory that is retrieved is the
one whose evidence accumulation passes the threshold first, just like the
direction of the saccade is determined by which cell's activity reaches
the threshold first. Placing the memory into the declarative buffer is a
discrete action done upon reaching the evidence threshold, just like a saccade is a discrete action taken after the threshold is reached.

Ratcliff et al. (2007) are able to model both the neural firing data
and the behavioral data, assuming that the growth in each accumulator can be described according to a leaky accumulator model (related
to the Ornstein-Uhlenbeck model of Busemeyer and Townsend, 1993).
This model assumes that information accumulates according to a fixed

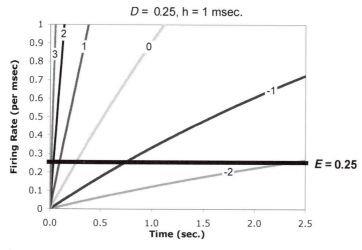

Figure 3.16. A representation of the growth in firing rates for different activation levels in the leaky accumulator model.

rate but that there is also a decay process. The model normally includes a
random component, but this will be ignored here to simplify the exposition.[29] If x reflects the firing rate—or, more abstractly, the evidence for
retrieving a chunk with activation A—the equation for change in x is

$$\frac{dx}{dt} = h(e^A - Dx)$$

where the activation is exponentiated to keep the values positive, D is
the decay rate, and h scales time. One can convert this differential equation into an equation specifying how firing rate changes with time:

$$x = \frac{e^A}{\beta}(1 - e^{-Dht})$$

Figure 3.16 shows how the firing rate increases with time for different
activation values, assuming the decay parameter D is 0.25 and the time
scale h is 1 ms. That figure also illustrates a threshold, E (for evidence),
of 0.25 and what this implies for the time to reach that threshold. As the
activation decreases, the time to reach the threshold increases. Increasing

29. However, the randomness in the evidence accumulation is an essential part of the
full conception. Its effects are reflected at a more aggregate level in ACT-R in terms of
the noise components added to the activations.

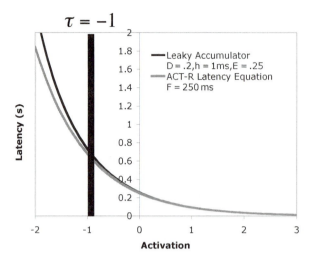

Figure 3.17. A comparison of the latencies produced by the leaky accumulator model and the ACT-R latency equation.

that threshold would increase the time; decreasing it would decrease the time.

One can convert the formula above into a formula giving time to threshold:

$$t = \frac{-\ln(1 - DEe^{-A})}{Dh}$$

This rather unattractive-looking expression has a simple approximation when the quantity with the logarithm is close to 1:

$$t \approx \frac{E}{h}e^{-A} \quad \text{for } DEe^{-A} < 0.1$$

which is the ACT-R latency equation where $F = E/h$. Figure 3.17 compares the ACT-R latency function against this latency function (not the approximation); the correspondence is quite good, particularly below the retrieval threshold. In conclusion, the latency function proposed in ACT-R fits well with current ideas about the neural basis of decision making.

4

The Adaptive Control of Thought

Chapter 3 reviews the argument that a flexible declarative memory is critical to our ability to adapt to a changing world. However, it is not enough to retrieve the relevant knowledge from our declarative warehouse; we must be able to use it. Using the knowledge to its full potential requires complex, deliberative processes in which we make inferences and predictions on the basis of that knowledge. For instance, if I have lost my wallet and remember that I have been to Starbucks I must elaborate on this knowledge to infer where my wallet might be and how to recover it. However, this complexity and deliberation can make it fatally flawed as a strategy when we have to act rapidly in situations where our cognitive resources are being stretched to their limits. Therefore, the development of effective cognitive procedures requires a process by which frequently useful computations are identified and cached as cognitive reactions that can be directly evoked by the situation. These cognitive reflexes need to be integrated with the more deliberative processes to yield adaptive control of thought.[1] The procedural module in figure 2.2 bears the responsibility of achieving the right balance of action and reflection. It con-

---

1. The title of this chapter is what the acronym ACT stands for. When I named it (Anderson, 1976), I was heavily influenced by both Allen Newell's emphasis on production systems as providing a model of control structure for thought and the need for control of thought to adapt with experience. At the time, the name seemed too close to "thought control" and its negative associations, so I did not reveal the meaning of the acronym until Anderson (1983) and have never emphasized that meaning. Perhaps now the theory has reached the point where it is beginning to live up to the positive implications of its title.

tains both the cognitive reactions and the more deliberative procedures. In this chapter I explain the procedural module and how it fits into the larger system, particularly how it relates to the knowledge in declarative memory and the intentional structure in the goal module.

The main portion of this chapter presents a description of the procedural module and evidence for it. However, it is important to recognize that this is not an isolated proposal but rather occurs in the context of a rich history of behavioral research and theory that extends back a full century, and in the context of a rich body of accumulated knowledge about the functions of relevant brain regions. The ACT-R proposal is just an attempt to summarize the lessons learned from all of these efforts, and thus the chapter begins by reviewing the relevant research.

The Relationship Between Thought and Action

The Behaviorist Debate

The last century was characterized by an ongoing and renewing debate about how what we know influences what we do. Chapter 3 discusses an early realization in the arguments of J. B. Watson (echoing many behaviorists of the time) that there was really no such thing as knowing separate from doing. As behaviorism advanced in the first half of that century, the issue of knowing versus doing became a point of disagreement within the behaviorist camp. This issue was enshrined in the debate between psychologists Clark Hull and Edward Tolman. Hull (e.g., Hull, 1952) had developed a much-envied mathematical theory that formalized the early arguments of Watson—knowledge was realized as S-R "habit strengths," which were connections between stimuli (the S) and responses (the R). His theory allowed an important role for drive and reinforcement, but fundamentally when the stimulus conditions were right, the response would be made. In Hull's world, you "just did it." Tolman, however, proposed that we learn two kinds of expectancies (e.g., Tolman, 1932). One is the S-R-S expectancy that if a certain response (R) is made in a certain situation (the first S), another event (the second S) will result. For instance, a bar press (R) in a Skinner box (S) will result in food (S). The other is the S-S expectancy that one stimulus will follow another. For instance, Tolman might argue that Pavlov's dogs developed the expectancy that food would follow a bell. Tolman proposed that these expectancies are put together to achieve various needs by "inference." While he spoke the language of behaviorism, his theory was correctly characterized as "cognitive."

There was another important difference between the two theories. According to Hull, habits build up their strength as a function of number of reinforcements. According to Tolman, reinforcement is not critical and the expectancies just reflect the frequency with which these contingencies are experienced in the environment. This reflects an old debate that psychologist Edward Thorndike had with himself in trying to sort out the law of effect and the law of exercise (Thorndike, 1927, 1932). The law of effect said that reinforcement was necessary to strengthen the bonds, and the law of exercise said that mere repetition of the behavior was enough. Initially, Thorndike thought that both laws were necessary, but in the end he decided in favor of the law of effect. However, Thorndike's decision did not end the matter, and the current evidence is that versions of both laws are at work—Thorndike had it right in the first place.

One of Tolman's classic demonstrations involved *latent learning*. The experiment by Tolman and Honzik (1930) involved three groups of rats running a maze with 14 choice points. Rats were put in at one end of the maze and were retrieved when they got to the other end. All rats ran the maze once a day for 17 days. For one group, food was always at the end of the maze. For another group, food was never at the end of the maze. For

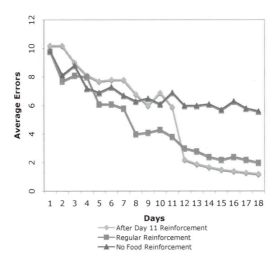

Figure 4.1. Average number of incorrect choices for three groups of rats that are running a maze. From Tolman and Honzik (1930).

a third group, food was introduced on the 11th day. Figure 4.1 shows the performance of the rats in terms of how many wrong choices they made before reaching the end of the maze. The group given food on the 11th day dramatically improved its scores on the 12th day and even performed slightly better than the group that was reinforced all along. According to Tolman, the nonreinforced rats were learning all the while. However, their learning was latent; only when a goal was introduced was the learning translated into performance. Thus, for Tolman, reinforcement was not necessary for learning but was necessary for performance.

Tolman's demonstrations did not end the matter (for a review of this research, see Kimble, 1961). A reasonable interpretation would be that sometimes learning took place in the way Tolman thought it did and sometimes as Hull thought it did, but the field was looking for an either-or answer. In that debate, Tolman tended to lose, though not really on the evidence. Rather, he lost because the theory that Hull proposed came closer to a mechanistic theory that explained how behavior came out of the organism. Tolman's theory never had that sort of character, although MacCorquodale and Meehl (1953) did try to "formalize" it. The attitude toward Tolman's theory was summarized in the famous criticism by Guthrie (1935):

> Signs, in Tolman's theory, occasion in the rat realization, or cognition, or judgment, or hypotheses, or abstraction, but they do not occasion action. In his concern with what goes on in the rat's mind, Tolman has neglected to predict what the rat will do. So far as the theory is concerned the rat is left buried in thought; if he gets to the food-box at the end that is his concern, not the concern of the theory. (p. 172)

The AI Legacy: Symbolic Planning Versus Reactive Agents

The solution to Guthrie's challenge came from the early work in artificial intelligence starting with Newell and Simon's general problem solver (e.g., Newell and Simon, 1961). They showed how one could take such expectancies (in the form of problem-solving operators) and reason about them, resulting in goal-directed behavior. Their theory was much more mechanistic than any earlier behaviorist theories. Newell and Simon produced computer simulation models that actually did the tasks. Their work was extended in the early generation of automated planning programs (Fikes and Nilsson, 1971), such as STRIPS (Stanford Research Institute Problem Solver). These systems worked from a symbolic representation of the relevant world and of the effects of different actions on that world. This was typically represented in some subset of formal logic. The actions in a system such as STRIPS are represented exactly like Tolman's S-R-S triples. In the language of planners, the first S is the precondition, R is the action, and the second S is the effect or postcondition.[2] Thus, in informal terms, a typical action might be "If I am in room 1, and go through the blue door, then I will be in room 2." The planners were capable of taking knowledge like this and planning paths to get from one place to another place—that is, they were quite capable of solving Tolman's maze.

However, this early work in artificial intelligence neither settled the matter in favor of Tolman nor brought any end to debate. It was argued that classic planning systems would not scale up (Chapman, 1987), and reactive architectures began to appear that just did tasks without any symbolic representation of knowledge (Agre and Chapman, 1987; R. A. Brooks, 1991). These reactive architectures avoided the efficiency problems because they did not have to discover a solution from first principles, but instead had the solution built in as instinct. The work of R. A. Brooks was particularly attractive in that he was able to use his ideas to build working robots. He developed a subsumption architecture in which more complex behaviors were layered over simpler ones. In some implementations there were mappings of perceptual states directly onto actions that are, in effect, Hull's S-R bonds. Brooks's research saw rapid progress in the late 1980s but seemed to hit a roadblock in achieving anything like human-level intelligence. Among the problems faced by this approach was achieving effective learning (Jennings et al., 1998). These kinds of architectures are a good way of implementing a policy in a known world, not of adapting to new information about the world.

The current emphasis in artificial intelligence seems to be on hybrid architectures (e.g., Ferguson, 1992; Firby, 1996; Georgeff and Lansky, 1987) that mix deliberative and reactive components. For instance, Georgeff and Lansky's procedural representation system consists of both a set of procedures that can be directly executed and a knowledge base of facts about the world that can be used to guide procedure selection. Its

---

2. Chapter 5 uses a version of this representation for instructions.

operation appears to have considerable similarity to ACT-R. In the guise of a rat running in Tolman's maze, such a system could plan a sequence of known procedures for traversing parts of the maze to achieve a novel path through the maze.

The design lessons from the AI research seem clear: to the degree one can anticipate how knowledge will be used, it makes sense to prepackage the application of that knowledge in procedures that can be executed without planning. To the extent that this cannot be anticipated, one must have the knowledge in a more flexible form that enables planning

The Struggle Between Action and Thought in the Individual Mind

In parallel with this century-long struggle of perspectives on the role of thinking versus acting, cognitive psychology has had a long tradition of studying how the struggle between thought and action plays out in the individual. The classic paradigm for studying this is the Stroop task first described by John Ridley Stroop (1935). The standard version currently used for this task is illustrated in figure 4.2a. Participants in the experiment are shown words in particular print colors. In the congruent condition, the print color of the word matches the word; in the conflict condition, they mismatch. Participants are asked to either read the word or name the print color. A neutral condition is created for word reading in which the word is in black ink, and a neutral condition is created for color naming when a nonword is presented. Figure 4.2b shows typical results (in this case from Dunbar and MacLeod, 1984). Through their years of reading, people have acquired a strong reflex to read the word. As a consequence, word reading is fast and not much affected by condition. On the other hand, if asked to name the ink color, their knowledge of what they are supposed to do has to fight with their reflexes. Participants take longer in the conflict condition and make more errors, occasionally saying the word rather than the color. This conflict basically involves the battle between Hull's S-R bonds (the urge to say the word) and Tolman's goal-directed processing (the requirement to comply with instructions). While there is this struggle, it is notable that, in the Stroop task at least, the goal usually wins. Someone who cannot do the task with few errors may be suffering from damage to the frontal cortex.

However, such conflicts are not immutable. With practice, the interference in the Stroop task decreases. It is unlikely an experiment will

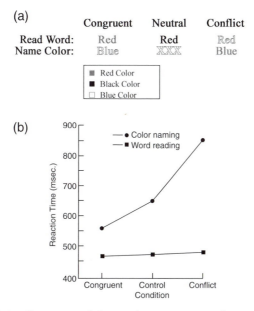

Figure 4.2. (a) An illustration of the conditions in a typical Stroop task; (b) data from Dunbar and MacLeod (1984).

ever be done that provides enough practice in color naming to match an adult's practice at word reading. However, in tasks where the reactive behavior is less engrained, it has been shown possible to reverse the direction of the interference. In one such task, MacLeod and Dunbar (1988) had participants learn color names for random shapes. They were shown these shapes in different colors and had to either give the color associated with the shape or say the ink color. The conditions are illustrated in figure 4.3a. In this case, the urge to describe the ink color is much stronger and interferes with saying the newly learned associations. However, over 20 days this effect reversed. Figure 4.3 shows the progression of this change (part b) and the results from an ACT-R model developed by Lovett (2005) (part c).

Another variant of the Stroop task presents participants with a display of numerals (e.g., five 3s) and pits naming the number of objects against indicating the identity of the numerals. The stronger interference in this case involves numeral naming interfering with counting (Windes, 1968). This paradigm has been used to compare Stroop interference in humans versus rhesus monkeys that had been trained to use the numerals (Washburn, 1994; see table 4.1). Both groups of participants were shown two arrays

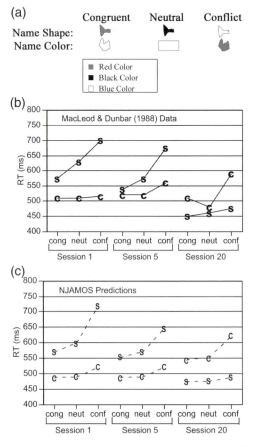

Figure 4.3. (a) An illustration of the conditions in McLeod and Dunbar (1988); (b) data from McLeod and Dunbar (1988); (c, color; s, shape; cong, congruent; neut, neutral; conf, conflicting); and (c) data from Lovett's (2005) simulation. c, color; s, shape; cong, congruent; neut, neutral; conf, conflict. From Lovett 2005. Reprinted by permission of the publisher. Copyright 2005 by Cognitive Science Society, Inc.

and were required to indicate which had more numerals independent of the identity of the numerals. Compared to a baseline where they had to judge which array of letters had more objects, both humans and monkeys performed better when the numerals agreed with the difference in cardinality and performed worse when the numerals disagreed. Both populations showed similar reaction time effects, but the humans made 3% errors in the incongruent condition, whereas the monkeys made 27% errors. The

Table 4.1.   Mean Response Times and Accuracy Levels
as a Function of Species and Condition

Condition	Accuracy (%)		Response Time (ms)	
	Mean	SD	Mean	SD
Rhesus Monkeys (N = 6)				
Congruent numerals	92	3	676	31
Baseline (letters)	86	4	735	49
Incongruent numerals	73	8	829	43
Human Subjects (N = 28)				
Congruent numerals	99	1	584	52
Baseline (letters)	99	1	613	59
Incongruent numerals	97	1	661	56

level of performance observed of the monkeys was like the level of perfor-mance observed with patients with damage to their frontal lobes.

On the practice view, one might expect that children would show less Stroop interference in naming the color of words than do adults, but in fact children (of an age at which they have already learned to read) show greater interference. This is attributed to the fact that children in general have greater difficulty in controlling their behaviors. One paradigm for studying the development of such control is the "Simon says" task. In one study, Jones et al. (2003) had children receive instructions from two dolls: a bear and an elephant. The instructions were such things as "Elephant says touch your nose." The children were to follow the instructions from one doll (the act doll) and ignore the instructions from another (the in-hibit doll). All children successfully followed the act doll, but many had difficulty ignoring the inhibit doll. From 36 to 48 months of age, children progressed from 22% success to 91% success in ignoring the inhibit doll. A few children used regulatory self-speech to control their behavior, as famously proposed by Luria (1961), but they also used strategies such as sitting on their hands or distorting their actions (e.g., pointing to their ear rather than their nose).

In summary, it seems that both Hull and Tolman were correct—be-havior is controlled by both reactions and reflections. Through various reflective processes, expectancies can be turned into behavior. With ex-tensive practice (e.g., either a child learning to read or a primate learning to use numerals), these reflections can turn into reactions. The ability for reflection to dominate reaction is something that appears to increase both phylogenetically and developmentally.

Relevant Brain Structures

Three brain systems are particularly relevant to achieving the balance between reflection and reaction. First, the basal ganglia are responsible for the acquisition and application of procedures (Hull's reactions). Second, the hippocampal and prefrontal regions are responsible for the storage and retrieval of declarative knowledge (Tolman's expectancies). This second set of structures was the focus of chapter 3, but they also play an important role in the service of achieving effective cognitive procedures. Third, the anterior cingulate cortex (ACC) exercises cognitive control in the selection of context-appropriate behavior (Newell and Simon's goals).

The Basal Ganglia

A number of researchers have proposed that the basal ganglia (see figure 2.1) perform the function of learning S-R associations and more advanced cognitive procedures (for a review, see Packard and Knowlton, 2002). Lesions to the basal ganglia impair learning in many instrumental-conditioning experiments. Patients with damage to the basal ganglia (from, e.g., Parkinson's disease and Huntington's disease) are impaired at such tasks as probabilistic classification and sequence learning.

One series of experiments implicating the basal ganglia in learning of procedures is described in Hikosaka et al. (1999). They had monkeys (and humans in some experiments) learn a sequence of responses to stimuli such as those in figure 4.4. The monkeys saw a sequence of five 4 × 4 grids in which two cells were lit up. They were to press the lit cells but had to select them in the correct order. Monkeys can learn such sequential tasks well and appear to show all the properties of human learning (Terrace et al., 2003). Given that they cannot be instructed in the task, there tends to be a period of getting the learning set for acquiring such sequences, but after that the monkeys learn new sequences relatively efficiently.

Hikosaka et al. (1999) had the monkeys learn such sets and then practice them over many months. They found interesting contrasts between

Figure 4.4. Example of material used in Hikosaka et al. (1995) to study serial memory in monkeys. Numbers (not shown to monkeys) indicate the order in which to press the cells. From Hikosaka, Rand, Miyachi, & Miyashita (1995). Used with permission of the publisher. Copyright 1995 by The American Physiological Society.

their knowledge of such sets early on and later after months of practice. Early on, they had no problem when the order of the five sets was reversed.[3] Also, regardless of whether they had been trained with their right or left hand, they had no difficulty in switching to the other hand. However, after months of practice they had become much faster but could key the set only with one hand and could not reverse the order of report. Their behavior gave all the appearance of switching from a flexible declarative representation to a classic S-R representation. Hikosaka et al. also reported a series of studies looking at the neural basis for the early versus late representations. Early on, the task activated prefrontal regions. They particularly focused on activation in supplementary motor area (SMA), which is close to the ACC. When they locally and reversibly inactivated SMA (by injecting muscimol), the newly learned sequences were disrupted but the highly practiced sequences were not. They found that the highly practiced sequences tended to produce activation in basal ganglia structures such as the striatum.[4] When they locally and reversibly inactivated these structures, they found that the highly practiced sequences were disrupted but not the newly learned sequences.

The basal ganglia region seems to display a variant of reinforcement learning (Thorndike's law of effect). Unlike Hebbian learning (Thorndike's law of exercise) associated with the hippocampus, which requires only contiguity, this learning requires feedback on the appropriateness of

3. In the tasks posed by Hikosaka et al. (1999), the monkeys had to key the two grid positions in the same order regardless of whether they were going through the matrices in forward or backward order.

4. The amount of learning involved in these tasks is at least an order of magnitude greater than the learning experiments we have performed (see figure 4.15) and must involve much more fundamental changes in the representation of the knowledge.

the behavior. The basal ganglia contain spiny neurons that many believe are involved in a process that learns to recognize favorable patterns in the cerebral cortex (e.g., Houk and Wise, 1995). These spiny neurons receive specialized inputs that appear to contain supervisory signals from dopamine neurons in other midbrain regions (Schultz et al., 1993, 1997).[5] Recent studies on the role of dopaminergic signals show that they do not simply report the occurrence of reinforcement. For example, Ljungberg et al. (1992) and Mirenowicz and Schultz (1994) show that the activation of dopamine neurons depends on the difference between expected and actual rewards. Moreover, this response is transferred back in time to the reward-predicting contextual patterns recognized by the striatum. These properties (responding to unpredicted reward and moving back in time) are exactly the properties of the so-called temporal difference learning that has become a popular reinforcement-learning algorithm in AI (e.g., Kaelbling et al., 1996; Sutton and Barto, 1998).

While most of this research has focused on nonhumans, where careful measurement can be obtained, imaging research indicates that similar effects are found with humans. The striatum adjusts its response in accordance with the valence (reward or punishment), magnitude of feedback (Breiter et al., 2001; Delgado et al., 2003), and difference from expectation (McClure et al., 2003; O'Doherty et al., 2003). For example, using a gambling paradigm, Delgado et al. (2003) found that the striatum differentiated both between the valence (a "win" or "loss" event) and the magnitude of reward or punishment (large or small).

The Hippocampus

As discussed in chapter 3, the hippocampus is a repository for declarative knowledge that can be used for multiple purposes. It is where the cognitive maps posited by Tolman are stored. It contains the "place cells" that fire when the animal is in a particular location in a known environment (O'Keefe and Nadel, 1978). The hippocampus will increase in size in many species as demands are made for increased spatial knowledge

---

5. While it is true that dopamine signals project to the cortex more generally, the dopamine modulation of the basal ganglia has a faster time constant and is plugged directly into the circuits that select actions. Also, the dopamine projections from the substantia nigra are controlled by the basal ganglia, so the basal ganglia receive a much more differentiated dopamine signal (Randy O'Reilly, personal communication).

(Jacobs et al., 1990). The hippocampal region, particularly in humans, stores much more than just spatial knowledge. Also, the neural learning in the hippocampus seems to be mainly Hebbian, which is a contiguity-based principal corresponding to Thorndike's law of exercise. This contrasts with the reinforcement learning in the basal ganglia corresponding to the law of effect (Atallah et al., 2004).

One line of research illustrating the difference between the hippocampus and basal ganglia involves maze learning in rats (for a review, see Packard and Knowlton, 2002). This involves a simple plus maze (see figure 4.5) that figured prominently in Tolman's debate with Hull. Rats are trained to start from position S1 and go to the food in R1. The question of interest concerns what rats will do when put in S2. Have they learned a place and continue to go to R1, or have they learned a right-turning response and now go to R2? As Restle (1957) reviewed, the behavioral results on this topic were ambiguous and varied from study to study depending on such things as the relative saliency of different cues. In a study by Packard and McGaugh (1996), after the rats had completed their learning, they were given either an injection that impaired their caudate or an injection that impaired their hippocampus. The animals with caudate impairment displayed place learning and went to R1, while the animals with hippocampal impairment displayed response learning and went to R2. The rats appear to have developed both a representation of where the location

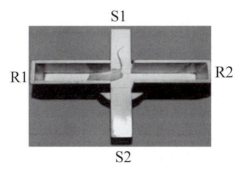

Figure 4.5. Example of a maze used to study place versus response learning. From Parle, M., Singh, N., & Vasudevan, M. (2005). Reprinted by permission of the publisher and author. Copyright 2005 by *Journal of Sports Science and Medicine.*

was in their hippocampus and a right-turning response tendency in their basal ganglia, and acted according to whichever was not impaired. In another study, Packard (1999) injected a memory-enhancing agent into either the caudate or the hippocampus. Rats with the hippocampal injection displayed a pattern of behavior typical of place learning; rats with a caudate injection displayed a pattern typical of response learning.

The Anterior Cingulate Cortex

The ACC plays a critical role in controlling behavior. It has undergone evolutionary changes that are found only in humans and the closely related great apes (Allman et al., 2001). These changes, which include a new class of spindle-shaped cells in much stronger concentrations in humans than in other apes, appear to be related to the ability to achieve appropriate behavior in the presence of conflicting stimuli. The amount of activation in the ACC appears to be correlated with the performance by children in tasks requiring cognitive control (Casey et al., 1997b). Developmentally, there also appears to be a positive correlation between performance and sheer volume of the ACC (Casey et al., 1997a).

There are a number of different theories in the literature on the role of the ACC. Some have postulated that it is involved in controlling cognition, much as is being proposed here. For instance, Posner and Dehaene (1994) have described the ACC as "involved in the attentional recruitment and control of brain areas to perform complex tasks" (p. 76). D'Esposito et al. (1995) have identified it with Baddeley's (1986) central executive, and Posner and DiGirolamo (1998) have related it to Norman and Shallice's (1986) supervisory activating system. However, there are other theories of the ACC. One theory relates it to error detection. This is supported by the error-related negativity (ERN) in event-related potentials that has been observed when errors are made in speeded response tasks (e.g., Falkenstein et al., 1995; Gehring et al., 1993). Dehaene et al. (1994) were able to localize the ERN as residing within the ACC. On the other hand, it responds more strongly in many tasks that do not involve errors. Botvinick et al. (2001), Carter et al. (2000), and Yeung et al. (2004) have argued that the ACC activity reflects response conflict and that error trials are just a special case of this. For instance, the ACC responds more strongly on a conflict trial in the Stroop task even though the participant does not make an error. More precisely, these researchers argue that the ACC is monitoring for conflict among potential responses, and they further argue that other regions of the prefrontal cortex respond to the conflict once detected. MacDonald et al. (2000) found that in the Stroop task, when participants are warned that it will be a difficult color trial, there is greater activation in dorsolateral prefrontal cortex (DLPFC) and not in the ACC in preparation for the task. In contrast, when the Stroop task is presented, the ACC responds to a difficult color trial. Thus, they argue that, unlike in the Posner and Dehaene (1994) proposal, the DLPFC[6] and not the ACC is responsible for control, with the ACC instead monitoring for conflict, as occurs in the Stroop task. This conflict is often interpreted as conflict among competing responses.

ACT-R's goal-module interpretation of the ACC is relatively close to the Posner and Dehaene (1994) proposal. The goal module is maintaining the abstract control states that allow cognition to progress in a correct path independent of the external situation. For instance, the goal must be set to a special color-naming control state to get correct performance on a color-naming trial in a Stroop task. When errors are made and detected, a separate control state is set to reflect on the nature of the error. Of course, it is possible that the ACC responds both to response conflict and to the need to set control states. For instance, Van Veen and Carter (2005) found evidence that response conflict was handled by a more anterior and ventral region rather than by a region that responded to what they called semantic conflict. Interestingly, the center of their semantic conflict region is quite close to our ACC region (indeed, our region is slightly farther posterior than their semantic conflict region).[7]

A study by Sohn et al. (2004, in press) provides evidence for the Posner and Dehaene (and ACT-R) view that the ACC serves a controlling function independent of errors or response conflict. They had people evaluate logical operators such as *and* versus *nand* and *or* versus *nor*. So, for instance, *and(true,true)* = *true* while *nand(true,true)* = *false*. As another example, *or(false,false)* = *false* while *nor(false,false)* = *true*. Table 4.2 shows

---

6. The prefrontal region we have been using to tap retrieval is only a small fragment of the overall human DLPFC, and other regions of DLPFC undoubtedly to play other roles, including roles involved in the higher level organization and execution of tasks (E. K. Miller and Cohen, 2001). The prefrontal cortex is much expanded in the human; chapter 5 includes speculation about one of the other functions it might perform.

7. Another interpretation is that ACC activity is just a reflection of task difficulty as indexed by errors or reaction time (Paus et al., 1998). There are variations on this position that tend to consider ACC activity artifactual, reflecting such things as sympathetic modulation of heart rate (Critchley et al., 2003).

Table 4.2.   Problems Presented to Participants by
Sohn et al. (2004, in press)

Positive		Negative	
And	Or	Nand	Nor
$ (I, I) = I	# (I, I) = I	^ (I, I) = B	% (I, I) = B
$ (I, B) = B	# (I, B) = I	^ (I, B) = I	% (I, B) = B
$ (B, I) = B	# (B, I) = I	^ (B, I) = I	% (B, I) = B
$ (B, B) = B	# (B, B) = B	^ (B, B) = I	% (B, B) = I

The single symbols stand for the operators ($, *and*; #, *or*; ^, *nand*; %, *nor*).
True (I) mapped onto the index finger, and *false* (B) mapped onto the
middle finger.

the full range of problems and how they were presented. The *nand* and
nor operators tend to involve inverting the arguments to get the response,
and they are more difficult behaviorally (Sohn and Carlson, 1998). One
can think of the *nand* and *nor* operators as creating a conflict between the
responses suggested by the stimuli and the required responses, just as in the
Stroop task. On the other hand, one can think of these operators as being
cognitively more complex. If *nand* is interpreted as *not and* (a proposal in
the spirit of Chase and Clark, 1972), then the participant must first evaluate
and and then reverse the evaluation. The Sohn et al. experiment served to
distinguish between the conflict and cognitive complexity interpretations of
the ACC. Participants either were or were not warned ahead of time which
operator they were going to have to evaluate. In either case they were given
9 s to prepare before seeing the problem. If they had a warning about an upcoming negative operator, participants could, among other things, prepare
to deal with the *not* portion, perhaps by mentally remapping their fingers.

Table 4.3 gives the latencies for positive and negative logical operators
with and without warning. With a warning about the upcoming operator, participants definitely were able to take advantage of the preparation

Table 4.3.   Latencies for Positive and Negative Logical
Operators with and without Warning in
the Sohn et al. Experiment

	Positive	Negative	Negative Cost
Warned	693 ms	763 ms	70 ms
Not Warned	1,306 ms	1,763 ms	457 ms

period to shorten their response times to the problems. Participants were also generally slower with negative operators, but with preparation they were able to reduce the cost of processing negatives from more than 400 ms to less than 100 ms. Thus, they were able to take advantage of a warning to largely eliminate the extra cost of the negative operators.

Figure 4.6 also shows the timing of the experiment and the response in the ACC. In the no-warning condition, the BOLD (blood oxygen level–dependent) response rises very little during the preparation period, presumably because participants can do little to prepare for the upcoming problem. On these unprepared trials, when the problem was presented, there was a greater response in the case of negative operators. This could be explained in terms of either response conflict or greater cognitive complexity. The two accounts can be discriminated by the results that occurred when participants were warned of the upcoming operator. When they were warned, there was a strong response in the preparatory interval that was greater in the case of negative operators. This is what would be predicted from a complexity perspective, but it would not be predicted by response conflict, since the participants did not yet know what their responses would be. Moreover, this preparation eliminated any difference between positive and negative problems during the response interval when the conflict could occur. Their preparation had removed the differential complexity of the two types of problems. Note also that all the data are from error-free trials. Thus, the difficulty registered in the ACC seems not an issue of responding to conflict or error, but rather an issue of dealing with a cognitively more

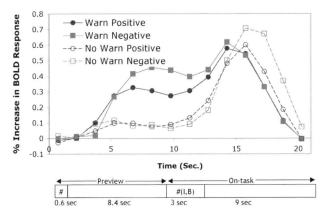

Figure 4.6. Effects of a warning on processing of positive and negative logical operators. From Sohn et al. (2004, in press).

complex condition. In the ACT-R interpretation, this extra cost involves setting an extra control state to process the implicit *not*.

The Sohn et al. study illustrates the lesson about the ACC that has come from every study we have done in our laboratory: it responds to manipulations of task complexity that correspond to the need to make extra distinctions in the control of the task. The effects of task complexity that we find are far too general and abstract to be just response conflict. However, Jonathan Cohen (personal communication) has stated that the conflict interpretation of the ACC is more general than just a matter of response conflict and extends to conflicts between things such as goals. While the ACC response that we see cannot be a matter of just response conflict, it could be interpreted as reflecting conflict between two lines of thought. Whenever there are multiple lines of thought to pursue (conflict), there is the need to set new control information to guide the path forward. It is not clear to me that these are not just two different ways of describing the same thing, one within a connectionist architecture that emphasizes interactions and the other within an architecture such as ACT-R that emphasizes discrete representations. So, as in many cases reviewed in this book, at an abstract level there seems to be an emerging consensus about the interpretations of brain and function.

Architecture

Production Rules

This chapter reviews both the declarative and procedural systems because they go hand in hand in most tasks. However, the principal focus in this chapter is on the procedural module; this section addresses the production system that provides the core of the procedural module and the learning processes associated with it. Table 4.4 provides an illustrative set of production rules for multicolumn subtraction taken from one of my textbooks (Anderson, 2000). Multicolumn subtraction is a task that has often been used to illustrate rule-based systems (Burton, 1982; Cooper, 2002; VanLehn, 1990; Young and O'Shea, 1981) and for which there is a striking absence of connectionist models.[8] It was one of the early success cases for rule-based approaches because it offered insight into what had

---

8. However, for interesting starts, see Dallaway (1994) and Noelle and Cottrell (1995).

Table 4.4.   Productions for Multicolumn Subtraction

Condition	Action
If the goal is to solve a subtraction problem	*Then* make the subgoal to process the rightmost column
If there is an answer in the current column, *And* there is a column to the left	*Then* make the subgoal to process the column to the left
If the goal is to process a column, *And* there is no bottom digit	*Then* write the top digit as the answer
If the goal is to process a column, *And* the top digit is not smaller than the bottom digit	*Then* write the difference between the digits as the answer
If the goals is to process a column, *And* the top digit is smaller than the bottom digit	*Then* add 10 to the top digit, *And* set as a subgoal to borrow from the column to the left
If the goal is to borrow from a column, *And* the top digit in that column is not zero	*Then* decrement the digit by 1
If the goal is to borrow from a column, *And* the top digit is zero	*Then* replace the zero by 9, *And* set as a subgoal to borrow from the column to the left

From Anderson (2000).

been a confusing pattern of errors in children's subtraction. A version of this model has been implemented in ACT-R so that it can be used to illustrate some important architectural features of the procedural system.

Readers may recognize many or all of the rules in table 4.4 as describing their own behavior.[9] Even though there are only seven rules, it produces solutions to all standard subtraction problems. If buggy rules are inserted to supplement or replace these rules, one can produce many of the error patterns that have been observed in children. However, because the focus of this section is on the architectural claims and not on these patterns of behavior, let us focus on just one production rule in that table, the rather bland rule for column subtraction when borrowing is not required:

If the goal is to process a column,
    And the top digit is not smaller than the bottom digit,
Then write the difference between the digits as the answer

9. There are variants of the subtraction algorithm, but table 4.4 captures the algorithm that is typically taught to American students.

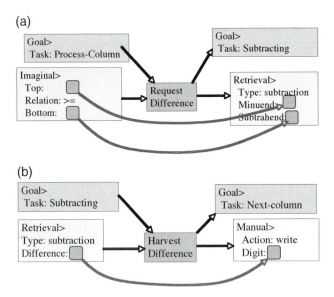

Figure 4.7. Graphical representation of the two ACT-R productions underlying subtraction from a column when borrowing is not required: (a) request-difference production; (b) harvest-difference production.

As it turns out, the ACT-R model requires two rules to produce the effect of this one rule that appeared in my textbook. The first ACT-R production must make a retrieval request for the difference between two numbers, and a second production must harvest the subtraction fact giving the difference. These two productions are illustrated in figure 4.7. The request-difference production (part a) responds to a combination of information in the goal and the imaginal buffer. The goal buffer holds the information that the intention is to process the column, and the imaginal buffer encodes the fact that the top number is greater than or equal to the bottom number. The production makes a retrieval request for the difference between the two numbers and changes the control state of the goal to note that it is subtracting. The harvest-difference production (part b) fires when the goal is in this state and when the declarative module has returned an answer. It requests that this answer be written out and updates the goal to note that it is ready to process the next column.

This one example illustrates all of the modules that are critical to the execution of cognitive procedures: the goal module holding control states, the declarative module retrieving critical information, and the procedural module executing the steps. In addition, there are connections to the outside world (the manual module) and the internal holding of external information (the imaginal module). As this example illustrates, production rules are just stimulus–response bonds that have "gone over to the cognitive side" because control states, mental images, and past memories are among the stimuli they respond to. Moreover, on their response side, the action repertoire includes changing the state of these internal buffers. Besides including mental stimuli and responses, these production rules illustrate a number of computational features that had been considered problematic in the history of stimulus–response theories:

1. The rules respond to conjunctions of information in that they require tests to be satisfied in multiple buffers. For instance, the first production fires only when the goal is in a certain state *and* the top digit is greater than or equal to the bottom digit. In the conditioning literature, it is usually harder to train lower organisms to respond to conjunctive cues than to simple cues, but there are ample demonstrations that many species have this capability (Kehoe and Gormezano, 1980; Sutherland and Rudy, 1991).

2. The rules respond to relations among elements. For instance, this rule will not respond simply when there are two numbers in a column, but rather when the top number is greater than or equal to the lower number. Again, there has been some controversy about whether lower organisms can respond to relationships among elements, but it seems clear that many species can (for a review, see Anderson, 2000).

3. As a more general description encompassing both 1 and 2 above, one can say production rules respond to *patterns* of elements. For instance, the first production in figure 4.7 is not specific to a particular pair of numbers. Rather, it will take whatever numbers appear in the column and use them to make a request of memory.

Production Compilation

Where did productions like those in figure 4.7 come from? Figure 4.8 illustrates the general analysis of the origin of production rules in ACT-R. The basic idea is that the system comes to some new situation for which

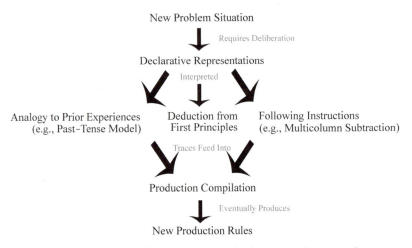

Figure 4.8. An illustration of the history by which new production rules are entered into the system.

it does not already have rules. This requires retrieval of declarative information and deliberation about what has been retrieved. Figure 4.8 illustrates various ways this might happen:

1. As discussed in chapter 3 (e.g., see the list of eight instance-based models in box 3.2), prior experiences can be retrieved and used in an instance-based process.
2. It is possible to reason from principles. For instance, young children will use counting to determine the sum of addition problems like 4 + 3, by counting three numbers beyond 4.
3. As discussed extensively in chapter 5, explicit instructions can be retrieved and followed.

In each case, declarative information is retrieved and interpreted by some general production rules. In any of these cases, the interpretative process can be compiled into new production rules, as described in this subsection.

In the case of the example in figure 4.7, the productions probably originated from explicit instruction. In particular, children are explicitly told that if the top number is bigger than the bottom number, they should subtract the bottom from the top. Processing this instruction does not directly result in the production rules in figure 4.7, but rather in some sort of declarative knowledge such as "If the bottom number is not larger than the top number, then subtract it from the top number." Initially, the child must retrieve this declarative knowledge and interpret it. The steps involved in doing this might be roughly as follows:

1. The child is looking at the column and tries to remember what to do next.
2. The child retrieves "If the bottom number is not larger than the top number, then subtract it from the top number."
3. The child determines that this instruction applies in the current situation and decides to retrieve a subtraction fact.

Eventually, these three steps get collapsed into a production rule such as the one in figure 4.7a. This collapsing can be achieved by a variation of the oldest idea in learning theory: learning by contiguity. Guthrie (1935) stated, in stimulus–response terms, the basic idea of learning by contiguity: "A combination of stimuli which has accompanied a movement will on its recurrence tend to be followed by that movement" (p. 26).

In the case of figure 4.7a, the "combination of stimuli" is the goal of processing a column and the state of the column, while the "movement" is the retrieval request for the difference between the two numbers. It is not trivial to get Guthrie's verbal statement to actually work, because the learning must uncover the relationship between stimulus and response. In the case of figure 4.7, that relationship is the copying of the numbers from the column to the retrieval request. However, it is by no means an unsolvable problem, and a number of well-defined solutions have appeared, including a process called chunking in Soar (Laird et al., 1986) and a related process called production compilation in ACT-R (Taatgen and Anderson, 2002; Anderson, Bothell et al., 2004).

Production compilation collapses two productions that follow each other into a single production. Appendix 4.1 provides some discussion of the technical issues in achieving this. One class of issues concerns what to do for different buffer combinations between the two productions. The most interesting case involves the situation where the first production makes a retrieval request for some declarative information, that information is retrieved, and the next production harvests that retrieval and acts upon it. The compiled production eliminates that retrieval step and builds a production specific to the information retrieved. This is the process by which the system moves from deliberation to action. Each time a new production of this kind is created, another little piece of deliberation is dropped out in the interest of efficient execution.

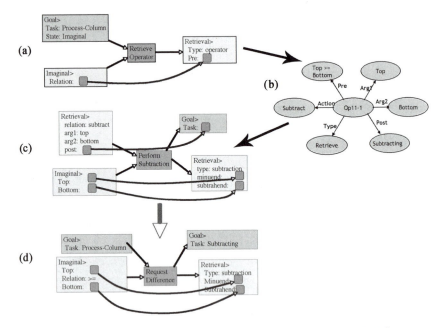

Figure 4.9. The process of compiling the production rule in figure 4.7: the production (a) retrieves the declarative representation of the operation (b). This operator is interpreted by the rule (c). This sequence is then collapsed into the rule (d).

Figure 4.9 illustrates the possible origins of the production rule in figure 4.7a. There are three steps corresponding to the three steps outlined above for the child:

1. The production "retrieve-operator" responds to the fact that the goal is to process the column and that the top number is greater. It requests retrieval of an instruction relevant to this situation. Note that this production is not specific to a situation where the top number is greater than or equal to the bottom. Rather, the production takes whatever relation is in the imaginal buffer (in this case it is "top >= bottom") and requests an instruction relevant to that relation. Thus, this is a general rule for finding relevant instructions.

2. The declarative chunk "Op11-1" is retrieved. This is a declarative structure that encodes an instruction in operator form. The nature of this operator representation is discussed in more detail in chapter 5, but basically it contains an action

appropriate to the situation. In the case of this operator for the situation, top >= bottom, that action is to subtract the top from the bottom.
3. The production "perform-subtraction" responds to the appearance of the operator and makes a request of the declarative module for the appropriate subtraction fact. It also changes the state of the goal to the post state in declarative operator, which in this case is "subtracting." This production is general to any request for subtraction and is not specific to instruction in the context of multicolumn subtraction.

Production compilation collapses such sequences (a production firing, a retrieval, and another production firing) into a single production, in this case the request-difference production rule in figure 4.9d. This rule is still general in the sense that it will apply to any pair of numbers in the column that satisfy the greater-than-or-equal relation, but it is much less general than the original pair of productions that gave rise to it. Production compilation can be seen as implementing Guthrie's basic idea of creating a link that goes from the initiating condition directly to the action.

The example in figure 4.9 reflects a single step of learning. One can imagine further collapsing of production rules. For example, the two rules in figure 4.7 would be collapsed if the first rule request-difference fired, a specific fact such as 7 − 2 = 5 was retrieved, and then harvest-difference fired. The rule that would result would be very specific: it would directly write out 5 when 7 and 2 were in the column without retrieving the intermediate arithmetic fact. This would be a further step in the direction of becoming a system that simply responds without thinking. However, as discussed in the next section, it requires multiple repetitions for any production to acquire enough strength to apply. This very specific rule is unlikely to receive enough practice to become a part of the child's repertoire, but it would if the child saw enough problems involving 7 and 2.

Utility Learning

Guthrie argued that such new rules would be learned in a single trial. However, the evidence is that they are learned much more slowly. This is in keeping with the general view that procedural memories are gradually acquired. In ACT-R models, these rules are gradually strengthened until they start to be used. The need to build up strength is what slows down the development of the very specific rules mentioned in the previous section: being so specific, they do not have many opportunities to be strengthened.

In the literature on reinforcement learning, the strengthlike quantity that determines what rules fire is often referred to as *utility*, since it is a measure of the value of the rule. When an organism finds itself in a situation where multiple rules apply, it chooses the rule with highest utility. There is some noise in these utility measures, and as a consequence it can vary from moment to moment which rule will be chosen. There is an approximate formula for the probability that one rule will be selected among a set of competing rules as a function of its utility relative to the utility of the other rules. If U_i denotes the utility of production i and U_j denotes the expected utility of the all applicable productions j (including i), then the probability that production i will be selected is given by the conflict-resolution equation[10]:

$$P_i = \frac{e^{U_i/s}}{\sum_j e^{U_j/s}} \tag{1}$$

In this equation, s is a parameter that reflects the noise in the utilities and is conventionally set in ACT-R to 1. This choice rule goes back to Luce (1959), serves as the selection mechanism in Boltzmann machines (simulated annealing stochastic recurrent neural network; Ackley et al., 1985; Hinton and Sejnowsky, 1986—where s is temperature), and has a wide variety of other applications in cognitive models, particularly those of a connectionist persuasion.

The utilities of productions are set according to the rewards they receive. They are updated according to a simple integrator model (e.g., see Bush and Mosteller, 1955).[11] If $U_i(n - 1)$ is the utility of a rule i after its $n - 1$st application, and $R_i(n)$ is the reward the rule receives for its nth application, then its utility $U_i(n)$ after its nth application will be given by the difference learning equation:

$$U_i(n) = U_i(n - 1) + \alpha[R_i(n) - U_i(n - 1)] \tag{2}$$

10. But it needs to be stressed that this formula is an approximate closed-form description of what happens on average. On any trial, noise is added to each utility and the rule with the highest utility is chosen.

11. This is a considerable simplification of the prior utility learning mechanism in ACT-R and better matches the general conception of neural learning in the basal ganglia.

where α is the learning rate and is typically set around 0.2. This is also basically the Rescorla-Wagner learning rule (Rescorla and Wagner, 1972) or the delta rule (developed for neural networks by Widrow and Hoff, 1960) and matches the evidence about dopamine signals in the basal ganglia. According to this equation, the utility of a rule will be gradually adjusted until it matches the average reward that the rule receives.

There are a couple of interesting issues about the reward itself. Rewards occur at various times not exactly associated with any production rule. For instance, when a monkey presses a button and receives a squirt of juice a second later, what productions get associated with this reward, and just how much reward do they receive? In ACT-R, all the productions that fired going back to the last significant event are rewarded, but they are given different rewards.[12] The reward for a production rule is the external reward received minus the time from the rule to the reward.[13] This serves to give less reward to more distant rules. This is like the temporal discounting in reinforcement learning but proves to be more robust.[14]

Another issue concerns what to do when a new rule is compiled. When a new production rule is first created, it has an initial utility of 0. Therefore, it is very unlikely to fire, because rules with higher utility exist (including the parent rule that gave rise to it in the first place). However, it can be recreated, and each time it is recreated its utility is increased according to the difference learning equation (equation 2). The reward attributed to the rule is the current utility of the first parent rule. For instance, in the case of figure 4.9, each time request-difference is created, it would receive the same reward as its parent, retrieve-instruction.

12. In ACT-R models, it is necessary to insert event markers so that this mechanism knows how far to go back in time in making reward. This is like using eligibility traces in reinforcement learning (see Sutton and Barto, 1990).

13. This promotes a utility scale in which rewards are to be expressed in time units—e.g., how much time is a monkey willing to spend to get a squirt of juice?

14. We have developed an application of a pure temporal difference learning to ACT-R (Fu and Anderson, 2006), but it has a limitation. This occurs when a critical choice between a correct rule and an incorrect (or lower utility) rule occurs early and is followed by common rules before the reward is received (which depends on that critical rule). There is no way in the simple reinforcement algorithm to propagate credit back to the correct rule and not the incorrect rule at the critical choice point. A discussion of this limitation is available in Anderson (2006), where I also describe the relationship between this utility calculation and the PG-C calculation that had been part of earlier ACT-R systems. As discussed there, the current ACT-R utility mechanism is just a simpler version that extends better to continuously varying rewards and has a clearer mapping to reinforcement learning.

To illustrate how these utility calculations work, consider how the following four rules might fare:

Retrieve-Instruction (Reward 10)
If the goal is to process a column,
Then retrieve an instruction for that kind of column.

Request-Difference-Subtract (Reward 14)
If the goal is to process a column,
    And the top digit is not smaller than the bottom digit,
Then subtract the bottom from the top

Request-Difference-Borrow (Reward 14)
If the goal is to process a column,
    And the top digit is smaller than the bottom digit,
Then borrow and subtract bottom from top.

Request-Difference-Wrong (Reward 14 or 0)
If the goal is to process a column,
Then subtract the smaller from the larger.

The first rule retrieves instructions appropriate for processing a column. The second[15] and third rules reflect alternatives that might be compiled from using correct instructions. The second and third rules have higher rewards because they produce the result (a correct answer in the column) without the effort of having to retrieve the original instructions and interpret them. The last rule represents the most common bug in children's subtraction. It has been argued that this bug originates essentially from incorrect self-instruction (J. S. Brown and VanLehn, 1980; VanLehn, 1990). It sometimes works, in which case it will be every bit as rewarding as the correct rule. When it leads to a wrong result, there is no reward. The exact magnitudes of reward assigned to these rules are hypothetical and are purely for illustration purposes.

We ran ACT-R with standard parameter settings through 100 subtraction experiences. The first rule, retrieve-instruction, started with its utility already at 10, and the other rules began with a utility of 0. Initially, the model will exclusively use the retrieve-instruction rule and apply the instruction. The correct and incorrect instructions were equally available,

---

15. Note that request-difference-subtract is basically request-difference in figure 4.7a.

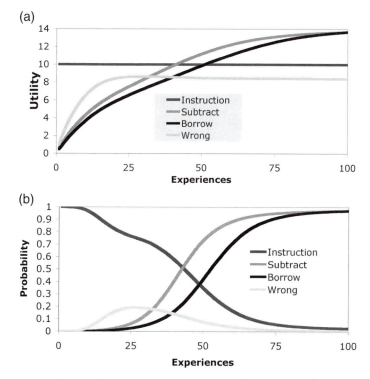

Figure 4.10. (a) The growth in the utilities of the four production rules with experience; (b) the change in the probabilities of selecting each rule.

making the model just as likely to compile the correct rule (request-difference-subtract or request-difference-borrow) as the incorrect interpretation (request-difference-wrong) each time retrieve-instruction applies.

Figure 4.10a shows the average utility over the 100 trials. The rule that retrieves instruction holds steady at 10 while the other three grow, initially collecting the utility of retrieve-instruction as their reward. Request-difference-wrong grows fastest because it applies in all situations, whereas the correct rules divide up the problems. Request-difference-borrow grows slowest because it applies in fewer cases than request-difference-subtract. Eventually the utilities of the learned rules reach a range (about eight) where they are sometimes selected rather than the instruction rule. This leads to a growth in actual experience, and the wrong rule suffers a slight depression in utility while the other two rules move past the instruction rule to their eventual steady-state utilities of 14. Figure 4.10b shows the probability that a rule will be selected when applicable (the instruction rule and wrong rule are always applicable; the other two are mutually exclusive).[16]

It is worth emphasizing some features of this treatment of utility:

1. *Gradual introduction of a rule:*   Initially, when a new rule is created, it has 0 utility, and it will not be tried. Rather, the system will continue to use the parent rule that gave rise to it. However, every time it is recreated, its utility will be increased until it is occasionally tried rather than its parent. Gradually, its utility will increase until it reaches a point where it can replace its parent if it is a superior rule.

2. *Ordering of rules by utility:*   When different rules lead to different outcomes, the system will learn to choose the rule with the highest outcome. For instance, in figure 4.10, faced with a choice between correct rules that always resulted in reward and a buggy rule that only sometimes resulted in reward, it came to choose the correct rules consistently.

3. *Sensitivity to solution time:*   Faced with two rules that produce the same result but one faster than another, it will come to prefer the faster because the utility of a rule is defined as the difference between the reinforcement and the delay. This is the basis for the preference for request-difference-subtract or request-difference-borrow over retrieve-instruction.

4. *Sensitivity to change:*   The system is not locked into one way of evaluating rules. Should the payoff for rules change, it can adjust. This does not seem to happen in a domain such as subtraction where the correct actions never change, but the next section considers a situation where people do adapt to changing probabilities of the success of an action.

Evidence

This final section reviews three lines of research that provide more specific evidence relevant to the mechanisms of procedural memory, going beyond the evidence already offered for the general view of cognitive

---

16. In figure 4.10, the probabilities in (b) can be calculated from the utilities in (a) using the conflict-resolution equation (equation 1) with a value of 1 for *s*.

procedures. It first examines a line of research that supports the utility computations just described; second, a series of fMRI (functional magnet resonance imagery) studies that support the mapping of the critical modules (declarative, procedural, and goal) onto brain regions; and third, a model of the acquisition of English past tense that shows how these pieces come together in a rather substantial learning effort.

Probability Learning

Back in the relatively early days of mathematical psychology, Friedman et al. (1964) completed an experiment on probability learning that is a marvel in detail of reporting. This task, a perfect case for illustrating utility learning, is an experimental version of guessing whether a possibly biased coin will come up heads or tails. Participants were to guess which of the two outcome lights (left or right) would come on. Task instructions encouraged participants to try to guess the correct outcome for each trial. The study changed the probability of the light on the right for each 48-trial block in the experiment. Specifically, for the odd-numbered blocks 1–17, the probability of the light on the right was 0.5. For the even-numbered blocks 2–16, the probability took on the values from 0.1 to 0.9 in one of 10 semirandom orders. In the first block, the two lights were therefore equally

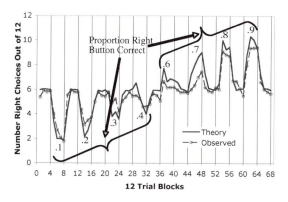

Figure 4.11. Results of Friedman et al. (1964): number of selections of the right button during various 12 trials of the experiment as affected by the probability of success of the button in odd blocks of the experiment.

likely. Starting from the second block and in each of the subsequent even-numbered blocks, one of the lights was more likely to be correct.

Friedman et al. (1964) report the exact sequence of trials participants saw in each of the even-numbered blocks. There were 48 trials in each block, and Friedman et al. reported the mean choice proportions of the light on the right in every 12-trial subblock. While they used 10 different orders, they kept track of the even-block that preceded each 0.5 odd block, and they classified the performance in each 0.5 block accordingly, so one can track the effect of prior experience on these 0.5 blocks. Figure 4.11 shows the correspondence between the data and what the model did using utility learning. The data reported are the numbers of choices of the light on the right out of 12 opportunities. The data are presented as if the even blocks systematically began with a 0.1 probability of the light on the right and incremented to 0.9. None of the 10 sequences used by Friedman et al. did this, but figure 4.11 sews the data back together as if this were the case. The 0.5 block after each even block is based on the average numbers for the 0.5 block that followed the even block with that probability.

The model assumed that the critical choice was between two rules for choosing the light.[17] The only parameter estimated in fitting the 68 data points in the figure was the reward for correctly guessing which was set at 2.0 units. The fit is quite remarkable. For instance, notice in the 0.8 block the model correctly predicts that the number of choices of the light on the right reaches a maximum in the second subblock and drops off a little. This is because the actual sequences used (there were two) for the 0.8 blocks had, by chance, a larger number of right choices correct in the first half of the block.

Friedman et al. (1964) also report a wide variety of statistics on sequential effects. For this purpose, they ran six 48-trial blocks after the set represented in figure 4.11 to get data on sequential changes when the overall probability was stable. The probability of the light on the right was 0.8 throughout these six blocks of trials. During these six blocks, they looked at how a run of lights all on one side affected the probability of

17. An actual ACT-R model that does the task is available as a solution to unit 6 in the ACT-R tutorial (available as part of the ACT-R download of ACT-R 6 at the main web site, act-r.psy.cmu.edu). That model is not presented in the exact sequence participants saw and has reward set to a value to give best fit to the subset of the data in that exercise. A LISP simulation of the full system reproducing all data (given the actual sequences), titled "Friedman model," is available under the book title from the Models link at the ACT-R website.

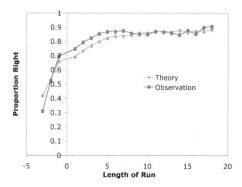

Figure 4.12. Results of Friedman et al. (1964): probability of selecting the right button as a function of the number of previous trials that the right button was successful. Negative numbers denote a string of trials during which the left button was successful.

guessing the next light would be on the right. This is plotted in figure 4.12, where a negative number reflects a run of lefts, and a positive number, a run of rights. The data are plotted for all cases where the total number of observations is greater than 100. There are many more cases of runs of rights than runs of lefts, so the plot is from –3 (three lefts in a row) to 18 (18 rights in a row). The behavior of the model is also given in the figure. Again, the correspondence is compelling. The figure shows that, unlike in some probability learning experiments, participants in this experiment were not displaying the gambler's fallacy and guessing the opposite after a long run. Friedman et al. took some effort to avoid this and so obtained a relatively pure test of utility learning without the complications of higher order hypothesis testing.

Figure 4.13 displays other measures of sequential statistics. Figure 4.13a displays the proportions of 32 trial types as a function of their choice and the feedback on the prior two trials. The correspondence is again good. Figure 4.13b collapses the data over the prior choices of the participant and just plots proportion of choices of the light on the right as a function of the prior two outcomes. When the first outcome was left and the second was right, participants were more likely to choose right than when this was reversed. Thus, participants are most strongly influenced by the most recent event. This recency effect is part of the nature of the utility updating: the most recent event has the strongest effect.

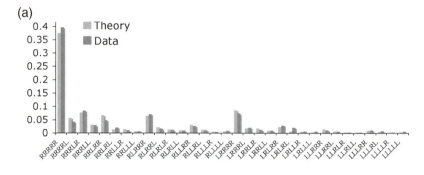

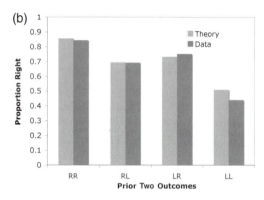

Figure 4.13. (a) The choice a participant makes on the current trial, C_0, as a function of their choice and the feedback on the prior trial (C_{-1} and F_{-1}) and the trial one prior to that (C_{-2} and F_{-2}). The points on the x-axis reflect the 32 combinations of $C_{-2}F_{-2}C_{-1}F_{-1}C_0$. For instance, LRRRL stands for the event where participants chose left two trials back and got right as feedback, chose right one trial back and got right as feedback, and now chose left. (b) The data in (a) collapsed and redisplayed to show the effect of the previous two outcomes.

The match between model and data in figures 4.11–4.13 is a testimony to (1) the success of Friedman et al. in getting a data set that would cleanly assess the issues of reinforcement learning (discouraging such things as hypothesis generation that can lead to the gambler's fallacy) and (2) the ability of the simple utility learning equations to capture how utility is tracked. These equations are not really unique to ACT-R; they are at most slight variants and elaborations of equations that go back more than 50 years, that have played a major role in accounting for conditioning, that have come to play a major role in machine learning, and for which there is neural evidence in the dopamine response. They are achieving the status of an established fact.[18]

fMRI Studies of Skill Acquisition

Production compilation collapses pairs of rules into one and frequently eliminates the need to retrieve declarative knowledge about the situation, achieving greater efficiency by eliminating unnecessary reflection. The general result is more rapid execution. The process of production compilation process is quite complex. Simply observing a speed increase does not seem to provide much evidence for production compilation. Many things could produce increased speed. This is a domain where the case has been substantially strengthened by brain imaging research.

This greater efficiency produced by production compilation should mean less metabolic cost and hence lower response in studies that track brain activity through fMRI measures. However, production compilation leads to more articulate predictions than simply a reduced fMRI BOLD response. Certain regions reflecting certain components should decrease in their activation, while other regions should remain constant. For instance, as a skill develops, fewer production rules need to be fired and less information is retrieved from declarative memory. Therefore, there should be less activation in the prefrontal regions involved in retrieval and the basal ganglia regions associated with productions. On the other hand, production compilation does not change the motor demands and often does not reduce the number of control states involved in performing a task. Therefore, there should not be decreases in motor region or ACC.

This prediction is different from the expectation that one frequently finds in the literature that there will be some shift in regions that are involved in the performance of a skill (for statements of this conventional view, see Anderson, 2005b). For instance, it has been suggested that with increased skill there will be a decrease in the involvement of more "cognitive" prefrontal regions and an increase in the involvement of more "stimulus–response" posterior regions. This view might predict decreases in the prefrontal and ACC regions and increases in the motor, sensory, and basal ganglia regions.

---

18. This is not to say that there will not be adjustments to their exact form or how they play out in an overall cognitive architecture.

Some evidence has been produced for the claim that there is a shift in activation, but much of it is subject to a serious artifact. In a paradigm where the participants are allowed to proceed at their own pace, learning can result in more production firing and perceptual and motor actions per unit time. However, when one controls the number of problems per unit time (as in a slow-paced event-related imaging procedure), there is often no evidence for increased motor or basal ganglia involvement.

Figure 4.14 illustrates changes in brain activation that I used in my 2005 textbook (data from Qin et al., 2003). It illustrates the regions that showed significant activation on the first versus the fifth day of practice in that experiment. Figure 4.14 clearly invites the inference that there are fewer active regions with practice, in line with the expectations of production compilation. However, figures such as this, which one often finds in the brain imaging literature, are potentially deceptive. What figure 4.14 illustrates are regions that show statistically significant effects of the task structure. Statistical significance is a measure of the size of an effect relative to the noise in the data. A region can switch from being significant to not (or vice versa) because of either a change in the magnitude of the effect or a change in the magnitude of the noise. Thus, the data may just be noisier on day 5, perhaps because participants are becoming bored and disengaged. Equally, experiments that show new significant regions on day 5 may simply reflect decreased noise (and decreased noise with practice seems a particularly likely possibility). One needs to look at the relative magnitude of the signal in the regions. Moreover, one needs to look at regions that are selected not because they reach some arbitrary threshold of statistical significance but because they have known functional significance.

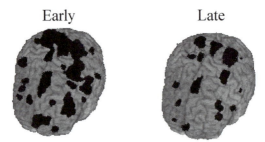

Early   Late

Figure 4.14. Regions activated in the symbol manipulation task of Qin et al. (2003): (a) early: day 1 of practice; (b) late: day 5 of practice. Note that these are "transparent brains" and that the activation is not just on the surface but also below the surface.

Production compilation predicts which regions should show reduced activations and which should not. Because there are fewer retrievals and production rule firings, there should be reduced activation in the prefrontal region (declarative module) and the caudate (procedural module). On the other hand, since compilation tends not to change the control structure of the task, there should not be reduced activation in the ACC, and since the manual requirements remain constant, there should not be reduced activation in the motor region. Our laboratory has completed four experiments that looked at changes in activation after many days of practice:

1. *Dual task*   This study is reported in Anderson and Anderson (in preparation). It involved a follow-up on the studies of Schumacher et al. (2001) and Hazeltine et al. (2002) (see figure 2.7). We contrasted performance on the second day of study, when participants were paying a substantial dual-task penalty, and on the fifth day, when it was largely eliminated.

2. *Fincham task*   This is reported in Fincham and Anderson (2006). It is an imaging follow-up to research by Anderson and Fincham (1994) and Anderson et al. (1997). The task involved learning examples of the timing of pairs of sports events and then determining the timing of new events by analogy. There is a dramatic speed increase over the course of days of practice, with participants often improving by a factor of 2. Participants were imaged on the first and fourth days of practice.

3. *Algebra*   This is the study described in figures 1.6–1.8. The original experiment was reported by Qin et al. (2004); a more detailed model is described in Anderson (2005). The experiment followed children learning to solve equations over five days and imaged them on the first and fifth days.

4. *Symbolic*   This was an experiment similar in design to the algebra system, but using an artificial algebra with adults. The artificial algebra was first developed by Blessing and Anderson (1996). The original imaging experiment was reported by Qin et al. (2003). It again involved five days of training, with the participants imaged on the first and fifth day. A model for this task is reported by Anderson (2007) using the same parameters that were used in Anderson (2005).

In each of these experiments, we collected data on five of our predefined regions: the ACC associated with the goal module, the parietal cortex associated with the imaginal module, the prefrontal cortex associated with the declarative module, the caudate associated with the procedural module, and a region of the motor cortex associated with the manual module.[19] The results in terms of average increase in the BOLD response on a trial are reported in figure 4.15 for the four experiments and the five regions, with the significant effects starred. While no two experiments agree entirely on which regions are significant, the overall trends are pretty consistent and are what would be predicted from the analysis of production compilation:

1. *Anterior cingulate*   This region shows a variety of effects but no consistent pattern: the dual-task experiment shows a significant reduction with practice, the Fincham task shows a significant increase with practice, and the other two experiments show no significant effects. An analysis of the overall effect across the four experiments is not even close to significant.[20] While this region does not show a consistent response to practice, it consistently increases with increases in task complexity (e.g., figures 1.8c, 2.12g, and 4.6). As argued in Anderson (2005a), practice does not have an effect because production compilation does not usually change the control demands of the task. Rather, it merely enables participants to move more rapidly through the control states. On the other hand, the number of control states will increase with cognitive complexity.

2. *Posterior parietal*   In contrast to the other regions, there are no strong predictions for this region. The models for the algebra experiment and the symbolic algebra experiment predict skipping of intermediate representations. As illustrated in figure 1.7 for the algebra task, the effect of production compilation can be to skip over intermediate steps of problem representation. There is no such expectation for the dual-task and Fincham experiments. The results in figure 4.15b show decreases in all experiments and significant effects in the dual-task and algebra experiments. The overall effect (just a test of reliability of the eight numbers displayed in figure 4.15b) is marginally significant.

---

19. While all four experiments used visual processing, the third and fourth experiments did not scan as low as the fusiform gyrus region that we use to monitor the visual module.

20. This is a test of reliability of the eight numbers displayed in the figure. The results of such a meta-analysis are reported for each part a–e in figure 4.15.

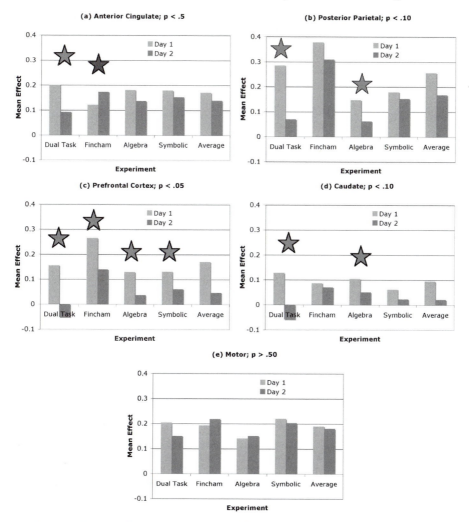

Figure 4.15. Results of four experiments looking at effects of practice in terms of average BOLD response of five brain regions: (a) ACC; (b) posterior parietal; (c) prefrontal cortex; (d) caudate; (e) motor region. Stars indicate effects that are significant (p < .05). The overall level of significance across the four experiments is given in the title associated with each figure.

3. *Prefrontal cortex*   The strongest expectation for a decrease involves the prefrontal cortex because the essence of production compilation is the dropout of retrieval of declarative information for deliberation. There were significant decreases in the prefrontal cortex associated with practice in all four of the studies, and the effect across the four experiments is also significant.

4. *Caudate*   Two of the experiments showed a significant decrease, and the effects in the other two experiments are in the predicted direction. A reduction is predicted in the caudate because compilation eliminates production firing. Often we have not gotten significant effects in the caudate (e.g., see figure 2.10), in part because its response is weak. The overall effect in the caudate across the four experiments is marginally significant.[21]

5. *Motor region*   While the motor region responds strongly in all experiments, in no experiment does it show an effect of practice even approaching statistical significance. Twice there are weak increases, and twice there are weak decreases. Each of these experiments had the characteristic that the number of manual actions per unit time did not change, so practice effects were not subject to the confound mentioned above.

In summary, these experiments display the textured effects predicted by production compilation. Unlike the common expectation, there is not a decrease in all prefrontal regions: while the region associated with retrieval shows a consistent and strong decrease, the ACC is relatively unchanged. Again in contrast to the common expectation, there is no increase in motor activation or caudate activation. The caudate appears to decrease as expected, and the motor region is basically unchanged.

Language Learning: Past Tense

The two previous examples are typical of attempts to capture learning in the laboratory—all the experiments involved less than 10 hours of learning. On the other hand, much of the significant learning humans do involves hundreds—sometimes thousands—of hours of learning. Perhaps the most ambitious learning enterprise in the human case is language acquisition, which takes tens of thousands of hours. It is just not feasible to examine in detail the complexity of learning that takes place over such a time scale. Researchers have attempted to come to grips with such large-scale learning in a number of ways. One common method has been to look at the learning of one small component of the overall competence. The classic example is the attempt to understand the acquisition of the past-tense inflection in English.

21. A potential problem with the caudate is that it should be always active to the extent the participants are thinking about something during the rest intervals, and what we are really looking at is evidence for an increase in its rate of involvement over this base rate.

While there is a clear set of inflectional rules for the English past tense (talk–talked, hunt–hunted, etc.), there are a great many exceptions (go–went, sing–sang, etc.). The acquisition of the past tense has been characterized as displaying U-shaped learning, in which three stages of learning are distinguished. In the first stage, when the child starts using past tenses, irregular verbs are used correctly. In the second stage, the child develops a sense for the regularity in regular past tenses. Now the child will continue to use regular verbs correctly, but will sometimes construct past tenses of irregular verbs in a regular way (e.g., go-goed as opposed to go-went). In the third stage, this overregularization diminishes until performance is without errors. Since performance on irregular verbs is worst in the second stage, the performance curve has a U-shape, hence the name of the phenomenon.

The appearance of overregularization errors in children's past tense had been originally taken as evidence that children were acquiring abstract rules (e.g., R. Brown, 1973). However, as reviewed in chapter 1, Rumelhart and McClelland (1986) showed that it was possible to produce a connectionist model that made overgeneralizations without building any rules into the model. Moreover, this model was able to produce the U-shaped learning curve. As noted in chapter 1, rather than just verbally describing how such a U-shaped learning function might happen, they produced a running computer simulation that actually generated the U-shaped function. This attracted a great many critiques, and while the fundamental demonstration of generalization without rules stands, the original model is acknowledged by all to be seriously flawed as a model of the process of past-tense generation by children. Many more recent and more adequate connectionist models (some reviewed in Elman et al., 1996) have been implemented; many of these have tried to use the backpropagation learning algorithm.

Despite the appearance of more adequate connectionist models, there remain reservations about these models. One class of issues relates to linguistic details; another class of issues concerns whether solutions to the learning problem have been in some way engineered into the way the problem is presented to the learning system (for both classes of issues, see, e.g., Marcus, 1995, 2001; Pinker and Prince, 1988; Pinker and Ullman, 2002). As an instance of the second class, it argued that the success of these models depends on training input that does not seem faithful to what a child receives. The original Rumelhart and McClelland model had artificially produced the onset of the U-shaped curve by switching from a training set of 10 items to 420 items. Later models (e.g., Plunkett and Juola, 1999) do not use such abrupt transitions but still change the relative frequency of the words over the training cycle. Other models distort the frequency of words in other ways, such as presenting verbs in proportion to the square root of their frequency in natural language (O'Reilly and Munakata, 2000) rather than their actual frequency. Another problem is that the connectionist models tend to use learning rules that require feedback on what the correct answer is. However, children often do not get feedback on their generations and do not seem to use it when they receive it (Pinker, 1984). While children do hear the forms that adults use, they are not told when the forms they use are incorrect.

The Taatgen and Anderson (2002) past-tense model avoids these problems and is a good illustration of how procedural learning works in ACT-R. The model simply learns from hearing adult past-tense generation and generating its own past tenses. It encounters verbs in proportion to their true rate of occurrence in the environment and requires no feedback on errors. This model was the first large-scale demonstration that this conception of procedural learning in ACT-R would really work. Since that time, there have been a number of additional demonstrations, particularly with respect to learning from instruction (e.g., Anderson, Bothell et al., 2004; Taatgen, 2005). Chapter 5 on algebra learning describes examples of learning from instructions.

Figure 4.16 illustrates the four ways that the model posits children can generate past tenses:

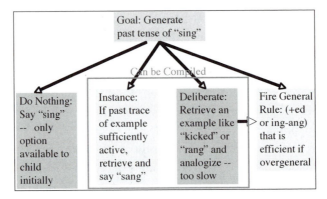

Figure 4.16. Illustration of the four ways the Taatgen and Anderson (2002) model could respond to the goal of generating a past tense.

1. They can just do nothing and use the present tense. For almost all words in English, this is the wrong thing, and the child risks a failure in communication and the loss of the reward associated with communication. Because it can lead to failures in communication, this is a low-utility option. Nonetheless, it probably happens with considerable frequency when the children are beginning their generation attempts because they do not have the basis for doing anything else. However, it is not detected in the records of their speech, and the child is typically just given credit with generating present tense verbs.

2. The child can attempt the instance-based strategies discussed in chapter 3 and try to retrieve a declarative instance of a past tense. Initially, such instances will come from memory of adults' (presumably correct) generations. Thus, this strategy will provide the initial correct instances of past-tense use, including irregular inflections. For a memory of a past tense to be retrieved, its declarative representation must be sufficiently active. Thus, this is a strategy most likely to work for words occurring with high frequency.

3. The child may not be able to retrieve a past tense of that particular verb (in this example, sing) but rather retrieves a past tense of some other verb such as "kicked" or "rang." Then, as discussed under instance-based strategies in chapter 3, the child can try to adapt this form to the current situation, presumably by some analogy process. The simplest analogy (and the only one modeled in Taatgen and Anderson) is when the example retrieved involves adding an inflection such as "ed."[22] While this process might result in a successful past-tense generation, it is rather laborious and not a good method in general for rapid speech. Because it takes a long time, it is a low-utility method that will tend not to be used if there are alternatives.

4. Production compilation can apply to either methods 2 and 3 to produce productions that just "do it." Applied to method 2, it would skip retrieval of the verb, and the new rule would only reflect a modest increment in utility. In contrast, applied to the

---

22. But this was extended to handle other inflections in a later model (Taatgen and Dijkstra, 2003).

analogy method 3, it would produce a rule that simply adds the "ed" suffix and result in a major gain in efficiency and hence utility. This general past-tense rule can compete quite successfully with the other alternatives, and when its utility has grown enough, it will produce overgeneralizations. This example of production compilation is interesting because what it produces is still a quite general rule, despite the fact that compilation moves procedures to more specific forms.

In the limit production compilation produces a dual-route model in which past tense can be produced by retrieving special case rules or by using general rules.[23] The special-case rules for irregulars come to be preferred over the general rules and result in the gradual elimination of overgeneralizations. These rules have higher utility than the general rule because irregulars are phonologically simpler (Burzio, 1999) than the regularizations and so cost less to produce.

Figure 4.17 displays the performance of the model for regulars and irregulars. Overgeneralization for the irregulars is defined as number of correct irregulars divided by the sum of correct irregulars and overgeneralizations,

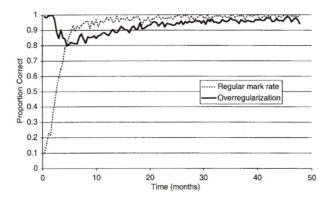

Figure 4.17. Performance of the Taatgen and Anderson (2002) model. Reprinted from *Cognition*, volume 86, Taatgen, N.A. & Anderosn, J. R., Why do children learn to say "Broke"? A model of learning the past tense without feedback, pages 123–155. Copyright 2002. With permission from Elsevier.

23. All of the approaches in figure 4.16 are implemented by production rules, evidence that the "rules" of the architecture are different than the "rules" that are part of the connections-versus-rules debate—to return to a theme of chapter 1.

which is the standard measure in the literature.[24] While the onset of overgeneralization is not all-or-none in either the model or the data, it is a relatively rapid transition in both model and data and corresponds to the first turn in the U-shaped function. Note that by this measure the overregularization is never more than 20% in the model. In fact, children do not seem to generate more than a minority of overgeneralizations.

The regular mark rate in figure 4.17 is defined as the number of correct inflections of regulars over the sum of correct inflections and failures to inflect. This is a statistic that is not reported in the literature, since it is nearly impossible to diagnose failures to inflect in children's speech because one does not really know if the child intended the past tense. Interestingly, the rate of overgeneralization only becomes relatively high when the model has reached the point of inflecting most verbs.

Note that the Taatgen model, unlike many other past-tense models, does not make artificial assumptions about frequency of exposure but instead learns given a presentation schedule of words (both from the environment and its own generations) like that actually encountered by children. Its ability to reproduce the relatively rapid onset of overgeneralization and slow extinction depends critically on both its symbolic and subsymbolic learning mechanisms. Symbolically, it is learning general production rules and declarative representations of exceptions. Subsymbolically, it is learning the utilities of these production rules and the activation strengths of the declarative chunks.

Beyond just reproducing the U-shaped function, the model explains why exceptions should be high-frequency words. There are two aspects to this explanation. First, only high-frequency words develop enough base-level activation to be retrieved. Indeed, the model predicts how frequent a word has to be in order to maintain an exception. Less obviously, the model explains why so many high-frequency words end up as exceptions. This is because the greater phonological efficiency of the irregular form promotes its adoption according to the utility calculations. Indeed, in another model that basically invented its own past-tense grammar without input from the environment, Taatgen showed that the model would develop one or more past-tense rules for low-frequency words but tend to adopt more efficient irregular forms for high-frequency words. In

24. This is really a measure of non-overgeneralization.

the model's economy, the greater phonological efficiency of the irregular form justifies its maintenance as a special case.

Note also that the model receives no feedback on the past tenses it generates, unlike most models, but in apparent correspondence with the facts about child language learning. However, it receives input from the environment in the form of the past tenses it hears, and this input influences the base-level activations of the past-tense forms in declarative memory. The model also uses its own past-tense generations as input to declarative memory and can learn its own errors (a phenomenon also noted in the memory for arithmetic facts; Siegler, 1988). The amount of overgeneralization displayed by the model is sensitive to the ratio of input it receives from the environment to its own past-tense generations.

I close this chapter with the Taatgen past-tense model because I continue to find it a compelling demonstration of how the ACT-R learning mechanisms work to produce a complex phenomenon. The model works without the artificial support that other past-tense models have had and behaves in a way that corresponds to the facts of the matter. Its sole fault is that it does not progress beyond the past tense to deal with full language generation. As noted in chapter 1, all of these past-tense models have set up rather convenient and artificial boundaries for their demonstrations. This is a strategy for dealing with the complexity of language learning, but eventually the field needs to go beyond such artificially constrained demonstrations.

Language in general nicely illustrates the issue of deliberation versus action that opened this chapter. Language is immensely complex and often requires careful deliberation, a fact that I am only too aware of as I try to craft this book. On the other hand, we have to speak and understand in real time, and there just is not the time to deliberate much over every word. In my own attempts at acquiring another language, I started out with much deliberation and little success in real-time processing. I got to the point where I was just starting to act without thinking and had some success, and then unfortunately gave up the effort to acquire the language before any permanent skill could set in. Perhaps I was taking too "cognitive" an approach to language learning, something I might have been spared when I learned my first language as a child. Perhaps, there is something special about language. Whether language really follows the course of other skills or it has the advantage of a special "language acquisition device" or other language module remains an issue that this book simply is not going to address.

Conclusions

As I noted at the beginning of this chapter, the issues presented here can be traced back to the debate between Hull and Tolman about the roles of thought versus action in behavior. Although cognitive science continues to recognize the centrality of these issues, it has advanced beyond this debate on many fronts. The field is no longer trying to settle an either-or issue, and the view I presented here emphasizes the importance of both reaction and reflection. There is now a much richer empirical base, including neuroscience evidence, to guide the theories. Perhaps most important, there now are running computational models that realize these ideas in much more mechanistic terms than Hull or Tolman ever imagined possible.

Learning can be conceptualized as a process of moving from thoughtful reflection (hippocampus, prefrontal cortex) to automatic reaction (basal ganglia). The module responsible for learning of this kind is the procedural module (or production system). I offer the procedural module as an explanation for behavior that embraces both Hull's reactions and Tolman's reflections and provides a mechanism for the postulated learning link between them. Through production compilation, thoughtful behaviors become automatized; through utility learning, behavior is modified to become adaptive. When combined with the declarative memory module discussed in chapter 3, the production system provides a mechanism by which knowledge is used to make behavior more flexible and efficient.[25]

Appendix 4.1: Notes on Production Compilation

A more complete, technical, and syntactic discussion of production compilation is available at the ACT-R 6 website (act-r.psy.cmu.edu/actr6/compilation.doc), but this appendix attempts to address the issues. There are two basic types of issues with combining a pair of production rules into a new compiled rule. The first addresses when different combinations of buffer and module actions in the two productions can be combined

---

25. I thank Jared Danker for help in fashioning this conclusion.

and how to combine them. The second issue concerns how to express the pattern in the resulting production rule. These two issues are addressed in the next two sections.

Combinations of Modules and Buffers

Different types of modules have different characteristics, with different consequences for production compilation. In the case of the motor modules (manual and vocal), it is not possible to compile two productions that both make motor requests of the same module because the two actions cannot be simultaneously performed by one module. Likewise, in the case of perceptual modules (visual and aural), it is also not possible for one module to make two attentional requests. Moreover, it is not possible to compile pairs of productions where one makes a request for a shift of attention and the second tests the contents of the buffer produced by that attentional shift. The reason is that one cannot know in advance what the result will be. These motor and perceptual restrictions place hard limits on how much information processing can be compiled into a single rule. One might imagine that learning processes exist that enable these boundaries to be bridged. So, for instance, one might combine individual motor actions into a larger macro action. Or, if a shift of perceptual attention always produced the same result, one might predict the result and skip the shift of attention. However, ACT-R does not yet have such motor or perceptual learning mechanisms. It is possible to imagine enhancing the modules in ACT-R to incorporate these elements, but until they are in place, the motor and perceptual actions will continue to place strict boundaries on how much can be compiled into a single rule.

As noted throughout the book, the declarative module can be seen as a special case of a perceptual module in which one perceives one's past. Analogous to making a request for an attentional shift, a production rule can request a retrieval, and a subsequent production can harvest the results of that retrieval in the declarative buffer. The difference is that because ACT-R's memory system is monotonic (memories are not deleted), a memory retrieved in response to a retrieval request remains something that can be retrieved if the request is repeated. In contrast, one cannot expect to see the same thing every time an attentional request is made of the visual module. This means that, in the case of declarative memory, one can safely drop out the request to memory and just build into the production the results of the retrieval.

The imaginal and goal modules behave differently than motor, perceptual, or declarative modules. The outcome of requests to these modules can be entirely predicted from the form of the requests. Basically, they are internal scratch pads on which notes can be written to oneself about the control state or problem state. This means they can be freely combined. If the first production involves a test C_1 of the contents of one of these buffers and an action A_1 on the buffer, while the other production involves C_2 and A_2, the resulting production can be given the condition $C_1 + (C_2 - A_1)$ and the action $A_2 + (A_1 - A_2)$ for this buffer, where $C_2 - A_1$ denotes all the conditions in C_2 that were not created by A_1 and so existed before the first production, $A_1 - A_2$ denotes all the actions in A_1 that were not overwritten by A_2 and so remained after the second production, and the + denotes the union of the two condition or action parts. Note that this implies a limit to the complexity of the productions that can be created by compilation. The conditions and actions can have, at most, one mention of each module, so no matter how many productions are eventually collapsed into a single production, there is a hard bound on the size of condition and actions. In actual practice, the combined rules often show no growth in size, as is true of the example in figure 4.9.

Creating the Eventual Production Patterns

Careful inspection of figure 4.9 will reveal some of the tricky issues involved in deciding the pattern of the resulting production. The resulting rule retains the abstract pattern of the original in mapping the contents of the top and bottom slots of the imaginal buffer into the retrieval request. However, the relation slot is no longer left as part of an abstract pattern but rather is now specific to the >= relation. This is because the instruction retrieved and compiled out was specific to that relationship. There are other tricky issues when the same slot is mentioned in both productions and one must track the dependency relationships.

In understanding how the new pattern is calculated, it is easier to consider first a situation without an intermediate retrieval that is being compiled out. Figure 4.18 illustrates such a case, representing abstractly two productions, production$_1$ (condition$_1$ → action$_1$) and production$_2$ (condition$_2$ → action$_2$), that are being compiled into production$_3$ (condition$_3$

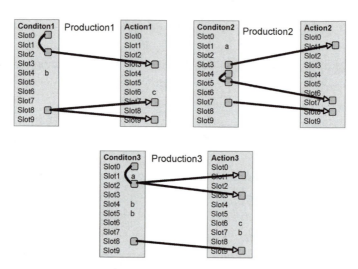

Figure 4.18. An illustration of how the patterns in production$_1$ and production$_2$ are compiled to produce the pattern in production$_3$.

→ action$_3$). Figure 4.18 represents the conditions and actions abstractly as single buffers with 10 slots, but these slots could be distributed across multiple buffers. This illustrates the various cases that production compilation has to deal with:[26]

1. *A network of mappings across the two productions*   The first production checks that the content of slots 0 and 2 are the same and maps this content to slot 3. The second production maps the content of slot 3 to slot 1. The resulting compiled production checks that the content of slots 0 and 2 are the same and maps this content to slots 1 and 3.

2. *Values appearing in the condition or action*   The second production checks that the content of slot 1 is *a*, and the first production sets the value of slot 6 to *c*. The resulting compiled production does both.

3. *A network of mappings intersecting a value*   The second production checks that the content of slots 4 and 5 are the same and maps this to

26. There is a way of treating all of these cases in a uniform formal framework as discussed in the technical documents associated with production compilation. This framework is similar to unification in first-order logic (see Russell and Norvig, 2002) and is the actual basis of the algorithm in the simulation. However, the more discursive description given here better describes what is happening at a qualitative level.

slot 7. However, the first production tested that the value of slot 4 was *b*. Therefore, the resulting production tests that the values of slots 4 and 5 are *b* and sets the value of slot 7 to *b*.

4. *Later mappings overwriting earlier mappings*   The first production maps the content of slot 8 onto slots 7 and 9. However, the second production maps the content of slot 5 onto 7 and overwrites the earlier mapping of slot 8 onto 7. Also, the second production maps the content of slot 7 onto 8, which combined with the first production just gets the content from slot 8 back to slot 8; therefore this mapping is ignored. All that is left is a mapping of the content of slot 8 onto slot 9.

Figure 4.19 illustrates what happens when retrievals are involved. Between production₁ and production₂ in figure 4.19 is the chunk that was retrieved in response to the first production and used by the second. Slots 3–6 in the productions are used to represent contents of the declarative buffer. The condition of production₁ contains a test of a prior retrieval—specifically, whether slot 4 of the retrieved chunk has *b* as its content. The action of the first production makes a new retrieval request, for a chunk with the same value in slot 3 that was in slot 2 and δ in its slot 6. As illustrated, the chunk that is retrieved is the one with values α, β, χ, and δ in its four slots. The second production harvests this chunk in its condition and maps the value from slot 4 of the retrieved chunk onto slot 3 and

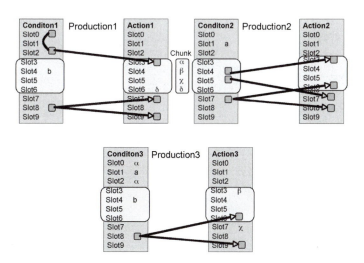

Figure 4.19. An illustration of how production₁, a retrieved chunk, and production₂ are compiled to produce the pattern in production₃.

the value of slot 5 onto slot 7. Just to complete the picture, the action of this production makes another retrieval request. The resulting production is specialized to the content of the chunk whose retrieval is being skipped. Because the first production mapped slots 0 and 2 onto slot 3 of the retrieval request and the value of the retrieved chunk in slot 3 was α, the resulting production has α in its condition slots 0 and 2. Because the second production mapped slot 4 of the retrieved chunk onto slot 3 and slot 5 of the retrieved chunk onto slot 7, the resulting production has β in slot 3 and χ in slot 7. Note that the resulting production is not entirely specific. It retains an abstract pattern where slot 8 is mapped onto slots 6 and 9. It also still processes the prior chunk that was retrieved and makes a retrieval request for a new chunk: it tests that slot 4 of the prior retrieved chunk is b and makes a request for retrieval of a chunk whose slot 3 is β and whose slot 6 is the same as the content of slot 8.

In all cases, production compilation produces a rule that maps the states of the buffers at the beginning of production$_1$ onto the state of the buffers at the end of production$_2$. If one were going to produce a rule that simply reproduced the mapping in a specific case, this would be a rule that tested for a set of specific elements in slots and put a set of specific elements in other slots. However, a general rule is produced that maps certain slots onto others. It may be the case that the reason it takes multiple trials for this rule to be learned is that this generalization is actually built up over multiple different instances.

5

What Does It Take to Be Human?

Lessons From High School Algebra

Allen Newell did not promise us rapid progress with respect to our query into the human mind. He said it was a question of such depth that it could hold us for an entire lifetime and we would be just a little ways into it. Reflecting on chapters 1–4, I have to conclude that his admonition to have modest expectations was good advice. With a few exceptions, the architectural features described in these chapters are not uniquely human. Rather than addressing the question of how the *human* mind can exist in the physical universe, the preceding chapters have largely addressed the question of how the *primate* mind can exist in the physical universe. All the brain regions associated with the eight modules in figure 2.2 have somewhat close homologues in the primate brain that perform similar functions. This invites the inference that primates have the competences reflected by these eight modules. In this book I emphasize the extreme plasticity of intellectual function that separates humans from all other creatures. Something is missing (a magical ninth module?) from the account so far of human intellectual function.

Some of the tasks described in chapters 1–4 are uniquely human. These include algebra, which is the focus of discussion here. However, the preceding chapters did not focus on what in the architecture enables only humans to perform such tasks. This chapter focuses on algebra and asks why it is something that almost all humans can acquire and no other creature can.

Algebra as the *Drosophila* for the Study of Human Cognition

The strategy in this chapter is to look in more detail at the acquisition of a competence that distinguishes humans from other creatures. Language is probably what most cognitive scientists would suggest as the distinguishing feature to investigate, but high school algebra[1] is a more strategic choice. In the case of language, it is often argued that evolutionary adaptations occurred to enable human linguistic proficiency. Algebraic proficiency was not anticipated in human evolutionary history. It is a recent human artifact[2] and illustrates the intellectual plasticity that has led to the fantastic growth of human culture and technology. So, if the goal is to understand how humans can acquire almost arbitrary intellectual competences, algebra is a purer choice.

Algebra is also a better choice methodologically for research. There are fairly crisp formal characterizations of what the target competence is. All competences are acquired against the background of prior knowledge. In the case of algebra, that prior knowledge can be restricted almost entirely to the middle-school mathematics that a child has mastered earlier in school, and there are fairly crisp characterizations of that. A suitably prepared student can master algebra in less than 200 hours[3]—about two orders of magnitude less learning time than goes into language—which

1. Algebra varies in exact content and when it is taught across countries and even within the United States. While there is nothing critical about this exact choice, this chapter focuses on what is referred to as Algebra 1, which is traditionally taught in the ninth grade in United States—although students often take that course in an earlier or later grade.

2. Traces of algebra can be found in "word problems" solved by early Babylonian, Chinese, and Egyptian mathematicians. Algebra similar to the modern form first appeared in the writings of the Greek mathematician Diophantus of Alexandria in the third century A.D. The Persian mathematician Al-Khwarizmi in the ninth century wrote *al-Kitab al-muhtasar fi hisab al-jabr wa'l-muqabala* ("Compendium on calculation by completion and balancing"). This book, which was the first systematic treatise on the solution of linear and quadratic equations, gave us the name algebra (derived from "al-jabr," meaning completion). Some time later during the twelfth century, Al-Khwarizmi's works were translated into Latin and became available to Europeans. Interestingly, Al-Khwarizmi's algebra and the early European algebra (but not the algebra of Diophantus) were all verbal. The algebraic notation we now know was developed by Renaissance scholars. For more information, see Press (2006), or visit www.geocities.com/mathfair2002/school/alg/alg0.htm.

3. If we were to focus just on linear and quadratic equations (the algebra set forth by Al-Khwarizmi but set in modern notation by the Renaissance scholars), we would be looking at something that can be mastered in about 50 hours.

means it is easier to encompass the total domain. Finally, the learners (near adolescents) are of an age where they make cooperative participants.

It is critical for the goals of this chapter that algebra be something that all and only humans can master. Presumably, there is little doubt that only humans can master algebra, but there might be some question about whether most humans can master algebra. For instance, American education has a tradition of streaming a significant fraction (sometimes more than 50%) of high school students into courses that do not involve much or any algebra. One of the justifications for this is the belief that these students are just not capable of learning algebra. However, there is now increased demand that all children be taught algebra. Bob Moses, the 1960s civil rights leader, has declared access to algebra to be the new civil right:

The Algebra Project seeks to impact the struggle for citizenship and equality by assisting students in inner city and rural areas to achieve mathematics literacy. Higher order thinking and problem solving skills are necessary for entry into the economic mainstream. Without these skills, children will be tracked into an economic underclass. (thealgebraproject.org)

Studies have found that having an algebra course is the best predictor of future earnings (Bednarz et al., 1996; Pelavin and Kane, 1990). This has spawned an "algebra for all" movement in American education, and many educational systems in America are now mandating that all of their children will learn algebra.[4] This raising of standards has been associated with considerable success, and children who were thought incapable of learning algebra can succeed (Porter, 1998). As further evidence that algebra is a competence that nearly all humans can acquire, it should be noted that some non-American societies achieve nearly universal competence in algebra.[5] This is not to say that the learning of algebra is not without difficulty; perhaps the research

4. Please note I am just reporting the "facts" about the current situation in America with respect to algebra. My opinions about them would be much more complex. The only opinion of relevance to this chapter is that almost every human can ("can" does not imply "should") learn algebra.
5. My non-American students and postdoctoral students often express extreme puzzlement about why this is an issue in America.

described in this chapter will someday have some positive impact on algebra education.

I have chosen to focus on algebra partly because I am looking where the light shines most brightly for me. In the 1980s and 1990s I was involved in the development of intelligent tutoring systems for a number of domains, but most focused on algebra (e.g., Anderson, Corbett et al., 1995; Koedinger et al., 1997). The work on algebra has subsequently advanced to become a modestly successful commercial product claimed to be used by 300,000 students (carnegielearning.com/; see also Koedinger and Corbett, 2006; S. Ritter et al., in press). Those tutors were based on the ACT theory of the time (Anderson, 1983, 1993). In particular, ACT models in these systems simulated how students solved the problems (correctly and incorrectly); these simulations were used to interpret student behavior and select instructional strategies. The relative success and robustness of these tutors are evidence for the basic correctness of the overall modeling approach.[6]

Despite the success of these tutors, there has not been a rigorous theoretical analysis of how algebra is learned and why these tutors would lead to more success. These systems have performance models embedded in them for displaying mathematical competence, not learning models of how the competence is acquired. If one were to look inside these competence models, one would find rules such as those in table 5.1. While these are not exactly production rules in the modern ACT-R sense, they nonetheless could be re-represented as ACT-R production rules. I believe that there is nothing uniquely human in these kinds of rules. What is uniquely human is how these kinds of rules are acquired.

Mathematical Competence From a Comparative Perspective

In order to identify what makes algebra unique to humans, we need to identify those mathematical abilities that humans share with other primates, so as to not confuse these with what is special about algebra.

---

6. However, there is a lot more to achieving success than just this, as is discussed in Koedinger and Corbett (2006) and S. Ritter et al. (in press). A critical reader of these sources might also find reasons to suspect that the success is qualified.

Table 5.1.   Example Production Rules

Production Rules in English	Example of Its Application
1. *Correct production possibly acquired implicitly* IF the goal is to find the value of quantity Q AND Q divided by Num1 is Num2, THEN find Q by multiplying Num1 and Num2.	To solve "You have some money that you divide evenly among 8 people and each gets 40," find the original amount of money by multiplying 8 and 40.
2. *Correct production that does heuristic planning* IF the goal is to prove two triangles congruent AND the triangles share a side, THEN check for other corresponding sides or angles that may be congruent.	Try to prove triangles *ABC* and *DBC* are congruent by checking whether any of the corresponding angles, such as *BCA* and *BCD*, or any of the corresponding sides, such as *AB* and *DB*, are congruent.
3. *Correct production for a nontraditional strategy* IF the goal is to solve an equation in x, THEN graph the left and right sides of the equation and find the intersection point(s).	Solve equation $\sin x = x^2$ by graphing both $\sin x$ and x^2 and finding where the lines cross.
4. *Correct but overly specific production* IF "$ax + bx$" appears in an expression AND $c = a + b$, THEN replace it with "cx."	Works for "$2x + 3x$" but not for "$x + 3x$."
5. *Incorrect, overly general production* IF "Num1 + Num2" appears in an expression, THEN replace it with the sum.	Leads to order of operations error: "$x * 3 + 4$" is rewritten as "$x * 7$"

From Koedinger and Corbett (2006).

Below is a partial list of mathematical competences that other primates appear to have:

1. Both human infants and primates appear to have an ability to represent exact magnitudes up to 3 or 4 without training (Brannon and Terrace, 2002; Hauser and Carey, 2003; Hauser et al., 2002).

2. Both human infants and primates (and indeed, many other species) appear to have an analogical numerical system that can represent larger quantities at least approximately. Again, this is

not something that seems to require training (for reviews, see Brannon, 2005; Hauser and Spelke, 2004).

3. Both humans and other primates are capable of spontaneously tracking the addition and subtraction of at least small numbers, and perhaps also larger numbers (Beran and Beran, 2004; Flombaum et al., 2005). Again, this is not something that seems to require training.

4. Both humans and other primates can be trained to compare quantities (e.g., two dots vs. four) or to order them in increasing sequence. They also appear to show comparable behavioral effects such as a distance effect where judgments are faster the farther apart the two digits are (Brannon, 2005).

5. Both humans and other primates can be trained to assigned symbols to different quantities. It does appear, however, that it is much more difficult to train nonhuman primates (Hauser and Spelke, 2004). Once trained, they tend to treat these symbols much the same as humans do. For instance, symbol-based Stroop numeric interference in monkeys is discussed in chapter 4. Primates are capable of counting in this system, as preschool children are; that is, they can point to the symbols in the order of their magnitude. Boysen and Bernston (1989) were able to get their chimpanzee Sheba to correctly perform addition of small quantities as indicated by symbols $(1+3, 2+2)$.

The study by Nieder et al. (2002) is particularly compelling in its evidence that nonhuman primates represent specific quantities such as 3 and 4. They trained monkeys to match samples on the basis of numerosity. The procedure, illustrated in figure 5.1a, was one in which the monkeys saw a number of items, a delay passed, and then the monkeys had to indicate whether a test stimulus had the same number of items. The researchers found about one-third of the neurons in the prefrontal cortex responded preferentially to different numbers during encoding and delay. Figure 5.1b displays responses of neurons that preferentially responded to numbers from 1 to 5. These neurons responded maximally when the number presented matched their preference, and their response rate dropped off monotonically as the number differed.

As an approximate statement, it may be said that the mathematical abilities of higher apes with extensive training like Sheba's appear to

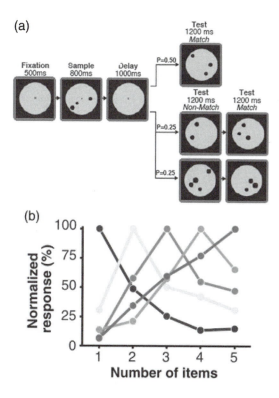

Figure 5.1. (a) An illustration of the procedure in Nieder et al. (2002).
(b) Normalized responses averaged for neurons displaying peak responses
for different preferred numbers. Figure a reprinted with permission from
Nieder, A. Freedman, D. J., & Miller, E. K. (2002). Representation of the
quantity of visual items in the primate prefrontal cortex, *Science, 297*,
1708–1711. Copyright 2002 AAAS.

match those of children before they enter school. This leaves them
far short of algebraic competence. Before they get to algebra, children
will have mastered addition and multiplication tables for single digits,
algorithms for multicolumn subtraction, addition, and multiplication
(and perhaps still the division algorithm, but that is fading from popu-
larity in education), and fractional arithmetic in both rational and deci-
mal notation. These competences could have been chosen as a target for
study rather than algebra. Algebra has the advantage of being so far from
primate mathematics that there can be no doubt that it is a uniquely
human competence. The age of the population makes experimentation

relatively easy. It is also a skill that relies less on the mastery of the addition and multiplication tables. Indeed, some mathematics educators advocate teaching algebra with calculators, thus completely eliminating the need for such massive memorization. In selecting a competence that is uniquely human, it is just as well to find one that does not depend on superior memorization skills.

Learning a Socially Transmitted Competence

This chapter focuses on learning by following verbal directions and, to a lesser extent, by following worked-out examples. However, a third way to learn is by discovery and invention. Cultural artifacts such as algebra came into being because of such a process. Some constructivist mathematics educators advocate having children learn in the same manner (e.g., Cobb et al., 1992). In the extreme, it is a very inefficient way to learn algebra or any other cultural artifact—we do not expect the next generation to learn to drive by discovery. However, when one looks in detail at what happens in the process of learning from instruction and example, one frequently finds many minidiscoveries being made as students try to make sense of the instruction they are receiving and their experience in applying that instruction.[7] Learning by discovery probably plays a more important role as a normal part of learning through social transmission (i.e., taking directions and following examples) than it does as a solo means of learning.

The distinction between learning from verbal directions and worked-out examples is somewhat artificial, and most learning situations involve some mix of the two. Verbal direction is restricted to linguistically enabled individuals, which would seem to restrict it to humans.[8] However, superior human learning cannot be explained simply by the human ability to process verbal directions. Many experiments have found that people learn as well or better from worked-out examples than from verbal directions (e.g., Cheng et al., 1986; Fong et al., 1986; Reed and Bolstad, 1991).

---

7. Indeed, many parents report observing beginning drivers having numerous near-accidents that serve as discovery experiences for learning to drive.

8. There is little evidence of learning by instruction even in language-trained apes, but the claim has been made that these language-trained animals are able to show examples of learning that non-language-trained animals are not (Oden et al., 2001; Premack, 1976)

When one tries to model learning from verbal directions (as described later in this chapter), it becomes apparent why this might be so. Here are two of the more problematic aspects of verbal instructions:

1. Verbal directions require understanding referring expressions such as "the innermost operation," whose reference is far from obvious to the novice learner. It can be easier to understand if the example just operates on the (9/3) in $[3+(9/3)]*x$.

2. Instruction typically describes tasks that involve multiple steps. Therefore, understanding the instruction also requires appropriately anticipating the intermediate state produced by a step so that one can appreciate the situation where the next step of instruction applies. The intermediate states are clearer if one is taken through a worked-out example.

On the other hand, worked-out examples have their own problems, as again becomes apparent when one tries to model learning from such examples. One big problem is inferring the appropriate generalization from an example. One is expected to apply what one sees (e.g., replacing $x+3=8$ by $x+3-3=8-3$) to other situations, but what are those situations, and exactly what is it that one is supposed to apply? The weakness of either mode by itself is probably why mathematics texts and mathematics teachers almost always choose to intermix the two modes of instruction.

Learning by Imitation

Because learning from a worked-out example does not require language, it is possible to compare different species as to their ability to succeed from such purely example-based instruction. There has been considerable comparative work on a similar (but ultimately different) issue, which is the ability of different species to learn by imitation. As R. Byrne and Russon (1998) comment, there has been a remarkable rehabilitation in the status of imitation in psychology. As they write:

> True intelligence, it used to be thought, is indicated by insight. The "cheap trick" of imitating allowed nonhuman species to simulate intellectual capacities they did not have. . . . Imitation's recent promotion to the status of an intellectual asset in cognitive science has been accompanied by a wealth of evidence that many

nonhuman species are unable to learn by imitating the actions
they see others perform, whereas even newborn humans are now
reported to show imitation. (p. 667)

Many things that might appear to be imitation in nonhumans have
been attributed to other, "lesser" factors. Consider a situation where one
chimp observes another breaking coconuts with rocks and comes to
do the same. To the naive observer, this would seem an obvious case of
imitation, but it is not so obvious to the comparative psychologist. Before
it will be declared true imitation, one has to rule out other explanations.
For instance, maybe the observation has just increased the salience of rocks
for the pseudo-imitator and this now becomes something it plays with,
thus discovering the relationship. Or perhaps the observation has just
instilled in the pseudo-imitator the goal of eating coconuts. Or perhaps
it has increased the tendency to swing rocks but with no attachment to
the goal of getting coconuts. The quest for "pure imitation" has led, in my
opinion, to a rather dumbed-down version of imitation that requires verbatim repetition of the actions without any inventive recombination.

This can be illustrated in the distinction noted by Whiten et al. (1996)
in the solution of two versions of what they called the artificial fruit task.
They compared the performance of young children and chimpanzees on
this task. The two versions of the apparatus are illustrated in figure 5.2, a
and b. The Plexiglas container had to be opened to get at the food contained
in it. In the case in figure 5.2a, two different techniques were demonstrated
for removing the plastic rods. The *poke* technique involved pushing a rod
out with the right index finger. The *twist* technique involved grasping the
rod and pulling it out with a twisting motion. Different techniques were
demonstrated to the participants, who then had their opportunity to open
the container. Independent observers who did not know which technique
had been used rated the solutions as pokes or twists. These ratings are
presented in figure 5.2c. Both chimpanzees and children showed a strong
tendency to imitate the action displayed to them. This is considered a paradigm that displays successful imitation by nonhuman primates.

Figure 5.2b illustrates a container that has a different locking device
and can again be opened in one of two ways: the handle could either be
pulled straight up out of the barrel that contained it or turned in a clock-
wise direction so that the lip swung away from the lid. Again, one of these
two techniques was demonstrated for the participant; the rated solutions
are given in figure 5.2d. The children continue to imitate, whereas the

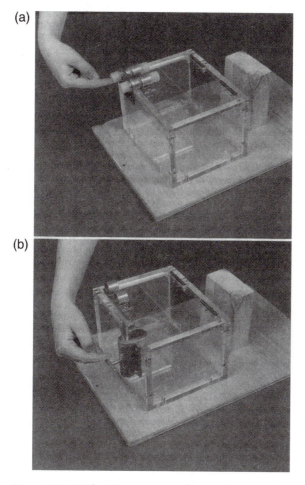

Figure 5.2. (a) Plexiglas container that can be opened
by a poke versus a twist. (b) Plexiglas container that
can be opened by a pull versus a turn.

chimpanzees show a strong tendency to pull independent of what had
been demonstrated. This is a frequent result—young children prove to
be very faithful imitators, while other primates are not. Some (Tomasello and Call, 1997) have argued that this reflects a fundamental species
difference. However, in the context of the experiment of Whiten et al.
(1996), the interesting question is why there is imitation on one task and
not on the other. It seems that chimpanzees can imitate but will adopt
their own choice of a method when that method is obvious (and pulling
is apparently an obvious method). However, young children often display

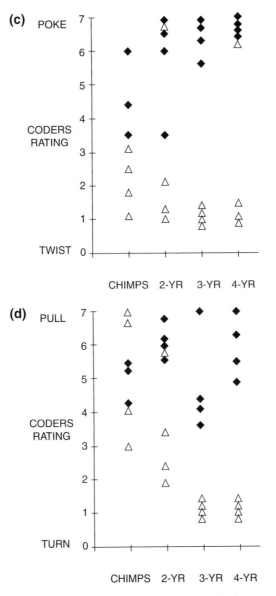

Figure 5.2. (*continued*) (c) Independent raters' scores for the actions in solving the problem in (a): solid diamonds are participants who had witnessed a poke; open triangles are participants who had witnessed a twist. (d) Independent raters' scores for the actions in solving the problem in (b): solid diamonds are participants who had witnessed a pull; open triangles are participants who had witnessed a turn. Ratings in (c) and (d) are on a 7-point scale where 0 is a perfect twist (c) or a perfect turn (d) and 7 is a perfect poke (c) or a perfect pull (d). From Whiten, Custance, Gomez, Texidor, & Bard (1996). Copyright American Psychological Association, and reprinted with permission.

an almost slavish attention to detail in their efforts to reproduce what was seen. Children appear to imitate verbatim less as they get older. Tomasello (2000) argues that young children may gain by their slavish imitation because the behavior they are observing may have critical details that they do not yet appreciate but will learn if they try exact copies of the behavior.

Learning Algebra From Examples Is Not Learning by Imitation

In any case, whether by the dumbed-down comparative definition or by more liberal definitions, imitation is inadequate to explain how humans learn from worked-out examples in algebra. Consider the following example of a relatively simple derivation:

$$x - 3 = 8$$
$$x - 3 + 3 = 8 + 3$$
$$x = 8 + 3$$
$$x = 11$$

Certainly, a child learning from this example needs to learn something more than how to solve just this specific problem. Suppose the child is given the problem $x-7=9$. The current verbatim repetition definition of imitation in the comparative literature would require that the child reproduce the next line as $x-3+3=8+3$, which would be bizarre. Children are quite capable of appreciating that the 3 in the example maps onto 7 in the current problem and the 8 maps onto the 9. Basically, the child must engage in analogy to extract anything useful out of this example. Most children, at the age they learn algebra, have no difficulty seeing this analogy.

And the analogy goes beyond simple mapping of elements. Consider what 11 in the example must be mapped to in the solution $x-7=9$. This requires seeing the relationship that 11 is the sum of 8 and 3. And relational inferences can get harder. Consider a child using this example to solve $x+7=9$. In this case, the child must recognize that 3 is added in the example to undo the subtraction, whereas the current problem requires subtracting to undo the addition. This is much more than mere imitation.[9]

9. Try solving the following analogy: "If g = 7Δr becomes g49r = Δ, what does 3Δa = b become?" I won't give you the "correct answer"; compare your solution with that of a partner solving it independently. You will probably discover that a consensus tends to exist in your species.

Of course, typical instruction does not depend entirely on the child's ability to identify the relations; it includes verbal directions pointing to the correct generalizations. But whether by direct example or by verbal direction, successful learning of algebra depends on formulating and using relatively complex generalizations. It is this capacity that is key to human learning and that seems missing from other species.[10] While children are capable of this by the age they come to algebra, they do not necessarily have this capacity at earlier ages. For instance, Loewenstein and Gentner (2005) document the development of preschool children at interpreting examples and in their ability to use linguistic descriptions accompanying the examples to help interpret these examples.

Interpreting Algebra Through the ACT-R Lens

In the remainder of this chapter, I review three efforts modeling algebra learning in ACT-R. The goal is to use the models for these algebra tasks to answer the question of what it is about human cognition that enables us to master algebra. While making no claim to having identified all that is unique about human cognition, in this chapter I identify three features. The first, the potential for abstract control of cognition, is a feature that has been part of ACT-R from its inception. The second, the capacity for advanced pattern matching, required a fundamental extension to the ACT-R architecture that is described below. The third, the metacognitive ability to reason about mental cognitive states, is a capacity that the expanded architecture allows, but one that has not received much attention within the ACT-R community. Each of the following three sections describes a modeling study that provides an opportunity to consider in detail one of these three features.

A Laboratory Study of Algebra Learning: Abstract Control

The first task is the Qin et al. (2004) experiment described in chapter 1. Data from this experiment have already been presented (figures 1.6, 1.8,

---

10. Chimpanzees have shown some ability to solve analogies (e.g., Oden et al., 2001), but not at a level sufficient to learn algebra. Their subject, Sarah, was achieving about 50% success on basic analogies, which is better than chance in this context but is nonetheless much less than can be accomplished by children ready for algebra.

and 4.15). The model for this task highlights the first feature that contributes to human success in algebra: the use of abstract control states. After describing the model, I discuss the importance of these abstract control states.

To review, the participants were children 11–14 years of age who had mastered middle-school math but who had not yet begun to solve equations. They were given an hour-long introduction to solving such equations as $7x + 3 = 38$ and then were given five days of practice at solving the equations. Figure 1.6 shows the behavioral speed-up over the five days; figures 1.8 and 4.15 show the results from fMRI imaging on days 1 and 5. Generally, participants get faster at performing this task. The cognitive regions show effects of problem complexity and tend to respond less with practice. A notable exception for the purposes of this section is the anterior cingulate cortex (ACC), which does show a robust effect of problem complexity but no effect of practice. This region is related to the goal module that maintains abstract control. The need for abstract control does not change over the course of the experiment.

The instruction-following model starts from an internal declarative representation of the instructions given to the children in this task. Table 5.2 shows the English rendition of the instructions that were published with the description of the model in Anderson (2005a). While the simulation starts from Englishlike instructions, the actual model did not parse these instructions. Rather, a LISP program converted these instructions into declarative chunks, and the model took over from there. This LISP program protected the model from having to produce the full flexibility that is required to use real instructions. The model in the next section actually dealt with the parsing and the extra demands that this creates.

Once the instructions are represented in declarative memory, ACT-R has interpretative productions for converting these instructions into behavior. The instruction is decomposed into actions that the participant already knows how to do: reading a number expression, performing an addition, keying a number, and so on. The instructions specify how to step through such known actions. The next section elaborates upon the nature of these instruction-following productions. This section focuses only on the overall flow of control among these productions.

Figure 1.7 contrasts the model's performance during a typical trial at the beginning of the day 1 (part a) with the performance during a typical trial at the end of day 5 (part b). That figure illustrates when the

Table 5.2.   English Rendition of Instructions Given to ACT-R Model for
             Equation Solving

Task	Conditional Execution
1. To solve an equation, encode it and	a. If the right side is a number, then imagine that number as the result and focus on the left side and unwind it. b. If the left side is a number, then imagine that number as the result and focus on the right side and unwind it.
2. To unwind an expression	a. If the expression is the variable, then the result is the answer. b. If a number is on the right, unwind-right. c. If a number is on the left, unwind-left.
3. To unwind-right, encode the expression (of the form "subexpression operator number") and	a. If the operator is + or − and the number is 0, then focus on the subexpression and unwind it. b. Otherwise, invert the operator, imagine it as the operator in the result, imagine the number as the second argument in the result, evaluate the result, and then focus on the subexpression and unwind it.
4. To unwind-left, encode the expression (of the form "number operator subexpression") and	a. If the operator is * and number 1, then focus on the subexpression and unwind it. b. Otherwise, check that the operator is symmetric, invert the operator, imagine it as the operator in the result, imagine the number as the second argument in the result, evaluate the result, and then focus on the subexpression and unwind it.

various modules were active during the solution of the equation and what they were doing. Processing of the instructions engages a pattern of activity involving the declarative module, the procedural module, and some more peripheral modules: basically, an instruction is retrieved, a production fires that interprets it, and it calls for activity by a module such as the manual module. A major dimension of learning in this task, and in all such models, is the dropout of instruction interpretation with practice. As can be seen by comparing figures 1.7a and 1.7b, fewer instructional steps are retrieved on day 5. This is due to production compilation that collapses these retrieve-instruction-and-interpret cycles into single production rules. As discussed in chapter 4, production compilation is a slow process, but eventually it can collapse multiple steps into a single rule.

Comparison With Primate Sequential Symbolic Behavior

It took well under an hour to instruct students on the equation-solving involved in this experiment. Corresponding to this, the amount of knowledge that the model must encode to perform the task is really rather little. The knowledge can be compactly communicated and represented because it just involves a few abstract bits of information such as performing the inverse arithmetic operation. To make such abstract bits work it is necessary for the model and the children to carry forward mental lines of computation that retrieve critical information from declarative memory and rerepresent the problem. The abstract control states enabled by the goal module are critical to the ability to carry forward these lines of thought without any external support. To bring out an essential function of these abstract control states, this subsection will compare a slight caricature of the model for this task with a slight caricature of a model for a similar task that nonhuman primates can do.

Solving these equations involves representing the sequential structure of the symbols and rearranging them. Primates are quite good at a number of tasks that require sequential processing. Consider the example of serial behavior that has been observed in the rhesus macaque. In the experiment reported by Terrace et al. (2003), monkeys learned four seven-item lists of pictures. On any particular trial, the monkeys were shown one set of seven pictures randomly arrayed on the screen, and they had to select them in the correct order. They were able to reproduce the seven items perfectly more than 65% of the time—a level of performance that is not much worse than humans would show in similar circumstances. Terrace et al. offer a number of varieties of evidence to argue that the monkeys are operating from a declarative representation of the list order and not some type of procedural representation. For instance, monkeys can correctly order two items from different lists that they have never seen paired before. These serial tasks are interesting because they bear certain superficial similarities to algebra symbol manipulation. In algebra symbol manipulation, a child is shown one array of symbols (the equation) and must produce another array of symbols (a rearranged equation—in the task described in this section, the response is reduced to a single key press, but it is typically more complex, as in the task described in the next section). Similarly, the monkey is shown one array of symbols and must produce a sequence of symbols or actions.

While the performance of monkeys in these serial tasks is in many ways remarkable, there are significant differences between transforming algebraic equations and manipulating serial lists. One major difference is in the generativeness of the child's algebraic capacity. The child is capable of responding to an arbitrary number of new expressions. Successfully solving equations requires being able to do more than generate a different behavior in the presence of a different equation. There is the requirement that the behavior result in the solution of the equation; this is like the well-formedness constraint of linguistic behavior. One particularly noteworthy aspect of the equation solving studied in this experiment is that the children had to do all the manipulation in their head—they only gave the final answer. This was not a particularly burdensome requirement for them; indeed, children often resent having to write out intermediate results. However, it does highlight the contribution of their mental structures to equation solving.

While the differences between children's algebraic symbol manipulation and monkeys' serial reproduction may seem obvious, the challenge is to identify what in the architecture is associated with this difference. ACT-R models for serial reproduction tasks such as those performed by Terrace et al.'s monkeys require visual, manual, and declarative buffers that work in ways formally similar to the models for the algebraic tasks. These, then, cannot be the source of the differences.

To facilitate a contrast between the sequential behavior in equation solving and the sequential behavior in the monkey task, figure 5.3 provides a simplified rendition of figure 1.7. It is basically the end state that production compilation would reach if given enough time. As in figure 1.7, the equation being solved is $7*x+3=38$. The simplified mental image of the equation just holds the intermediate result, but it is the critical piece of information in that it is what is not supported by external information. For instance, at one point the image in figure 5.3 holds an internal representation of 35 that is intermediate between the original equation and the final answer of 5. Being able to hold onto such an internal representation, detached from either stimulus or action, is critical to the model's algebraic competence. It is tempting to point to the parietal cortex as what is human-unique in this algebra problem solving, since the parietal cortex is postulated to correspond to the imaginal module. The region of parietal cortex that corresponds to the imaginal module may not have an exact homologue in the monkey brain (Zilles and Palomero-Gallagher, 2001).

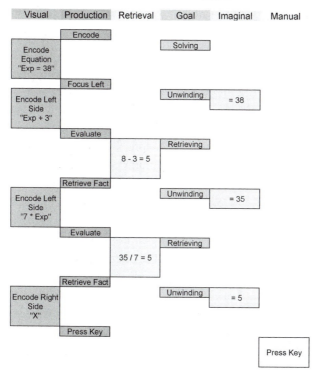

Figure 5.3. A representation of the basic buffer operations required to implement the unwind strategy in ACT-R to solve the equation $7 * x + 3 = 38$.

While human ability to hold such intermediate results may have some special properties, it is not totally discontinuous from the ability of the monkey. This becomes apparent when one tries to develop an ACT-R model for the monkey task of ordering two items from two lists. Terrace et al. have shown a generative capacity to the monkey's serial knowledge in that it can take a pair of elements from different lists that it has not seen together, and correctly order them with high accuracy. Figure 5.4 is a similar flow-chart for a model for this ordering task. The model assumes that the monkey retrieves the location of each item in the pair, creates an image that synthesizes the two locations, and then picks the item that is first in this image. While the imaginal module in this example may not have all of the flexibility of human imagery in equation manipulation, it does synthesize two objects in order to make an appropriate decision. A comparison of figures 5.3 and 5.4 indicates that the two tasks do not differ in their capacity demands on the imaginal representation. Both require a relatively small amount to be held in the imaginal buffer. In fact, the algebra task really requires holding just one number at any time, whereas two items have to be synthesized in the image for the serial task.

Comparing figures 5.3 and 5.4, however, does reveal a striking difference. The model in figure 5.4 does not require any state tests against the goal buffer. Perhaps humans in doing the task use such control tests, but they are not necessary to accomplish the task. Control elements in the goal generally serve to disambiguate which production to fire when the states of all the other buffers are the same. However, it turns out that each production that fires in figure 5.4 is uniquely determined by the states of the other buffers. The conditions for each production are reviewed in table 5.3. Note that there is a distinct state of the buffers that uniquely selects each production.

In contrast, because of the iterative nature of the algebra algorithm, it is not possible to find unique states of the nongoal modules for each production in the model. The model is faced with multiple situations where it has focused on an element in the equation, has retrieved an arithmetic fact, and has an image of an intermediate result. Without the help of the control element in the goal, the model would not know whether it is time to retrieve another arithmetic fact or perform another transformation of the equation. Therefore, it would sometimes skip retrievals or trans-

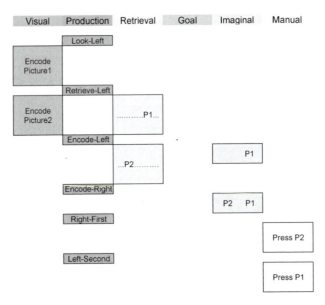

Figure 5.4. A representation of the basic buffer operations required to implement the serial ordering task. P1 and P2 are the pictures.

Table 5.3.   Buffer Conditions for the Firing of Each of the Productions in
Figure 5.4

Production	Buffer Condition
1. Look-left	The presentation of the stimulus (not shown) is the condition for this production that requests the encoding of the first element.
2. Retrieve-Left	The appearance of the left element in the visual buffer is the condition for this production that requests both the encoding of the second element and the retrieval of the position of the left element in its list.
3. Encode-Left	The appearance of positional information in the retrieval buffer and an empty imaginal buffer are the conditions for this production that positions the left element in the image and requests retrieval of the right element.
4. Encode-Right	The appearance of positional information in the retrieval buffer and an incomplete image are the conditions for this production that similarly places the right element in the image.
5. Right-First	The appearance of information in the imaginal buffer in which the right element is first is the condition for this production that selects the right element with a manual press.
6. Left-Second	The manual selection of that element and an imaginal buffer in which the left element is second are the conditions for this production that selects the left element with a manual press.

formations and would repeat them at other times. In the current model, repeats are innocuous, but skips mean that it fails to solve the problem. For instance, in a model that does not use the control information, faced with the equation $3x+9=15$, it can respond 6 because it omitted retrieving $6/3=2$ or because it omitted to use the fact when retrieved.[11]

Throughout this book, the goal buffer that holds control elements is associated with the ACC. The ACC is particularly active in studies where participants have to direct their behavior in a way that violates typical response tendencies. The ACC has undergone major evolutionary changes

11. These problems can be avoided if one puts control information into the image, but then this loses the separation of control state and problem state. One might try to take advantage of the fact that the declarative buffer empties on retrieval in ACT-R 6.0, and one can do a test for whether the buffer is empty. However, this is somewhat technical (not something that is easy to learn). It also only deals with this situation and is not a solution to the problem of having to take different actions in states where all buffers but the goal buffer are identical. However, I should note that questions of when abstract control elements are needed in human models have become an issue of some interest in the ACT-R community (e.g., Taatgen, 2005), and within my own research group it has become something of a challenge to see how much algebra can be done without control elements.

that are found only in humans and the closely related great apes (Allman et al., 2001). These changes, which include a new class of spindle-shaped cells in strongest concentration in the human ACC, appear to be related to the ability to achieve appropriate behavior in the presence of conflicting stimuli. While these cells appear in the higher apes, they are much more frequent in the human ACC.[12]

So, where does this leave the question of what enables the human-unique aspects of algebra-problem solving? A critical mental ability is the capacity to maintain abstract control states that allow the human to take different courses of action when all the other buffers are in identical states. While there is no justification for saying that this capacity is totally lacking in nonhuman primates, it does seem vastly improved in humans, at least by the age when they begin to learn algebra. Two other capacities that are critical to the learning of algebra are considered in the next two sections.

Learning to Solve Linear Equations: Dynamic Pattern Matching

Modeling a Full Course of Learning

The second study was considerably more ambitious: we taught students to solve the full range of linear equations that appear in the classic Algebra 1 textbook by Foerster (1990). This is still only a fragment of a full algebra course; the critical material spans 15 sections in the first four chapters of the Foerster text, and students solved all the "odd" problems in the Foerster text. Table 5.4 gives the 15 sections and shows examples of the problems that students solved. We looked at two populations: 10 children just starting algebra working with the standard linear form, and 15 adults (Carnegie Mellon University undergraduates) working with a novel data-flow isomorph to algebra that we developed (see figure 5.5).[13]

---

12. These neurons also are found in the frontal insular (FI) cortex, again only in higher apes. K. K. Watson et al. (2006) note that these neurons have structural properties that suggest they "provide a rapid relay to other parts of the brain of a simple signal derived from information processed within FI and ACC" (p. 1112). Reflecting the wide range of opinions about the function of the ACC, Allman et al. (2005) suggest that these neurons are especially involved in making social judgments.

13. This section describes unpublished work with Shawn Betts. While the data shown in figure 5.7 were generated with earlier versions of the tutor and model, we have made a version, titled "Linear Equations," available at the ACT-R website. This version has the advantage over the earlier versions of allowing one to use both the linear tutor and the data-flow tutor and allowing instructions or examples.

Table 5.4. The Algebra Sections From Foerster (1990) and Overall Performance Measures[a]

Section	Number of Problems	Representative Problem	Children Time per Problem (s)	Children (Standard) Mean Errors per Problem	Adults Time per Problem (s)	Adults (Data Flow) Mean Errors per Problem
1.1	16	$(16 - (3 * 2)) - 4$	43.9	0.38	25.4	0.18
1.2	16	$(x - 31) * 4$ if $x = 80$	36.0	0.44	17.2	0.11
1.7	25	$x + 5 = 4$	34.9	0.64	28.7	0.27
2.1	17	$35 + -11$	15.2	0.15		
2.3	19	$(((45 - 7) - 58) + 11) - 21$	38.0	0.58		
2.4	13	$(-3 * -5) * -7$	19.8	0.24		
2.5	28	$(5 - -3)/(3 - -3)$	25.9	0.28		
2.6	20	$(-18 - (3 * x)) + 7$	35.9	0.75	32.9	0.20
2.7	20	$13 - (4 * x) = 25$	53.3	1.38	32.7	0.40
3.1	6	$(2 * ((3 * x) + 8)) + 40$			83.9	0.45
3.2	9	$8 - (5 * (4 - (6 * x)))$			67.6	0.36
3.4	23	$(8 * ((2 * x) + 3)) - (4 * ((3 * x) + 6))$			97.5	0.95
4.1	11	$((9 * x) - 14) - (5 * x) = -10$			59.7	0.43
4.2	21	$(2 * ((3 * x) - 7)) + (4 * x) = 26$			82.9	0.64
4.3	18	$((6 * x) + 7) - (2 * x) = (3 + (2 * x)) - 9$			92.5	0.62

[a]The times are calculated by summing median times per problem across students. If the errors on a problem are greater than 3, this measure is truncated to 3 (a bound introduced in Anderson et al., 1989). Both of these statistics are used in the hope of eliminating the undue influence of outliers.

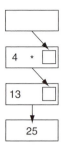

Figure 5.5. The data-flow isomorph of 13 − (4 * x) = 25. In this representation, some number enters the top box, and that number flows down to the second box, where it is multiplied by 4; that result flows down to the third box, where it is subtracted from 13, and that result flows down to the bottom box, where it is displayed as 25. To solve this, the student would try to determine what number had entered the top box.

The children and the adults did somewhat different sections. Because we could not count on the children knowing the arithmetic for negative numbers, we included four sections from Foerster that reviewed this material for them. In two sessions, the children got to section 2.7. In contrast, adults were able to get to section 4.3 in two sessions.

We created an interface in which either students or the model could interact with the same instruction and solve problems in identical ways. This meant that it was possible to put solutions of students and the model in close correspondence. Figure 5.6 illustrates that interface: part a is the linear form that was used with the children; part b is the data-flow form used with adults. In both cases it is the same equation being solved: 13 − 4x = 25. The two parts of the figure capture the state of the screen at the same point in the middle of problem solving. While normally no instruction is given at points like this, the figures display the instruction that a student might get if he or she requested a hint. The reader can confirm that the hint constitutes rather minimal instruction. The beginning of the section contains some general instruction for that section. The interface uses a combination of mouse selections and typed entries that enable the student to perform these transformations relatively efficiently.

For purposes of illustration, table 5.5 gives the general instruction at the beginning of section 1.7, the first section on solving such simple one-transformation equations as x + 3 = 8. The section begins with the introduction to equations. Then in the interface the student walks through

(a)

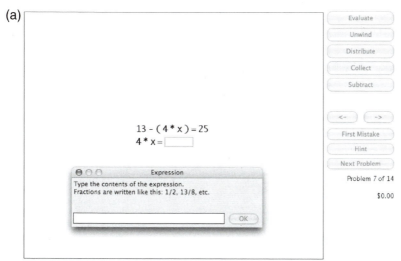

Evaluate

Unwind

Distribute

Collect

Subtract

<-   ->

First Mistake

Hint

Next Problem

Problem 7 of 14

$0.00

$$13 - (4 * x) = 25$$
$$4 * x = \boxed{}$$

Expression

Type the contents of the expression.
Fractions are written like this: 1/2, 13/8, etc.

OK

The result of subtracting something from 13 is 25.
To find out the value of that something, subtract 25 from 13.
Click the green box and type 13 - 25.

(b) The result of subtracting something from 13 is 25.
To find out the value of that something, subtract 25 from 13.
Click the green box and type 13 - 25.

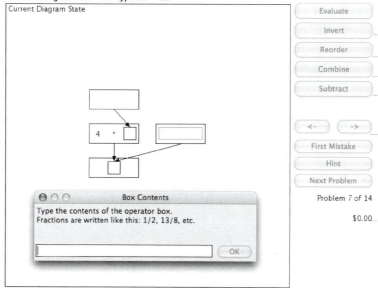

Current Diagram State

Evaluate

Invert

Reorder

Combine

Subtract

<-   ->

First Mistake

Hint

Next Problem

Problem 7 of 14

$0.00

4   *

Box Contents

Type the contents of the operator box.
Fractions are written like this: 1/2, 13/8, etc.

OK

Figure 5.6. Tutor interface: (a) the linear condition for use with children; (b) the data-flow condition for use with adults solving the problem that started out as figure 5.5.

Table 5.5.   Instructions for Transforming an Equation

Step	Task
Introduction	An equation is a sentence that says an expression with x is equal to a number. To solve an equation, find the value of x that would make this true. To do this, the equation must be transformed so that x is alone on one side of the equal sign and a number is on the other side. You can do this by unwinding the operations on the side of the equation that contains x.
Step 1	Find a equal sign with just a number on one side; then click the equal sign; then click the operator that is nearest the equal sign.
Step 2	Click the button labeled "unwind."
Step 3	Click the box that is green.
Step 4	Key the number isolated by the equal sign; then key the new operator, which is the inverse of the operator; then enter the number associated with the operator.

the mechanics of the four steps involved in transforming an equation such as $x+3=8$ into $x=8-3$. Table 5.5 gives the instruction accompanying each step. The first step indicates what part of the equation is being transformed, the second selects the unwind operation, the third selects a box for entering the new value, and the fourth specifies the value to be entered.

Unlike the previous model, this model started with the verbal directions on the screen and parsed these into an internal declarative representation of the instructions that it then used. The parsing rules were rather ad hoc, and I would not want to claim much psychological plausibility for them. However, the requirement that the internal declarative representation of the instructions be derived from general verbal directions made it impossible to craft the internal declarative representation for the task. This exposed a limitation in the ACT-R architecture that is discussed below.

Before discussing this modeling issue in detail, I first review the overall performance of the participants and the ability of the model to reproduce at least one aspect of that performance. As shown in table 5.4, children made more errors than did the adults, and they took much longer on common sections because they had to retry their solutions until they got the right answer. An inspection of the children's solutions and verbal protocols did not reveal any deep misunderstandings; they were just more prone to slips and less able to determine where their slips had occurred.

The number of errors and times both tended to increase for later sections. This is not surprising, since the problems were more complex in later sections and so required more steps of transformation.

Figure 5.7 looks at a measure that normalizes for problem complexity. This is the time to perform a single step of transformation of the equation. The number of keystrokes and mouse clicks was the same in this interface, independent of problem complexity. This is unlike paper and pencil solution, where more complex equations require more transcription of notation. The number of keystrokes and mouse clicks is also the same for the regular algebra and the data-flow isomorph. Figure 5.7 shows the performance of the adults over the 11 sections of the curriculum and the performance of the children on the five sections they had in common with the adults. The x-axis is the 181 problems that make up the 11 sections, and the y-axis is the measure that normalizes for problem complexity. The measure given is the median time per transformation. There are long times at the beginning of each section that speed up to near-asymptotic times by the last three sections. The children and adults show nearly identical times per cycle despite the fact that they were working with two different systems. The model predicts this because it responds to the abstract structure of the problems that is common for the linear representation and the data-flow representation.

As shown in figure 5.7, the model does a pretty good job of matching up with participant performance. The behavior of the model as dis-

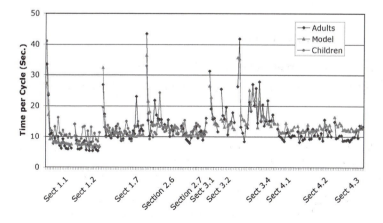

Figure 5.7. A comparison of the performance of the model with that of children learning the linear form of algebra and adults learning the data-flow form.

played in this graph is largely a result of the subsymbolic processes that were the topic of chapters 3 and 4. On the declarative side, there is the issue of retrieving the instructions. After first reading the instructions, the declarative representations will be weak. Therefore, the time to recall the instructional steps will be slow, and there will be many failures of recall. The failures of recall are particularly costly in time because the model will have to request help and spend time reading that help. Thus, the parameters controlling base-level learning are largely responsible for the rapid initial learning. The model will reach an asymptotic speed when it has compiled and is using the most compact production rules possible. The rate of this learning is determined by the learning rate parameter for production utility. The parameters controlling both the base-level learning and the production utility learning were set at the values described in the preceding chapters and are the default values for the model.[14]

While this match between model and data is reassuring, the more important outcome was that the model could learn from this instruction at all. This required a significant extension to the pattern-matching capabilities of the ACT-R architecture. While these extensions contributed to a number of aspects of the behavior of the model, they made their largest contribution to interpreting the instructions. As noted above, the instructions are no longer hand crafted but instead arise from parsing productions operating on the English sentences. This new feature that we had to add is called "dynamic pattern matching" and is discussed in the following section. Appendix 5.1 gives a more thorough exposition of the approach to instruction interpretation.

Dynamic Pattern Matching

Dynamic pattern matching can be illustrated in the processing of the one phrase in step 4 in table 5.5 ("Key the number isolated by the equal sign")

---

14. Recently, we have completed an imaging study of students learning from this curriculum. We found effects of complexity and learning remarkably similar to the pattern displayed in figure 1.8 for the simpler fragment of algebra (the experiment described immediately above). The one surprise came from the fusiform region that we associate with the visual module (we scanned low enough in the brain to pick up this area, whereas we had not in the earlier study). There were practice-based reductions of activation in the left fusiform gyrus, which is a region associated with reading of detailed material. Mathematics educators (e.g., Kirshner and Awtry, 2004) have speculated that part of developing mastery in algebra involves effectively learning to see new patterns in algebraic expressions, and this result seems to support them.

in the context of solving $x-5=3$. The parsing of the instruction breaks this down into two commands:[15]

1. Find the number isolated by the equal sign.
2. Key the number.

The critical feature in this instruction is the appearance of the referring expression "the number." Command 1 results in this expression referring to the number 3 while command 2 uses this expression to designate the 3. Instructional language is replete with situations where a referring term acquires a reference and this reference is used one or more times downstream. This same basic capacity is required in a learning-from-example model that was also developed for this task. So, for instance, if one wants to use a solution for $x-8=4$ as a model for solving $x-5=3$, one has to create a role for the 4 in the example that will map to the 3 in the problem in the same way that "the number" in the instruction is designating 3 in the problem. Dynamic pattern matching is a mechanism recently added to ACT-R to support these sorts of mappings. Without it, there is no tractable way to maintain the correspondence between the terms (created either in understanding the example or in understanding the verbal directions) and their references in the problem.

Figure 5.8 illustrates two of the productions that fired in processing this instruction: part a illustrates the instantiation of the first rule, and part b the abstract form of this rule used in the key step of interpreting the first command. Figure 5.8, c and d, similarly illustrates a rule used in the interpretation of the second command.

In the case of figure 5.8a, one rule has already applied in response to the first command and requested visual attention go to the region right of the equal sign. This has resulted in the encoding of the number 3 in the visual buffer. The production in figure 5.8a processes the result of this attentional move. The production copies the 3 in the visual buffer to the number slot of the goal buffer, where it can be found for later use, such as in the interpretation of the second command.[16] This rule might look innocent in its instantiated form, but when we look at its abstract form in

---

15. We could have given the instruction in this two-phrase form, but it seemed more natural to merge them into a combined sentence. Nothing in the discussion to follow depends on this choice of sentence structure.

16. It is not clear whether the goal module should be used to hold such temporary references or whether a separate module ought to be used for this purpose.

figure 5.8b, we see something old and something new. The old is what we
call static pattern matching; the new is dynamic pattern matching:

- *Static pattern matching:* The rule is not specific to number 3
  but is capable of applying to any number. Therefore, figure
  5.8b shows that the content of the visual buffer is moved to
  the goal buffer. This is the kind of pattern used in productions
  throughout the book, starting with figure 1.10b.
- *Dynamic pattern matching:* The slot into which the number is
  copied is determined from the role slot of the goal, which had
  been set to number as part of the instruction interpretation.
  Thus, the location in the goal to which the number is copied is

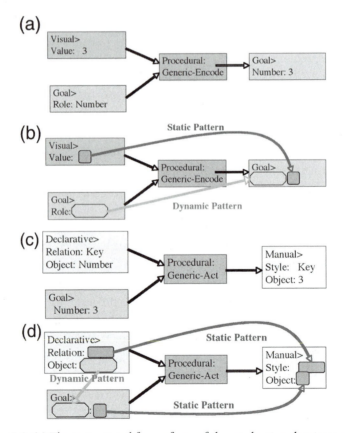

Figure 5.8. (a) The instantiated form of one of the production that interprets
"Find the number isolated by the equal sign" applied to $x-5=3$; (b) the abstract pattern behind (a); (c) the instantiated form of a production that interprets "key the number"; (d) the abstract pattern behind (c).

dynamically set in response to this instruction. This is a more powerful kind of pattern matching because the positional slots involved in the production can change depending on the situation—in this case, depending on the instruction.

Figure 5.8c illustrates the rule used in interpreting the second command, "Key the number." That production responds to retrieval of the command, which is to key the number; determines that the number is 3; and requests the execution of a motor program to key 3 (which, given that ACT-R models a skilled typist, will result in a finger movement to the appropriate key). As figure 5.8d illustrates, this production again mixes dynamic pattern matching with static pattern matching. The dynamic pattern matching in this case involves having the value in the object slot of the declarative buffer tell the system where to look in the goal buffer. In the case of figure 5.8c, that location is the number slot, but in other cases it will be other locations.

Dynamic pattern matching is interesting because, in contrast to static pattern matching, it cannot be implemented by simple neural pathways. In the case of static pattern matching, one can interpret the connections as pathways between fixed neural regions. In contrast, with dynamic patterns the regions from or to which the information is being moved are being determined dynamically.

One might wonder if this functionality could not be achieved without dynamic pattern matching. For instance, dynamic pattern matching was not part of the instruction interpretation model for the earlier laboratory experiment described (figure 1.7) or other instructional models we have developed (e.g., Anderson, Bothell et al., 2004; Anderson, Taatgen, and Byrne, 2005; Taatgen, 2005). It was not needed because we did not work from actual instruction but instead shaped by hand the internal representations of the instructions so that they could work with fixed slots. Such ad hoc rendering of the instructions does not generalize when one has to process arbitrary verbal instructions rather than preencoded internal instructions. It also does not extend to general models that learn from examples. Of course, ACT-R is Turing equivalent even without dynamic pattern matching, and it is possible to program in solutions, but these solutions would take too long and would be too error prone. For instance, one might imagine a system that committed facts such as "number is 3" to declarative memory and had general interpretive machinery for retrieving and using these facts. However, this would spread out over potentially many production cycles what can be done in a single cycle, and it would be quite prone to errors of declarative memory.

Dynamic pattern matching is one step in the direction of giving the ACT-R pattern matching the much greater power of the Soar Rete pattern matcher (Forgy, 1982). The Rete matcher can engage in search to match a pattern; potentially this search can explode into an NP (nondeterministic polynomial time) complete problem (Doorenbos, 1995). Dynamic pattern matching does not involve any search, and more generally, the ACT-R pattern matcher never engages in search. Interestingly, within the Soar community, patterns that involve search are disapproved of (John Laird, personal communication). That is, in the Soar world, the pattern matching in figure 5.8 is not viewed as problematical, but the more powerful patterns that require search are discouraged. Thus, a consensus seems to be emerging about how much information can be brought together in the pattern matching that involves one 50-ms cycle of cognition.

Possible Neural Implementation of Dynamic Pattern Matching

While dynamic pattern matching requires more of the brain than does static pattern matching, it is by no means beyond the scope of ideas put forth for neural information processing. For instance, there are proposals for tensor product representation (Smolensky, 1990) and temporal synchrony (Shastri and Ajjanagadde, 1993). As discussed in these references, dynamic pattern matching moves us in the direction of the full power of variables and all the controversy associated with that in cognitive science.[17] However, dynamic pattern matching is still a very contained sense of variable use compared to what is possible.

With respect to the brain realization of dynamic pattern matching, I am attracted to an idea suggested by Randy O'Reilly based on O'Reilly and Frank (2006; see their figure 12). His suggestion concerns how to deal with the fact that in dynamic pattern matching, one does not know ahead of time which brain region will be needed as the source or destination of the information. O'Reilly suggests mapping information between all potential regions and then dynamically gating the paths between the regions. Figure 5.9 provides an expanded version of the productions in figure 5.8 that illustrate this. There are two regions in the goal buffer,

---

17. Dynamic pattern matching gives the ACT-R system some of the power associated with higher order logic.

slot1 and slot2, which can be dynamically allocated to two different roles. In the context of step 4 in table 5.5, slot1 might be serving the number role and slot2 might be the operator role. However, in other contexts, they might be serving other roles. In Figure 5.9a the contents of the visual buffer are sent to both slots in the goal. The big addition to these figures is a mapping structure that maps between roles and slots (at the bottom of figure 5.9a). This stores that in the current context, slot1 is number and slot2 is operator. The contents of the role slot in the goal are tested against the two slots of the mapping structure. Whichever matches then opens the gate to the corresponding slot in the goal buffer and allows the content from the visual buffer to enter that slot. Similarly, in figure 5.9b, both slots from the goal have their contents mapped to the object slot of the manual buffer, and the mapping structure will determine which one to enable according to which of its slots matches the object slot in the declarative buffer. The use of these gating operations and an intermediate mapping structure can enable dynamic pattern matching with fixed neural pathways. O'Reilly and Frank suggest that this capacity for gating

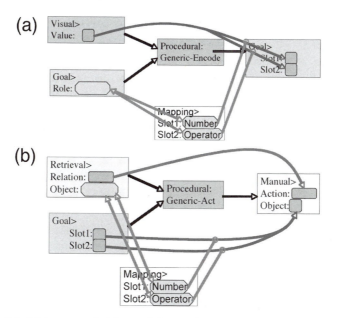

Figure 5.9. (a) An expanded form of the production in figure 5.8b to include a mapping structure that gates the values from the visual buffer; (b) an expanded form of the production in figure 5.8d to include a mapping structure that gates the values from the goal buffer.

involves prefrontal structures.[18] Given the greatly expanded prefrontal cortex of humans, this might explain human ability to make flexible use of instructions and examples.

Concluding Observations About Dynamic Pattern Matching

While dynamic pattern matching enables the instructions to be processed efficiently, eventually production compilation eliminates the need for dynamic pattern matching. Consider the production in figure 5.10 that results from a compilation of the two productions in figure 5.8. This rule has only a static pattern that copies the number from the visual buffer to the manual buffer. These are the kinds of production rules that one can imagine any primate having, and it could be trained through operant measures to hit the appropriate key in response to a visual stimulus (which is what that production reflects). Indeed, any of the productions ultimately learned by the model for this task could be trained to a monkey through operant techniques. However, this would be a very slow way to learn compared to human ability to follow directions or to interpret examples.

In summary, to follow instructions (verbal directions and examples), humans need general rules that are able to process the relational structure that appears in these instructions. Architecturally, this requires a capacity to match more general patterns than other primates can. Specifically, the human architecture can process rules in which the specific pattern matched changes with the context. While this section has discussed dynamic pattern matching with respect to the processing of verbal directions, this same capacity is essential to modeling the analogical processing of examples. As discussed in the introduction to this chapter, the ability to process complex relational structures seems to be exactly what is missing in nonhuman primates and what is essential to the learning of algebra. Therefore, dynamic pattern matching joins the ability to exercise abstract cognitive control as another architectural feature distinguishing humans from other primates. The model would not have been able to display successful learning in this task without it, let alone match up with the performance data in figure 5.7 as well as it did.

18. This also seems related to Ericsson and Kintsch's (1995) proposal for a long-term working memory, something that has the efficiency of working memory but the capacity of long-term memory.

Figure 5.10. The production that results from the compilation of the two productions in figure 5.8, b and d.

Mastery of an Algebraic Concept: Does Metacognition Require Special Architectural Features?

Solving linear equations has a particularly algorithmic quality. One might wonder whether learning the more conceptual aspects of mathematics would pose additional architectural demands. In this section I describe unpublished work with Jennifer Ferris of one exploratory study that looks at the learning of a more conceptual aspect of algebra.[19] In dealing with this problem, we were struck by the fact that metacognitive activities were playing a major role in the learning of the students. One might wonder whether dealing with metacognition would require new architectural features of ACT-R. For instance, the Soar architecture is often advertised as being especially designed for dealing with metacognition. It turns out that we found nothing in the metacognitive activities that required architectural additions to ACT-R. However, our ability to model metacognition did require the two architectural features we have already identified: abstract control and dynamic pattern matching. While hardly definitive, this study invites the inference that metacognition is not an architecturally distinguished activity.

Pyramid Problems

This investigation into the strengths and weaknesses of ACT-R took place in an algebra domain we invented called *pyramid problems*. Table 5.6 gives

---

19. We have made the model, titled "pyramid model," available at the ACT-R website (act-r.psy.cmu.edu) under the models link and the title of this book. This also contains a Soar model developed with John Laird and a comparison of the two models.

Table 5.6.   Pyramids: Bases and Heights

Instruction

There is a notation for writing repeated addition where each term added is one less than the previous. For instance:

   5 + 4 + 3 is written as 5 $ 2

   Since 5 + 4 + 3 = 12, we would evaluate 5 $ 2 as 12 and write 5 $ 2 = 12

The parts of 5 $ 2 are given names:

   5 is the base and reflects the number you start with

   2 is the height and reflects the number of items you add to the base

   5 $ 2 is called a pyramid

Problems

Evaluate the following:

   1. 5 $ 3
   2. 10 $ 4
   3. 8 $ 1
   4. 3 $ 4
   5. 5 $ 7
   6. 0 $ 4
   7. 13 $ 0
   8. 1000 $ 2000

Write pyramid expressions to describe the following:

   9. 6 + 5 + 4 + 3
   10. 9 + 8 + 7
   11. 1 + 0 + (–1) + (–2)
   12. $x + (x - 1) + (x - 2) + (x - 3) + (x - 4)$
   13. 20 + (20 – 1) + . . . + (20 – 11)
   14. 15 + (15 – 1) + . . . + (15 – x)
   15. $z + (z - 1) + . . . + (z - y)$

Find the height x for the following pyramid expressions:

   16. 6 $ x = 15
   17. 10 $ x = 55
   18. 912 $ x = 912
   19. 3 $ x = –9
   20. 100 $ x = –101

Find the base x for the following pyramid expressions:

   21. x $ 2 = 15
   22. x $ 1 = 15
   23. x $ 4 = 35
   24. x $ 6 = 35
   25. x $ 6 = 0
   26. x $ 6 = –7

---

the complete text of the instruction and the problems that participants receive. To get a sense of what participants in this experiment experienced, you might try to read these instructions and solve the problems before reading on. As you do so, ask yourself whether your cognition stretches beyond what has been discussed so far. As noted in chapter 2, one reason for studying these problems was to create a situation that required knowledge to be brought together in novel ways. Recall that this is the intellectual activity that philosopher Jerry Fodor sees as beyond computational modeling.

A few comments are needed on the choice of domain, instruction, and problems. These pyramid problems were created on analogy to the instruction on powers and exponents in the classic algebra text of Foerster (1990, section 1.3). We did not want to use exponents because it is hard to control prior knowledge on this topic, and we also wanted to experiment with college students who would already know about exponentials. The text of the examples and instructions in table 5.6 is based on what appears in Foerster. However, the Foerster text contained a lot of additional instructional material that we eliminated because we judged it as not productive. Like the problems in the original text, the problems we used are a mixed bag in both difficulty and content. Problem 8, which will be the principal topic of discussion in this section, was inspired by the 1^{1000} problem that appears in the Foerster text. As in the Foerster text, the initial problems are all evaluation problems; later problems require using the knowledge in different ways. The expression-writing problems 13–15 with ellipsis notation were inspired by analogous problems in Foerster. Foerster also has problems that give the base and require finding the exponent (analogous to problems 16–20). No problems in Foerster give the exponent and require finding the base (which would be analogous to problems 21–26), but we could not resist including them at the end, and they proved informative.

The instruction in table 5.6 is quite minimal and involves only definitions of terms, a simple statement of how to evaluate pyramid expressions, and one example. We gave this instruction to six Carnegie Mellon University undergraduates and to six high school students who were receiving As in introductory algebra. One thing that is remarkable is that all these students were able to solve these problems with relatively little difficulty, little guidance, and extremely few errors. Both the college students and the high school students averaged only about one error on the 26 problems. In a reduced study in one of my Carnegie Mellon classes, I gave six students only the verbal directions below with no worked-out example:

$N \, \$ \, M$ is a pyramid expression for designating repeated addition where each term in the sum is one less than the previous.

N, the base, is first term in the sum.

M, the height, is number of terms you add to the base.

and I gave six students only one worked-out example with no verbal directions:

$$7 \$ 3 = 7 + 6 + 5 + 4$$

with arrows that connected the 7 on the left to the first term on the right and 3 on the left to the number of terms added. Both groups were then asked to solve the two evaluation problems:

$$10 \$ 2$$
$$3 \$ 4$$

Five students out of the six in both groups were able to successfully solve the problems given just one or the other source of information. So, suitably prepared students are capable of mastering this material with even less instruction than is in table 5.6.

Table 5.7 summarizes the performance of the original set of 12 students on the problems. There were no significant differences between college students and high school students, so we combined these. Because of a problem with the recording device, the data of one juvenile were lost for the last seven problems. Table 5.7 gives the number of participants who required experimenter help on each problem, the number who incorrectly solved the problem, and the median time that students spent on each problem, the minimum time of any student, and the maximum time. The table also gives the times for an "old" ACT-R model and a "new" ACT-R model. The "old" model is the same one used in the first study described in this chapter. That model solved simple linear equations, but since it worked from instructions, it could be tasked to solve other problems such as these pyramid problems. This model did not actually process verbal instructions but instead was given handcrafted declarative information. The "new" model is an extension of the model used for the second study in this chapter. It started from the written instructions that it parsed and then used (which requires dynamic pattern matching). The instructions provided to the model were easier to parse than what is in table 5.6 and were somewhat more explicit:

To evaluate a pyramid,
    first set the term to the base;
    then set the sum to the base;

Table 5.7. Performance of the Original Set of 12 Students on the Problems in Table 5.6

Problem	N	Assisted	Errors	Time (s)			ACT-R Model	
				Median	Minimum	Maximum	New	Old
1. 5 $ 3	12	4	0	16	5	135	18	21
2. 10 $ 4	12	0	1	30	20	52	21	27
3. 8 $ 1	12	0	1	7	1	26	9	10
4. 3 $ 4	12	0	0	25	10	34	21	27
5. 5 $ 7	12	0	1	29	9	43	33	44
6. 0 $ 4	12	0	0	16	6	43	21	27
7. 13 $ 0	12	0	2	5	2	8	5	4
8. 1000 $ 2000	12	3	0	72	7	176	Long	73
9. 6 + 5 + 4	12	0	0	7	1	10	6	5
10. 9 + 8 + 7	12	0	0	5	2	9	5	5
11. 1 + 0 − 1 − 2	12	1	0	6	2	10	6	5
12. x ... x − 4	12	0	0	6	2	13	7	5
13. 20 ... 20 − 11	12	0	0	15	8	49	XXX	11
14. 15 ... 15 − x	12	0	0	11	3	54	XXX	11
15. z ... z − y	12	0	0	7	3	10	XXX	11
16. 6 $ x = 15	12	0	0	28	7	133	XXX	17
17. 10 $ x = 55	12	0	1	71	23	103	XXX	57
18. 912 $ x = 912	12	0	0	6	2	7	XXX	5
19. 3 $ x = −9	12	0	1	49	6	126	XXX	51
20. 100 $ x = −101	12	5	1	127	23	166	XXX	101
21. x $ 2 = 15	11	3	1	32	14	149	XXX	28
22. x $ 1 = 15	11	0	0	15	3	98	XXX	12
23. x $ 4 = 35	11	0	0	48	26	153	XXX	39
24. x $ 6 = 35	11	0	0	59	13	94	XXX	51
25. x $ 6 = 0	11	0	0	32	6	120	XXX	51
26. x $ 6 = −7	11	0	1	57	13	195	XXX	51
						Correlation	0.929	0.957
						Deviation	6.15	7.28

then repeat as many times as the height:
　　first decrement the term,
　　　and then add the term to the sum;
　　when done with the repetition, write the sum.
To write a pyramid,
　　first write the base;
　　then write $;
　　and then write the height.

　　As can be determined from table 5.7, the new ACT-R model was much more successful than the old model. However, this success had relatively little to do with processing written instructions. Rather, it turned on giving the new model a set of metacognitive abilities. Elsewhere (Anderson and Ferris, in press), we describe a number of details about these abilities, but here I focus on just a couple.

The 1000 $ 2000 Problem

This section focuses on how the model solved the 1000 $ 2000 problem as it exemplifies the fundamental challenges to the architecture. Modeling the solution of this problem made heavy use of the architectural support for abstract control of cognition and advanced pattern matching, both of which have already been discussed. These architectural features proved important in a number of places, but here I focus on two episodes in the solution of the 1000 $ 2000 problem that involved metacognitive capabilities. One capability is to reflect on ongoing cognition, and the other is to maintain multiple cognitive states.

　　Before discussing the architectural challenges and how they were met, it would be a good idea to note some facts about the context of this problem and its solution. After the first problem, no students suffered any real difficulties with problems 2–7 (table 5.6), and all solved these by the process of iterative addition.[20] Thus, students had been succeeding by using iterative addition immediately for each of the previous problems,

---

20. Although there are closed-form formulas for the sum. Indeed, pyramid problems are a generalization of triangular numbers, about which there is a famous story. It is reported that Carl Friedrich Gauss discovered the formula in response to a busywork assignment by his elementary school teacher. None of our students came up spontaneously with such closed-form formulas. Nonetheless, our college students were able to when tasked (after the problems in table 5.6) with doing so.

and one might have expected an Einstellung effect (Luchins, 1942) such that students would have started trying to solve 1000 $ 2000 this way. However, no student did so—all showed near-immediate recognition of a difficulty. Some registered this difficulty with silence, but from some we got such comments as:

(3:14)[21] ah 1000 out 2000 places
(3:17) hum
(3:19) there is probably an easier way to write this out, huh?

or

(7:00) okay, it's just that one problem on 8, I don't know what the hell that adds up to
(7:06) I'm not going to spend my time crunching numbers

These cases are typical in that students gave evidence within a few seconds of reading the problem that they recognized the difficulty. After recognizing that they had a problem, students averaged about half of their time in unproductive attempts before they tried a method that worked. (An unproductive path tried by many was to find an analogy to what they knew about factorial.) Five students reasoned about simpler problems such as 2 $ 4. Others reasoned more abstractly:

(5:05) we'd go all the way to 0
(5:06) <um-hum>
(5:06) and then we'd go all the way to negative 1000
(5:09) so those cancel out and = 0, right?

A number of students confirmed the answer (0) by a second method before giving it as their final answer. The new model tried factorial, then abstract reasoning, and finally confirmed the answer of 0 by solving 2 $ 4. This corresponded to the protocol of one student.

Interrupting Normal Processing

The first metacognitive challenge raised by this problem is recognizing the difficulty and then interrupting the normal processing. Detecting a problem in normal cognitive processing might seem to require a second

---

21. These numbers are the time in minutes and seconds from when the student started solving the problems.

mind to be minding what the first mind is doing. However, it falls naturally out of the existing control structure in ACT-R. Figure 5.11 illustrates the processing in the model during the critical point in time, approximately between 1.5 and 3.0 s into the solving of the problem. In the first 1.5 s, the model had already encoded the base, and it begins the next 1.5 s doing normal processing: initializing the sum and the term to this base. Then at 2.0 s it starts to interpret the next step of instruction directing it to test whether the count is the height. It has not yet encoded the height, so the next 0.5 s is spent encoding the height as 2000. It is at this point that a rule Too-Much? fires. This rule simply notes that the height controls the number of iterations and that it is very large. In some situations, doing something many times is acceptable (e.g., counting out cards from a deck), but sometimes it is not. Therefore, this rule requests some further information about exactly what the iteration is. It

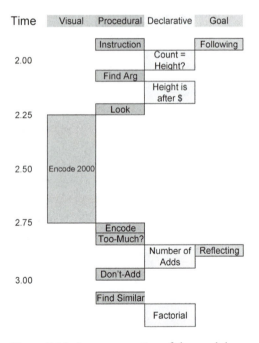

Figure 5.11. A representation of the module activity during the critical period of time when cognition is redirected in solving the 1000 $ 2000 problem. Time goes down the figure. Represented in the various columns are the activities of some of the modules.

sets the control state to "reflecting" to prevent the normal operators from applying at least for a moment. The fact is retrieved that the height is the number of additions. The system regards any task requiring so many additions as unacceptable and sets about looking for some way to deal with this situation. As a first (and unproductive) step along a long path to solution, it tries to retrieve something similar to the current concept and retrieves factorial. Note that as soon as it sets the control element from following to reflecting, it is prevented from continuing along its normal course of processing. This illustrates the potential of these abstract control elements to "apply the brakes" to the normal information processing.

The critical event in this episode is that the model is able to divert its course of processing in response to the appearance of 2000 in the problem. There is nothing special in the ability to change behavior in response to an unexpected stimulus. Any primate might change its behavior in response to the appearance of a dangerous predator. However, there is something quite different between reacting to a cheetah as a dangerous animal and reacting to 2000 as a dangerous iterative bound. In one case we are responding to an external stimulus; in the other case we are responding to an external stimulus in conjunction with an internal intention. Note that it is not simply the number 2000 that is causing the problems: these subjects would have had no difficulty evaluating 2000 $ 1. It is the 2000 as an iterative bound that is the problem. This requires that we represent states of intention (the intention to perform 2,000 additions) in the same terms that we represent external stimuli. This is the abstract control that is achieved by the goal module.

Figure 5.12 illustrates the production Too-Much? that achieves this diversion of processing. We can see that it involves the two features emphasized in this chapter. First, illustrating the abstract control, this production is responding to an iterative bound in the goal and sets the goal

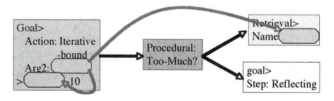

Figure 5.12. An illustration of the production Too-Much? that applies in figure 5.11.

to reflecting. Second, it involves an instance of dynamic pattern match-ing: it takes the identity of the iterative bound (height in location arg2) and looks in that location to find the value of the iterative bound. If that bound is greater than 10, then the production fires.[22] This production nicely illustrates how the architectural features of abstract control and dynamic pattern matching enable a metacognitive activity.

Maintaining Multiple States of Mind

Another architectural challenge raised by this problem is maintain-ing multiple states of mind. Figure 5.13 illustrates some of the state information that the model has near the end of solving this problem. At the point it has determined that 2 $ 4 is 0. The figure represents three substates:

1. The top goal is waiting on the check with the simple problem. It is holding a pointer to an image of the hypothesized answer: 1000 $ 2000 = 0.
2. It has already processed the subgoal of abstract addition and has an image of that result.
3. It is currently focused on the goal of solving 2 $ 4 = 0 and has finally reached a point where it is ready to check with the parent.

Each state in figure 5.13 is illustrated with its last control element (checking simple, return result, checking parent). The structures in figure 5.13 are maintained in declarative memory, and successful performance at this point depends on being able to retrieve the parent goal to perform the check.[23] It is critical that the system can maintain more than one internal state so that it can compare results and keep straight different internal control states. Essentially, the capacity to represent the structure in figure 5.13 depends on the fact that chunks can contain pointers to other chunks. This allows hierarchical structures and other more complex structures to be represented.

---

22. Setting 10 as the threshold is clearly ad hoc, but it reflects the idea that we have learned to be suspicious of being asked to do something more than some threshold value. One could imagine this rule being acquired and the value being set through a sequence of such learning experiences.
23. Memory for the state of the abstract addition is really no longer necessary at this point.

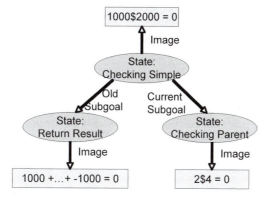

Figure 5.13. A representation of the structure interconnecting three goal chunks towards the end of the solution of the 1000 $ 2000 problem.

Comparison with Soar

In January 2006, I created with John Laird a Soar model that solved these pyramid problems in parallel with developing the ACT-R model just described. The two systems solved the problems in basically the same way. This was an interesting exercise because the Soar architecture is more explicitly designed to support metacognition. Seeing how to develop a model for this task in Soar helped guide the ACT-R model and vice versa. At each step, Soar has the capacity to deliberate on what to do next, whereas ACT-R just fires the next production—Rick Lewis, who has worked with both ACT-R and Soar, has characterized Soar as the "worried thinker" and ACT-R as the "mellow doer." Soar has special architectural support for impasses where it can step aside from the current processing and reflect on that processing, while ACT-R has no such architectural support. Nonetheless, the architectural mechanisms in ACT-R were sufficient to support metacognition that produced equivalent behavior. Figures 5.11 and 5.13 illustrate how: a production could respond to the current state and redirect cognition in figure 5.11, and the architectural primitive in ACT-R for storing buffer contents gave it the information it needed in figure 5.13 to relate different states of mind.

While metacognition does not seem to require any additional architectural primitives, the ACT-R model of it in this task does depend on the two architectural features of abstract control through the goal module and dynamic pattern matching in the procedural module. To the extent that these architectural features are unique to humans, these sorts of metacognitive capabilities may well be unique to humans.

Final Reflections

Marcus (2001)[24] identifies three features that he defines as constituting the "symbol manipulation hypothesis":

1. The mind represents abstract relationships between variables.
2. The mind has a system of recursively structured representations.
3. The mind distinguishes between mental representations of individuals and mental representations of kinds.

While not claiming that connectionist models are incapable of these attributes, he does claim that a class of connectionist models, which he calls "multilayer perceptrons," are incapable of displaying these features.

It is interesting to consider how the first two items on Marcus's list relate to the two architectural features highlighted in this chapter. Marcus's features are really representational claims, while the concern in this chapter has been with process capacities of the architecture. However, representational and process claims are not really independent (Anderson, 1978). Marcus considers only the second of his features, recursively structured representations, to reflect a uniquely human feature. When Marcus writes of variables as a pan-species capability, the kind of tasks he is referring to, such as match-to-sample tasks, require only static pattern matching where an item is moved from one buffer (perhaps visual) to another (perhaps motor). Dynamic pattern matching and recursive representations are connected. Dynamic pattern matching is only useful in a system that has powerful, interlinked representations. Processing recursive representations can be much easier with dynamic pattern matching.

The human brain is expanded over that of other primates, and it is not just a matter of more brain. There are new prefrontal and parietal regions, and in the case of some regions such as the ACC, there are new kinds of cells. While brain lateralization is also a common feature of

---

24. Marcus gave his 2001 book the interesting title *The Algebraic Mind*. However, he is using "algebra" to refer to the abstract computations of the mind and not high school algebra, which is in comparison a rather mundane course of study.

many species, its connection with language seems unique (Halpern et al., 2005), and Marcus's second feature is strongly motivated by considerations of language processing. So, it seems pretty clear that there have been some changes to the structure of the human brain that enable the unique functions of human cognition. As Newell prophesized, we are only a little ways into understanding how to characterize this connection at the architectural level.

Appendix 5.1: Some Details of Instruction Processing

Figure 5.14 illustrates the two declarative structures that are created by the parsing of the instruction "Key the number isolated by the equal sign" in step 4 of table 5.5. These two structures encode the two commands that this instruction is parsed into:

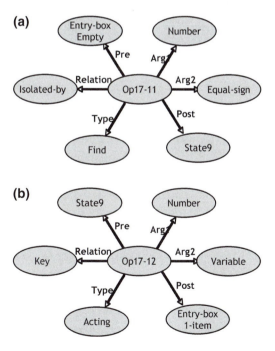

Figure 5.14. Declarative representation of the two operators created from the parsing of "Key the number isolated by the equal sign."

1. Find the number isolated by the equal sign.
2. Key the number.

These are encoded according to an operator structure that we have been evolving for representing instruction.[25] Each operator consists of a number of slots. The six slots in these examples can be broken down into three types:

1. *Pre and post slots* point to representations of the state of the problem before and after the operator applies. These states can be references to either external states of the world or internal states. So, for instance, Op17-11 (figure 5.14a) has as its pre state the external appearance of an empty entry box in which to type, and it has internal "State9" as its post state, while Op17-12 (figure 5.14b) has State9 as its pre state and an entry box with one item as its post state. State9 is an internal state that bridges between the perceptual act in command (a) and the motor action in command (b) that changes the external state. Referring as much as possible to external states enables flexible performance. This allows the system to recognize when things have gone awry, replan in the middle, and reason back from desired states. However, there are those occasions where the external environment does not signal where one is and abstract control states such as State9 are required.
2. *A type slot* indicates the general class of which the operator is an instance. Different classes require different principles for interpretation. Op17-11 is a "find" operator that requires a production to request a shift of attention to the desired object and another production (generic-encode illustrated in figure 5.8, a and b) to harvest the result of that shift of perceptual attention. Op17-12 is an "acting" operator that requires a production (generic-act in figure 5.8, c and d) to perform a manual action on some object.

25. Niels Taatgen has been developing this representation, and I suspect it will continue to be fine-tuned after the publication of the book. These ideas are also discussed in unit 7 on the online ACT-R tutorial (part of the ACT-R 6.0 download available from the ACT-R 6 link at the ACT-R website: act-r.psy.cmu.edu).

3. *Relation, arg1, and arg2 slots* specify the actual behavior to be performed. Op17-11 specifies finding a number isolated by an equal sign, and Op17-12 specifies keying that number.

Notice that these operators assume abilities that are part of the student's existing repertoire. Op17-11 assumes the student has the ability to find a number isolated by a symbol such as "=" (obviously not a perceptual primitive). Presumably, for students this represents a product of their previous mathematics experience; Foerster definitely just assumes this ability without any instruction. Similarly, Op17-12 assumes the ability to key a number into the interface; modern-day students definitely have this ability.

This operator representation gives the system a robustness such that it can pick up after errors. Sometimes students will mistype something or the interface might act strangely and get them into an unexpected state. If this happens in the model, it can look at the screen and determine what state it is in and start back down the correct path. Thus, unlike some models, it does not get stuck when something unexpected happens, as long as that unexpected event still leaves it processing the same basic algebra interface that the instructions refer to.

Because the model has to process instructions crafted without consideration of the internals of the system, it has to process referring terms such as "number" that can bridge multiple operators. This creates the representational challenge that requires dynamic pattern matching. In our earlier projects, where we could craft the declarative representation of the instruction to fit assumptions about internal processing, this was not required. I have not discussed the parsing productions here because they are ad hoc and apply to only a restricted language subset. Nonetheless, the discipline of having to parse from natural language exposed this weakness of our earlier approach.

6

How Can the Human Mind Occur?

The title of this book can create the wrong expectations. One might interpret the title as posing a near-paradox, as in "How can God allow so much suffering?" Or one might expect a full answer, as in "How can birds sit on power lines without being electrocuted?" Perhaps the most misleading expectation created by the title of this book is that it will address the mind–body problem. Curiously, it was only relatively late in the writing this book that I realized that its title was creating this expectation. To understand how I could exhibit such a blind spot, you need to understand the mindset with which I come at this problem, a mindset inherited from Allen Newell. The best way to explain that is to quote some more from Newell's last lecture, where he enumerates the things that his ultimate scientific question does not include:

> It is also not the issue of the mind–body problem. That's the
> philosopher's question. Now they may have the same answer.
> It may be that the answer to my question and the answer to their
> question is the same. But it turns out, of course, that my question
> is a simple scientific question. It may be an ultimate one and hard
> to get at, but it is a scientific question. And the mind-body is
> not. It is a philosophical question. And, in fact, if the mind-body
> question were cast as a scientific question, all of philosophers
> would do different things than they now do about it. They would
> go out in the laboratory, for instance. (Newell, 1993)

So we have been pursuing a scientific question, and one about which we should have modest expectations for our progress at answering. This final chapter is the place to summarize what progress we have made in answering that question.

The Answer So Far

Each of the preceding chapters offers a piece of the answer:

1. The answer takes the form of a cognitive architecture—that is, the specification of the structure of the brain at a level of abstraction that explains how it achieves the function of the mind.
2. For reasons of efficiency of neural computation, the human cognitive architecture takes the form of a set of largely independent modules (e.g., figure 2.2) associated with different brain regions.
3. Human identity is achieved through a declarative memory module that, moment by moment, attempts to give each person the most appropriate possible window into his or her past.
4. The various modules are coordinated by a central production system that strives to develop a set of productions that will give the most adaptive response to any state of the modules.
5. The human mind evolved out of the primate mind by achieving the ability to exercise abstract control over cognition and the ability to process complex relational patterns.

The summary above is just a bunch of one-liners; as Newell said, the true answer must have the details—"how the gears clank and how the pistons go." These chapters and the many publications from the ACT-R community have laid out some of those details. They have shown how the modules can interact to achieve adaptive cognition and behavior in tasks as varied as driving a car and solving an equation. They elaborated, at considerable length, how the declarative and procedural modules work and how they acquire new knowledge. They provided evidence for the association of these modules with various brain regions and even speculated a bit about how they might be implemented in the brain. In this book, I have also discussed what computational features distinguish the human cognitive architecture from the cognitive architectures of other primates.

There is an unfortunate tendency to view the progress summarized in this book as a growth in the success of ACT-R rather than a growth in knowledge about the human mind. Herbert Simon in his last years complained about what he saw as the brand-naming of theories.[1] In the abstract for a talk he gave on February 24, 1998, Simon wrote:

> We typically (and properly) implement our research with large complex systems that employ a collection of interacting mechanisms to achieve their results. Hence, we often think of advances in terms of the names of such programs: e.g., LT, GPS, EPAM, PRODIGY, Soar, BACON, ACT-R—just to mention a few of local origin. However, it can be argued that the real "action" lies largely in the mechanisms embedded in these programs, and in issues about how such mechanisms can be combined effectively. The "brand names" tend to make difficult the analysis and comparison of these mechanisms or the exchange of knowledge between research groups. One can argue that it has caused and causes an enormous amount of duplication of effort. Physicists did not divide quantum mechanics into the Heisenberg Brand, the Schrodinger Brand, and the Dirac brand.

One of the goals in writing this book was to show that these accomplishments are not just successes of ACT-R, but also growth in general scientific knowledge. Sometimes when I present these ideas, I get the comment, "but we already knew that," as in "we already knew the anterior cingulate was involved in control," or "those ideas about utility learning are commonplace in the reinforcement learning community." To such comments, I respond, "That's terrific." This means that ACT-R is showing how what we already know is starting to add to an understanding of the human mind. If the term "ACT-R" were to disappear and we came to celebrate a scientific understanding of the human mind, we would all be well served. However, to return to Newell's admonition, whether or not the term ACT-R survives, we are still only a little ways into understanding the answer to the question he posed.

The Newell Criteria

Anderson and Lebiere (2003) introduced the Newell test as a way of both identifying progress toward a satisfactory knowledge of the human mind

---

1. There is a certain irony here, given that it was Simon and Newell who introduced the first brand names into psychology (the names of their early computer simulations).

and seeing where more work was needed. It consists of 12 criteria based on two lists published by Newell (1980, 1990). In line with Simon's admonition, it is worth reviewing what this book has had to say about these criteria in a way that is not specific to ACT-R:

1. *Behave as an (almost) arbitrary function of the environment:* Anderson and Lebiere (2003) operationalized the first criterion as being able to behave with great flexibility. As chapter 5 emphasizes, this requires an ability to dynamically match patterns and guide our cognition independent of our environment. It is these abilities that have enabled the human mind to acquire nearly arbitrary competences that were not anticipated in its evolutionary history.

2. *Operate in real time:* It is not enough for a theory of cognition to explain the great flexibility of human cognition. It must also explain how humans can do their thinking in what Newell referred to as "real time," which means human time. As emphasized in chapter 2, human cognitive architecture has been strongly constrained by the need to achieve real-time behavior within the constraints of neural tissue.

3. *Exhibit rational, that is, effective adaptive behavior:* Humans do not just perform marvelous intellectual functions. The computations they perform serve their needs. How the subsymbolic level of computation is adaptively tuned to the environment was particularly stressed in chapters 3 and 4. How humans can reflect on the adaptiveness of the actions they are planning and exercise suitable control is discussed in chapter 5.

4. *Use vast amounts of knowledge about the environment:* One key to human adaptivity is the vast amount of knowledge that can be called upon. The subsymbolic computations described in this book are supposed to help the human system manage large databases. Nonetheless, I do not think ACT-R or any other system has yet given us a real understanding of how humans manage their large databases of knowledge.

5. *Behave robustly in the face of error, the unexpected, and the unknown:* Living in the real world is not like solving a puzzle such as the Tower of Hanoi. The world can change in unexpected ways. Even human efforts to control the world by acting upon

it can have unexpected effects. People make mistakes and have to recover. The ability to deal with a dynamic and unpredictable environment is a precondition to survival for all organisms. Given the complexity of the environments that humans have created for themselves, the need to be constantly sensitive to their world (e.g., a car moving into one's lane) is one of the major cognitive stressors that they face. In this book, I have emphasized the basal ganglia as a system that brings the perceptual modules and central modules together to select appropriate action.

6. *Integrate diverse knowledge:* Anderson and Lebiere (2003) interpreted this criterion as the ability to bring together distal knowledge to come up with novel conclusions. This is what philosopher Jerry Fodor thinks is beyond computational models (see chapter 2). The exploration of pyramid problems in chapter 5 is an exercise intended to stress this ability. We not only developed an ACT-R model capable of doing this but also developed a Soar model. This issue just may not be the problematical one that Fodor thought it was.

7. *Use (natural) language:* This is a topic that this book has neglected, much as Newell neglected the topic. However, it has not been ignored by the ACT-R community (or the cognitive science community as a whole).[2] One big issue in the field remains the degree to which there is special neural support for language processing (the same issue raised by Fodor's proposal for a language module). Looking at many cognitive science efforts from a considerable distance, they seem to involve general-purpose processing mechanisms operating on language-specific representations. These general-purpose mechanisms are often what I would characterize as subsymbolic, such as ACT-R's activation calculus. It seems that

---

2. Given that the book has so ignored this topic, I feel obliged to point out some of the work done by others in the ACT-R community. For instance, Lewis and Vasishth (2005) have produced a detailed theory of real-time parsing, and R. L. Lewis (personal communication) has ideas about how this could be scaled up to full natural language. Another application to language processing is Jerry T. Ball's Double-R theory (see doublertheory. com/index.html). Emond (2006) has made the WORDNET database (Fellbaum, 1998; G. A. Miller, 1998) available for ACT-R use. There is now available a representation of similarities between words for ACT-R use (Royer et al., 2005) that has been abstracted using a technique similar to LSA (latent semantic analysis; Landauer and Dumais, 1997).

something like the symbolic–subsymbolic distinction is playing out in this domain where the symbolic is language specific but the subsymbolic is not.

8. *Exhibit self-awareness and a sense of self:* Newell connected this eighth criterion most with the concept of consciousness. I have ignored this even more than language in this book, but I will end with some brave remarks on this topic.

9. *Learning from environment:* One striking feature of the brain is that almost all of its tissue is capable of changing with experience. This book has been about understanding the learning changes associated with declarative and procedural memory. These two combine to produce complex learning, as discussed in chapter 5. While these learning processes are important, there are also important perceptual and motor learning processes. These are the kinds of learning that have tended to be more successfully modeled with connectionist-like computations rather than at the higher level allowed in ACT-R. It is an interesting question whether there are useful higher level characterizations of perceptual and motor learning.

10. *Acquire capabilities through development:* Another goal is to characterize the kind of changes that occur through development. While there are lots of learning models in different architectures that address specific events in development, such as acquisition of the past tense, we lack a real grip on the changes that occur with development. Like the issue of vast amounts of knowledge, the challenge is finding a way to deal with the scale of the phenomena.

11. *Arise through evolution:* If the scale of development remains overwhelming, the scale of evolution is even more so, compounded by the real lack of hard data (whereas there is no lack of potential hard data in the case of development). While evolution still seems a pipe dream for computational models, it is possible to begin to produce useful comparative computational models. A little of that was displayed in chapter 5.

12. *Be realizable within the brain:* Clearly the dimension of greatest growth in recent cognitive science has been our understanding of the neural basis of cognition. It is also the greatest dimension of growth within ACT-R, even since we introduced the Newell

test in 2003. The book has summarized a small fraction of this knowledge and how it has influenced modern ACT-R . Perhaps the biggest contribution of our own laboratory to this topic is showing how to relate detailed cognitive models to detailed brain imaging data. This methodology is not at all tied to the ACT-R theory; it can be used in general to test any explicit theory of cognition.

The Question of Consciousness

In venturing into the question of consciousness, I might be seen as not following Newell's practice of leaving the philosophers' domain to the philosophers, but Newell's eighth criterion is concerned with at least aspects of consciousness. Other psychologists have not left the topic alone, either, and they have found ways to study it in the laboratory. It is also the case that, along with emotion, it is the favorite filler for X in the question "How does ACT-R deal with X?" that I am asked when I describe ACT-R to general psychology audiences.

Consciousness refers to our sense of awareness of our own cognitive workings. It was introduced into Western thought in this sense by Descartes; previously, the Latin term *conscientia* was used to refer to knowledge we possessed, possibly shared with others and with God. The pre-Descartes sense of consciousness might more fit the contents of declarative memory in ACT-R. It is interesting to wonder whether, if not for Descartes, there would be any question about whether ACT-R could deal with consciousness.

I have always felt ill at ease in addressing the topic of consciousness, and Christian Lebiere and I would not have addressed it in 2003 if it were not on Newell's list. Even Newell felt compelled to remark that "it is not evident what functional role self-awareness plays in the total scheme of mind" (Newell, 1990, p. 20). In 2003, we noted that in ACT-R consciousness has an obvious mapping to the buffers that are associated with the modules. The contents of consciousness are the contents of these buffers, and conscious activity corresponds to the manipulation of the contents of these buffers by production rules. The information in the buffers is the information that is made available for general processing and is stored in declarative memory. ACT-R models can generate introspective reports by describing the contents of these buffers. In 2003 we did not think this was much of an answer and gave ACT-R low marks on this dimension. I have subsequently come to the conclusion that this is indeed what consciousness is and that running ACT-R models are conscious. They may not be conscious in the same sense as humans, but this is probably because ACT-R gives a rather incomplete picture of the buffers that are available in the human system. Moreover, typical ACT-R models tend to give a rather incomplete picture of the operations on the buffers that ACT-R does have. Still, identifying ACT-R buffers with consciousness is a significant conclusion because consciousness is very much caught up in the popular conception of the mind.

This is not a particularly novel interpretation of consciousness; it is basically the ACT-R realization of the global workspace theory of consciousness (Baars, 1988; Dehaene et al., 1998; Dehaene and Naccache, 2001).[3] Some of ACT-R's buffers, such as the visual and aural buffers, hold information about the external world; others, such as the goal and imaginal buffers, hold information about internal states. From the point of view of ACT-R, our knowledge of the external world is not fundamentally different than our knowledge of our internal workings. This denies that the mind knows itself in any way other than it knows the external world. It also denies any special status for introspective reports, since our internal perceptions could be subject to illusions just as our external perceptions are. This is a viewpoint with a long tradition in psychology; it conflicts with an even longer tradition in philosophy. As far as ACT-R is concerned, Descartes might as well have said, "I perceive, therefore I am."

Many will find the identification of consciousness with the contents of the buffers in ACT-R to be problematic. By this definition, it might seem that any computational system that put some information out in globally accessible registers would be conscious. Moreover, if one looks

---

3. According to Dehaene and Changeux (2004):

We postulate the existence of a distinct set of cortical "workspace" neurons characterized by their ability to send and receive projections to many distant areas through long-range excitatory axons. These neurons therefore no longer obey a principle of local, encapsulated connectivity, but rather break the modularity of the cortex by allowing many different processors to exchange information in a global and flexible manner. Information, which is encoded in workspace neurons, can be quickly made available to many brain systems, in particular the motor and speech-production processors for overt behavioral report. We hypothesize that the entry of inputs into this global workspace constitutes the neural basis of access to consciousness. (p. 1147)

at the information that flits in and out of the ACT-R buffers, one would wonder whether much of it deserves to be put in correspondence with the contents of consciousness. The goal buffer in the ACT-R model for equation solving (figure 5.3) switches back and forth every second or less between the control states for unwinding and retrieving. No student in that experiment reported this experience. After (or during) solving $7x + 3 = 38$, a student might report remembering the arithmetic facts $8 - 3 = 5, 35/7 = 5$, and maybe a little more. However, no student would report anything like the detail in figure 5.3, which is already an abstraction from the more detailed model in figure 1.7. However, just because something is in a buffer does not mean it will be reported. It only means that it could be reported if a reporting procedure were executed that looked for information in that buffer and knew how to translate the contents of that buffer into a linguistic description. ACT-R is not like just any machine that makes information available in globally accessible buffers because of what is placed in those buffers. These are products of powerful modules that have been shaped by evolution to produce functionally adaptive results that can work with each other.

Probably more bothersome than the claim that everything in the buffers is part of consciousness is the claim that there is nothing more to consciousness. Here ACT-R is following Dennett's (1991) lead. He refers to belief that there is something more to consciousness as the idea of a "Cartesian theater" where things must appear for presentation to the mind. He argues instead that the contents of consciousness are, indeed, often fleeting and, at best, momentarily noted. He compares this to the multiple drafts that a paper goes through, only a few of which are ever archived and recorded. More recently, he has come to also use the metaphor of fame (Dennett, 1993) and argues that all these drafts (contents of buffers in ACT-R) compete for fame and only a few ever get noticed—but they were all there at one time.

There are a host of philosophical objections to this view involving things such as the possibility of zombies (Kirk, 1974), qualia (Block, 1978), and a Chinese room (Searle, 1980). Here I am willing follow Newell's admonition and leave the philosopher's domain to the philosopher. However, I will note that Dennett (1991) discusses these various objections, and I find his dismissal of these objections persuasive. He argues that we have been so ingrained to think in terms of something like a Cartesian theater that we find it hard to think in terms of something like this buffer theory (much as our naive physics makes it hard for us to think about things in terms of modern physics).[4] But if we can just suspend our disbelief and carry through the interpretation, it does account for all the facts and avoids the contradictions of the prescientific views. I do not want to imply that Dennett has silenced all critics—there have been recent counterarguments. Chalmers (1997) claims that the perspective being espoused here has just ignored the hard problem of consciousness, which he defines as answering why our cognitive processes are accompanied by any phenomenal experience at all. However, our phenomenal conscious experience is just the exercise of our ability to access and reflect on the contents of our buffers. Most information-processing models in ACT-R are fixated on doing a single task and do not reflect generally on the contents of the buffers, but this is just an incompleteness of the models. The last model in chapter 5 for the pyramid task (see figure 5.11) showed how such reflection can be essential to success in tasks. Perhaps this model's use of reflection points to an answer to Newell's puzzlement about the functionality of consciousness.

If we resist the temptation to believe in a hard problem of conscious-ness, we can appreciate how consciousness is the solution to the funda-mental problem of achieving the mind in the brain. As noted in chapter 2, efficiency considerations drive the brain to try to achieve as much of its computation as possible locally in nearly encapsulated modules. How-ever, the functionality of the mind demands communication among these modules, and to do this, some information must be made globally available. The purpose of the buffers in ACT-R is to create this global access. The contents of these buffers will create an information trail that can be reported and reflected upon. As in the last example in chapter 5, adaptive cognition sometimes requires reflection on this information trail. Thus, consciousness is the manifestation of the solution to the need for global coordination among modules. It is a trademark consequence of the architecture in figure 2.2. That being said, chapters 1–5 develop this architecture with only oblique references to consciousness. This is be-cause the information processing associated with consciousness is already described by other terms of the theory. It still is not clear to me how invoking the concept of consciousness adds to the understanding of the

---

4. It is interesting to speculate on whether this is built into us by our internal experi-ences, in the same way naive physics reflects our external experiences, or whether this is something we have acquired as part of our post-Descartes enculturation.

human mind, but taking a coherent reading of the term consciousness, I am willing to declare ACT-R conscious.

Appendix 6.1 The Future of ACT-R

Upon rereading appendix 1.1 on the history of ACT-R, I was struck by two observations. The first is that I have had a very poor history of predicting where ACT might go next. Therefore, I am wise to make this appendix short to minimize the embarrassments of my mispredictions. The second observation is that the evolution of the ACT theory has really been driven by external inputs (the right branches in figure 1.11). Some of these were from outside our laboratory, and some were essentially parallel activities within my laboratory at Carnegie Mellon University.

What are the current parallel research threads that might drive the future development of ACT-R? Within my own laboratory, the parallel strands of research have already been reflected in this book—the fMRI research mapping of ACT-R modules onto the brain and the work on algebra to identify what enables us to master new competences. Both are active strands of research pursuing interesting questions, but I am not sure that either is going to bring new, profound changes to the architecture.

However, ACT-R is no longer an activity localized at Carnegie Mellon, and one can look to things happening within the larger ACT-R community. There are substantial efforts afoot to develop new modules within ACT-R or to improve existing ones. These include efforts to develop modules for spatial processing and navigation, multimodal integration of episodic memories, more effective motor modules, language processing components, and temporal (timing) modules. These efforts are ongoing, and the reader is directed to the ACT-R website for information (act-r.psy.cmu.edu). These efforts can be seen as incremental, but they can also result in changes that would be judged as fundamental. For instance, the emergence of ideas about how to process time in ACT-R has led to novel ideas about the basic control of cognition (e.g., Salvucci et al., 2006). Basically, as Newell suspected, efforts to improve the functionality of an architecture can have profound effects on that architecture.

New structural efforts are complementing these functional efforts. In collaboration with the Leabra group (Attallah et al., 2004; O'Reilly, 2006), we have been trying to find mappings between the Leabra architecture and the ACT-R architecture. This is possible because of deep compatibilities between the ways these two systems view the role of the basal ganglia in implementing procedural competence and the hippocampus in implementing declarative knowledge. There is also a more general agreement in their conceptions of the role of different parietal and prefrontal regions. We hope these efforts will deepen our understanding of the mapping of ACT-R onto brain structures and the computational underpinnings of ACT-R modules. Our previous explorations in ACT-RN (Lebiere and Anderson, 1993) had such a stimulating impact on theory development. If consideration of the more abstract ACT-R level of description leads to a better Leabra system, so much the better. It would be even better if both systems could simply be absorbed into that brand-free understanding of the human mind that Herbert Simon wanted in the end.

References

Ackley, D. H., Hinton, G. E., & Sejnowsky, T. J. (1985). A learning algorithm for Boltzmann machines. *Cognitive Science, 9*, 147–169.

Aggleton, J. P., & Brown, M. W. (1999). Episodic memory, amnesia, and the hippocampal-anterior thalamic axis. *Behavioral and Brain Sciences, 22*, 425–489.

Agre, P., & Chapman, D. (1987). PENGI: An implementation of a theory of activity. In *Proceedings of the Sixth National Conference on Artificial Intelligence (AAAI-87)* (pp. 268–272). San Francisco, CA: Morgan Kaufmann.

Aha, D. W., Kibler, D., & Albert, M. (1991). Instance-based learning algorithms. *Machine Learning, 6*, 37–66.

Allman, J. M., Hakeem, A., Erwin, J. M., Nimchinsky, E., & Hof, P. (2001). Anterior cingulate cortex: The evolution of an interface between emotion and cognition. *Annals of the New York Academy of Sciences, 935*, 107–117.

Allman, J. M., Watson, K. K., Tetreault, N. A., & Hakeem, A. Y. (2005). Intuition and autism: A possible role for von Economo neurons. *Trends in Cognitive Science, 9*(8), 367–373.

Amos, A. (2000). A computational model of information processing in the frontal cortex and basal ganglia. *Journal of Cognitive Neuroscience, 12*, 505–519.

Anderson, J. A. (1973). A theory for the recognition of items from short memorized lists. *Psychological Review, 80*, 417–438.

Anderson, J. R. (1976). *Language, Memory, and Thought*. Hillsdale, NJ: Erlbaum.

Anderson, J. R. (1978). Arguments concerning representations for mental imagery. *Psychological Review, 85*, 249–277.

Anderson, J. R. (1980). *Cognitive Psychology and Its Implications*. San Francisco, CA: Freeman.

Anderson, J. R. (1983). *The Architecture of Cognition*. Cambridge, MA: Harvard University Press.

Anderson, J. R. (1990). *The Adaptive Character of Thought*. Hillsdale, NJ: Erlbaum.

Anderson, J. R. (1991a). Is human cognition adaptive? *Behavioral and Brain Sciences, 14,* 471–484.

Anderson, J. R. (1991b). The adaptive nature of human categorization. *Psychological Review, 98,* 409–429.

Anderson, J. R. (1993). *Rules of the Mind*. Hillsdale, NJ: Erlbaum.

Anderson, J. R. (2000). *Learning and Memory,* 2nd ed. New York: Wiley.

Anderson, J. R. (2005a). Human symbol manipulation within an integrated cognitive architecture. *Cognitive Science, 29,* 313–342.

Anderson, J. R. (2005b). *Cognitive Psychology and Its Implications,* 6th ed. New York: Worth Publishing.

Anderson, J. R. (2006). *A New Utility Learning Mechanism.* Paper presented at the 2006 ACT-R workshop, act-r.psy.cmu.edu/workshops/workshop-2006/actr-ws-proceedings2006-pn.pdf.

Anderson, J. R. (2007). Using brain imaging to guide the development of a cognitive architecture. In W. D. Gray (ed.), *Integrated Models of Cognitive Systems*. New York: Oxford University Press, 49–62.

Anderson, J. R., Albert, M. V., & Fincham, J. M. (2005). Tracing problem solving in real time: fMRI analysis of the subject-paced Tower of Hanoi. *Journal of Cognitive Neuroscience, 17,* 1261–1274.

Anderson, J. R., & Anderson, J. F. (in preparation). Perfect Time Sharing: Attempts to Compare ACT-R and Epic.

Anderson, J. R., & Betz, J. (2001). A hybrid model of categorization. *Psychonomic Bulletin and Review, 8,* 629–647.

Anderson, J. R., Bothell, D., Byrne, M. D., Douglass, S., Lebiere, C., & Qin, Y. (2004). An integrated theory of mind. *Psychological Review, 111,* 1036–1060.

Anderson, J. R., & Bower, G. H. (1973). *Human Associative Memory*. Washington, DC: Winston & Sons.

Anderson, J. R., Conrad, F. G., & Corbett, A. T. (1989). Skill acquisition and the LISP tutor. *Cognitive Science, 13,* 467–506.

Anderson, J. R., Corbett, A. T., Koedinger, K. R., & Pelletier, R. (1995). Cognitive tutors: Lessons learned. *Journal of the Learning Sciences, 4*(2), 167–207.

Anderson, J. R., & Ferris, J. (in press). *Learning Algebra: Can ACT-R Be as Smart as a Human?*

Anderson, J. R., & Fincham, J. M. (1994). Acquisition of procedural skills from examples. *Journal of Experimental Psychology: Learning, Memory, and Cognition, 20,* 1322–1340.

Anderson, J. R., Fincham, J. M., & Douglass, S. (1997). The role of examples and rules in the acquisition of a cognitive skill. *Journal of Experimental Psychology: Learning, Memory, and Cognition, 231,* 932–945.

Anderson, J. R., Fincham, J. M., & Douglass, S. (1999). Practice and retention: A unifying analysis. *Journal of Experimental Psychology: Learning, Memory, and Cognition, 25,* 1120–1136.

Anderson, J. R., John, B. E., Just, M. A., Carpenter, P. A., Kieras, D. E., & Meyer, D. E. (1995). Production system models of complex cognition. In *Proceedings of the Seventeenth Annual Conference of the Cognitive Science Society* (pp. 9–12). Hillsdale, NJ: Erlbaum.

Anderson, J. R., & Lebiere, C. (1998). *The Atomic Components of Thought.* Mahwah, NJ: Erlbaum.

Anderson, J. R., & Lebiere, C. L. (2003). The Newell test for a theory of mind. *Behavioral and Brain Science, 26,* 587–637.

Anderson, J. R., Qin, Y., Jung, K.-J., & Carter, C. S. (2007). Information-processing modules and their relative modality specificity. *Cognitive Psychology, 54,* 185–217.

Anderson, J. R., Qin, Y., Stenger, V. A., & Carter, C. S. (2004). The relationship of three cortical regions to an information-processing model. *Cognitive Neuroscience, 16,* 637–653.

Anderson, J. R., & Reder, L. M. (1999). The fan effect: New results and new theories. *Journal of Experimental Psychology: General, 128,* 186–197.

Anderson, J. R., & Schooler, L. J. (1991). Reflections of the environment in memory. *Psychological Science, 2,* 396–408.

Anderson, J. R., Taatgen, N. A., & Byrne, M. D. (2005). Learning to achieve perfect time sharing: Architectural implications of Hazeltine, Teague, & Ivry. *Journal of Experimental Psychology: Human Perception and Performance, 31,* 749–761.

Attallah, H. E., Frank, M. J., & O'Reilly, R. C. (2004). Hippocampus, cortex and basal ganglia: Insights from computational models of complementary learning systems. *Neurobiology of Learning and Memory, 82*(3), 253–267.

Baars, B. J. (1988). *A Cognitive Theory of Consciousness.* New York: Cambridge University Press.

Baddeley, A. D. (1986). *Working Memory.* Oxford: Oxford University Press.

Badre, D., Poldrack, R. A., Paré-Blagoev, E. J., Insler, R. Z., & Wagner, A. D. (2005). Dissociable controlled retrieval and generalized selection mechanisms in ventrolateral prefrontal cortex. *Neuron, 47,* 907–918.

Basso, M. A., & Wurtz, R. H. (1998). Modulation of neuronal activity in superior colliculus by changes in target probability. *Journal of Neuroscience, 18,* 7519–7534.

Bednarz, N., Kieran, C., & Lee, L. (1996). *Approaches to Algebra: Perspectives for Research and Teaching.* Dordrecht, Netherlands: Kluwer Academic Press.

Bell, C. G., & Newell, A. (1971). *Computer Structures: Readings And Examples.* New York: McGraw-Hill.

Beran, M. J., & Beran, M. M. (2004). Chimpanzees remember the results of one-by-one addition of food items to sets over extended time periods. *Psychological Science, 15*(2), 94–99.

Berry, D., & Broadbent, D. A. (1984). On the relationship between task performance and associated verbalizable knowledge. *Quarterly Journal of Experimental Psychology, 36A,* 209–231.

Best, B. J., Schunn, C. D., & Reder, L. M. (1998). Modeling adaptivity in a dynamic task. In M. A. Gernsbacher & S. J. Derry (eds.), *Proceedings of the 20th Annual Conference of the Cognitive Science Society* (pp. 144–159). Hillsdale, NJ: Lawrence Erlbaum Associates.

Blessing, S., & Anderson, J. R. (1996). How people learn to skip steps. *Journal of Experimental Psychology: Learning, Memory and Cognition, 22,* 576–598.

Block, N. (1978). Troubles with functionalism. Reprinted in N. Block (ed.), *Readings in the Philosophy of Psychology* (Vol. 1). Cambridge, MA: Harvard University Press.

Bogacz, R., Brown, E. T., Moehlis, J., Hu, P., Holmes, P., & Cohen, J. D. (2006). The physics of optimal decision making: A formal analysis of models of performance in two-alternative forced choice tasks. *Psychological Review, 113,* 700–765.

Botvinick, M. M., Braver, T. S., Carter, C. S., Barch, D. M., & Cohen, J. D. (2001). Conflict monitoring and cognitive control. *Psychological Review, 108*(3) 624–652.

Boysen, S. T., & Bernston, G. G. (1989). Numerical competence in a chimpanzee. *Journal of Comparative Psychology, 103,* 23–31.

Boyton, G. M., Engel, S. A., Glover, G. H., & Heeger, D. J. (1996). Linear systems analysis of functional magnetic resonance imaging in human V1. *Journal of Neuroscience, 16,* 4207–4221.

Brannon, E. M. (2005). Quantitative thinking: From monkey to human and human infant to adult. In S. Dehaene, J. Duhamel, M. D. Hauser, & G. Rizzolatti (eds.), *From Monkey Brain to Human Brain* (pp. 97–116). Cambridge, MA: MIT Press.

Brannon, E. M., & Terrace, H. S. (2002). The evolution and ontogeny of ordinal numerical ability. In M. Bekoff, C. Allen, & G. M. Burghardt (eds.), *The Cognitive Animal* (pp. 197–204). Cambridge, MA: MIT Press.

Breiter, H. C., Aharon, I., Kahneman, D., Dale, A., & Shizgal, P. (2001). Functional imaging of neural responses to expectancy and experience of monetary gains and losses. *Neuron, 30,* 619–639.

Brewer, J. B., Shao, Z., Desmond, J. E., Glover, G. H., & Gabrieli, J. D. (1998). Making memories: Brain activity that predicts how well visual experience will be remembered. *Science, 281,* 118–120.

Brooks, F. P., Jr. (1962). Architectural philosophy. In W. Buchholz (ed.), *Planning a Computer System* (pp. 5–16). New York: McGraw-Hill.

Brooks, R. A. (1991). Intelligence without representation. *Artificial Intelligence*, *47*, 139–159.

Brown, J. S., & VanLehn, K. (1980). Repair theory: A generative theory of bugs in procedural skills. *Cognitive Science, 4*, 379–426.

Brown, R. (1973). *A First Language*. Cambridge, MA: Harvard University Press.

Brunwik, E. (1955). Representative design and probabilistic theory in a functional psychology. *Psychological Review, 62*, 193–217.

Buckner, R. L. (2000). Functional neuroimaging of human memory. In M. S. Gazzaniga (ed.), *The Cognitive Neurosciences* (2nd ed., pp. 817–828). Cambridge, MA: MIT Press.

Buckner, R. L., Kelley, W. M., & Petersen, S. E. (1999). Frontal cortex contributes to human memory formation. *Nature Neuroscience, 2*, 311–314.

Buckner, R. L., & Koutstaal, W. (1998). Functional neuroimaging studies of encoding, priming, and explicit memory retrieval. *Proceedings of the National Academy of Sciences of the USA, 95*, 891–898.

Budiu, R., & Anderson, J. R. (2004). Interpretation-based processing: A unified theory of semantic processing. *Cognitive Science, 28*, 1–44.

Burton, R. R. (1982). Diagnosing bugs in a simple procedural skill. In D. Sleeman & J. S. Brown (eds.), *Intelligent Tutoring Systems*. New York: Academic Press.

Burzio, L. (1999). Missing players: Phonology and the past-tense debate. *Lingua, 112*, 157–199.

Busemeyer, J. R., & Townsend, J. T. (1993). Decision field theory: A dynamic cognitive approach to decision making in an uncertain environment. *Psychological Review, 100*, 432–459.

Bush, R. R., & Mosteller, F. (1955). *Stochastic Models for Learning*. New York: Wiley.

Byrne, M. D., & Anderson, J. R. (2001). Serial modules in parallel: The psychological refractory period and perfect time-sharing. *Psychological Review, 108*, 847–869.

Byrne, R., & Russon, A. (1998). Learning by imitation: A hierarchical approach. *Behavioral and Brain Sciences, 21*, 667–721.

Cabeza, R., Dolcos, F., Graham, R., & Nyberg, L.(2002). Similarities and differences in the neural correlates of episodic memory retrieval and working memory. *Neuroimage, 16*, 317–330.

Card, S., Moran, T., & Newell, A. (1983). *The Psychology of Human-Computer Interaction*. Hillsdale, NJ: Erlbaum.

Carew, T. J., Hawkins, R. D., & Kandel, E. R. (1983). Differential classical conditioning of a defensive withdrawal reflex in Aplysia californica. *Science, 219*, 397–400.

Carter, C. S., MacDonald, A. W., Botvinick, M., Ross, L. L., Stenger, V. A., Noll, D., & Cohen, J. D. (2000). Parsing executive processes: Strategic versus evaluative functions of the anterior cingulate cortex. *Proceedings of the National Academy of Sciences of the USA, 97*, 1944–1948.

Casey, B. J., Trainor, R., Giedd, J. N., Vauss, Y., Vaituzis, C. K., Hamburger, S., Kozuch, P., & Rapoport, J. L. (1997a). The role of the anterior cingulate in automatic and controlled processes: A developmental neuroanatomical study. *Developmental Psychobiology, 30* (1), 61–69.

Casey, B. J., Trainor, R. J., Orendi, J. L., Schubert, A. B., Nystrom, L. E., Cohen, J. D., Noll, D. C., Giedd, J., Castellanos, X., Haxby, J., Forman, S. D., Dahl, R. E., & Rapoport, J. L. (1997b). A developmental functional MRI study of prefrontal activation during performance of a Go-No-Go task. *Journal of Cognitive Neuroscience, 9*, 835–847.

Chalmers, D. (1997). Moving forward on the problem of consciousness. *Journal of Consciousness Studies, 4*(1), 3–46.

Chapman, D. (1987). Planning for conjunctive goals. *Artificial Intelligence, 32*, 333–377.

Chase, W. G., & Clark, H. H. (1972). Mental operations in the comparisons of sentences and pictures. In L. W. Gregg (ed.), *Cognition in Learning and Memory*. New York: Wiley.

Chater, N., & Oaksford, M. (1999). Ten years of the rational analysis of cognition. *Trends Cognitive Science, 3*(2), 57–65.

Cheng, P. W., Holyoak, K. J., Nisbett, R. E., & Oliver, L. M. (1986). Pragmatic versus syntactic approaches to training deductive reasoning. *Cognitive Psychology, 18*, 293–328.

Cherniak, C. (1990). The bounded brain: Toward quantitative neuroanatomy. *Journal of Cognitive Neuroscience, 2*, 58–68.

Clark, A. (1997). The dynamical challenge. *Cognitive Science, 21*(4), 461–448.

Cobb, P., Yackel, E., & Wood, T. (1992). A constructivist alternative to the representational view of mind in mathematics education. *Journal for Research in Mathematics Education, 23*, 2–33.

Cohen, M. S. (1997). Parametric analysis of fMRI data using linear systems methods. *Neuroimage, 6*, 93–103.

Cohen, N. J., Eichenbaum, H., DeAcedo, B. S., & Corkin, S. (1985). Different memory systems underlying acquisition of procedural and declarative knowledge. *Annals of the New York Academy of Sciences, 444*, 54-71.

Collins, A. M., & Quillian, M. R. (1972). How to make a language user. In E. Tulving & W. Donaldson (eds.), *Organization of Memory*. New York: Academic Press.

Cooper, R. P. (2002). *Modelling High-Level Cognitive Processes*. Mahwah, NJ: Erlbaum.

Cosmides, L., & Tooby, J. (2000). The cognitive neuroscience of social reasoning. In M. S. Gazzaniga (ed.), *The new cognitive neurosciences* (2nd ed., pp. 1259–1272). Cambridge, MA: MIT Press.

Critchley, H. D., Mathias, C. J., Josephs, O., O'Doherty, J., Zanini, S., Dewar, B.-K., Cipolotti, L., Shallice, T., & Dolan, R. J. (2003). Human cingulate cortex and autonomic control: Converging neuroimaging and clinical evidence. *Brain, 126,* 2139–2152.

Daily, L. Z., Lovett, M. C., & Reder, L. M. (2001). Modeling individual differences in working memory performance: A source activation account in ACT-R. *Cognitive Science, 25,* 315–353.

Dale, A. M., & Buckner, R. L. (1997). Selective averaging of rapidly presented individual trials using fMRI. *Human Brain Mapping, 5,* 329–340.

Dallaway, R. (1994). *Dynamics of Arithmetic: A Connectionist View of Arithmetic Skills.* Cognitive Science Research Papers 306. Brighton, UK: University of Sussex, citeseer.ifi.unizh.ch/dallaway94dynamics.htm.

Dehaene, S., & Changeux, J. P. (2004). Neural mechanisms for access to consciousness. In M. Gazzaniga (ed.), *The Cognitive Neurosciences* (3rd ed.) (pp. 1145–1158). Cambridge, MA: MIT Press.

Dehaene, S., Kergsberg, M., & Changeux, J. P. (1998). A neuronal model of a global workspace in effortful cognitive tasks. *Proceedings of the National Academy of Sciences of the USA, 95,* 14529–14534.

Dehaene, S., & Naccache, L. (2001). Toward a cognitive neuroscience of consciousness: Basic evidence and a workspace framework. *Cognition, 79,* 1–37.

Dehaene, S., Piazza, M., Pinel, P., & Cohen, L. (2002). Three parietal circuits for number processing. *Cognitive Neuropsychology, 20,* 487–506.

Dehaene, S., Posner, M. I., & Tucker, D. M. (1994). Localization of a neural system for error detection and compensation. *Psychological Science, 5,* 303–305.

Dehaene, S., Spelke, E., Pinel. P., Stanescu, R., & Tsivkin, S. (1999). Sources of mathematical thinking: Behavior and brain-imaging evidence. *Science, 284,* 970–974.

Delaney, P. F., Reder, L. M., Staszewski, J. J., & Ritter, F. E. (1998). The strategy-specific nature of improvement: The power law applies by strategy within task. *Psychological Science, 9,* 1–7.

Delgado, M. R., Locke, H. M., Stenger, V. A., & Fiez, J. A. (2003). Dorsal striatum responses to reward and punishment: Effects of valence and magnitude manipulations. *Cognitive, Affective, and Behavioral Neuroscience, 3*(1), 27–38.

Dennett, D. C. (1991). *Consciousness Explained.* Boston, MA: Little & Company.

Dennett, D. C. (1993). The message is: There is no medium. *Philosophy and Phenomenological Research, 53,* 919–931.

D'Esposito, M., Piazza, M., Detre, J. A., Alsop, D. C., Shin, R. K., Atlas, S., & Grossman, M. (1995). The neural basis of the central executive of working memory. *Nature, 378,* 279–281.

Dienes, Z., & Fahey, R. (1995). Role of specific instances in controlling a dynamic system. *Journal of Experimental Psychology: Learning, Memory, and Cognition, 21*(4), 848–862.

Donges, E. (1978). A two-level model of driver steering behavior. *Human Factors, 20*, 691–707.

Doorenbos, R. (1995). *Production Matching for Large Learning Systems.* Ph.D. dissertation, Carnegie Mellon University, School of Computer Science, Pittsburgh, PA.

Duchaine, B., Cosmides, L., & Tooby, J. (2001). Evolutionary psychology and the brain. *Current Opinion in Neurobiology, 11*, 225–230.

Dunbar, K., & MacLeod, C. M. (1984). A horse race of a different color: Stroop interference patterns with transformed words. *Journal of Experimental Psychology: Human Perception and Performance, 10*, 622–639.

Ebbinghaus, H. (1913). *Memory: A Contribution to Experimental Psychology* (H. A. Ruger & C. E. Bussenues, Trans.). New York: Teachers College, Columbia University. (Original work published 1885)

Eichenbaum, H. (1997). How does the brain organise memories? *Science, 277,* 330–332.

Eichenbaum, H., Otto, T., & Cohen, N. J. (1994). Two functional components of the hippocampal memory system. *Behavioral and Brain Sciences, 17,* 449–518.

Elman, J. L., Bates, E., Johnson, M., Karmiloff-Smith, A., Parisi, D., & Plunkett, K. (1996). *Rethinking Innateness: A Connectionist Perspective on Development.* Cambridge, MA: MIT Press.

Emond, B. (2006). WN-LEXICAL: An ACT-R module built from the WordNet lexical database. In *Proceedings of the Seventh International Conference on Cognitive Modeling* (pp. 359–360). Trieste, Italy: Edizioni Goliardiche.

Ericsson, K. A., & Kintsch, W. (1995). Long-term working memory. *Psychological Review, 102,* 211–245.

Falkenstein, M., Hohnbein, J., & Hoorman, J. (1995). Event related potential correlates of errors in reaction tasks. In G. Karmos, M. Molnar, V. Csepe, I. Czigler, & J. E. Desmedt (eds.), *Perspectives of Event-Related Potentials Research* (pp. 287–296). Amsterdam: Elsevier Science.

Feldman, J. A., & Ballard, D. H. (1982). Connectionist models and their properties. *Cognitive Science, 6* (3), 205–254.

Fellbaum, C. (1998). *WordNet: An Electronic Lexical Database.* Cambridge, MA: MIT Press.

Ferguson, I. A. (1992). *TouringMachines: An Architecture for Dynamic, Rational, Mobile Agents.* Ph.D. dissertation, Clare Hall, University of Cambridge, UK. (Also available as Technical Report No. 273, University of Cambridge Computer Laboratory)

Fikes, R. E., & Nilsson, N. J. (1971). STRIPS: A new approach to the application of theorem proving to problem solving. *Artificial Intelligence, 2,* 189–208.

Fincham, J. M., & Anderson. (2006). Distinct roles of the anterior cingulate and prefrontal cortex in the acquisition and performance of a cognitive skill. *Proceedings of the National Academy of Sciences of the USA, 103,* 12941–12946.

Firby, R. J. (1996, May). Modularity issues in reactive planning. In *Proceedings of the Third International Conference on AI Planning Systems* (pp. 78–85). Menlo Park, California: The AAAI Press.

Fletcher, P. C., Frith, C. D., & Rugg, M. D. (1997). The functional neuroanatomy of episodic memory. *Trends in Neuroscience, 20,* 213–218.

Fletcher, P. C., & Henson, R. N. A. (2001). Frontal lobes and human memory: Insights from functional neuroimaging. *Brain, 124,* 849–881.

Flombaum, J., Junge, J., & Hauser, M. D. (2005). Rhesus monkeys (Macaca mulatta) spontaneously compute large number addition operations. *Cognition, 97,* 315–325.

Fodor, J. A. (1983). *The Modularity of Mind.* Cambridge, MA: MIT/Bradford Books.

Fodor, J. A. (2000). *The Mind Doesn't Work That Way: The Scope and Limits of Computational Psychology.* Cambridge, MA: MIT Press.

Fodor, J., & Pylyshyn, Z. (1988). Connectionism and cognitive architecture: A critical analysis. *Cognition, 28,* 3–71.

Foerster, P. A. (1990). *Algebra I,* 2nd ed. Menlo Park, CA: Addison-Wesley.

Fong, G. T., Krantz, D. H., & Nisbett, R. E. (1986). The effects of statistical training on thinking about everyday problems. *Cognitive Psychology, 18,* 253–292.

Forgy, C. L. (1982). Rete: A fast algorithm for the many pattern/many object pattern match problem. *Artificial Intelligence, 19*(1), 17–37.

Frank, M. J., Loughry, B., & O'Reilly, R. C. (2001). Interactions between the frontal cortex and basal ganglia in working memory: A computational model. *Cognitive, Affective, and Behavioral Neuroscience, 1,* 137–160.

Friedman, M. P., Burke, C. J., Cole, M., Keller, L., Millward, R. B., & Estes, W. K. (1964). Two-choice behavior under extended training with shifting probabilities of reinforcement. In R. C. Atkinson (ed.), *Studies in Mathematical Psychology.* Stanford, CA: Stanford University Press.

Friston, K. J. (2003). Introduction: Experimental design and statistical parametric mapping. In R. S. J. Frackowiak, K. J. Friston, C. Frith, R. Dolan, K. J. Friston, C. J. Price, S. Zeki, J. Ashburner, & W. D. Penny (eds.), *Human Brain Function* (2nd ed.). San Diego, CA: Academic Press

Fu, W.-T., & Anderson, J. R. (2006). From recurrent choice to skilled learning: A reinforcement learning model. *Journal of Experimental Psychology: General, 135,* 184–206.

Gabrieli, J. D., Milberg W., Keane, M. M., & Corkin, S. (1990). Intact priming of patterns despite impaired memory. *Neuropsychologia, 28*(5), 417–427.

Gehring, W. J., Goss, B., Coles, M. G. H., Meyer, D. E., & Donchin, E. (1993). A neural system for error detection and compensation. *Psychological Science, 4*, 385–390.

Gentner, D., Holyoak, K. J., & Kokinov, B. (eds.). (2001). *The Analogical Mind: Perspectives from Cognitive Science.* Cambridge, MA: MIT Press.

Georgeff, M. P., & Lansky, A. L. (1987). Reactive reasoning and planning. In *Proceedings of the Sixth National Conference on Artificial Intelligence (AAAI–87)* (pp. 677–682), San Francisco, CA: Morgan Kaufmann.

Gibson, J. J. (1966). *The Senses Considered as Perceptual Systems.* Boston, MA: Houghton Mifflin.

Gigerenzer, G., Todd, P. M., & the ABC Research Group (eds.). (1999). *Simple Heuristics That Make Us Smart.* New York: Oxford University Press.

Gilboa, I., & Schmeidler, D. (2000). Case-based knowledge and induction. *IEEE Transactions on Systems, Man, and Cybernetics, Part A, 30*(2), 85–95.

Glass, A. L. (1984). Effects of memory set on reaction time. In J. R. Anderson & S. M. Kosslyn (eds.), *Tutorials in Learning and Memory* (pp. 119–136). New York: Freeman.

Glover, G. H. (1999). Deconvolution of impulse response in event-related BOLD fMRI. *Neuroimage, 9*, 416–429.

Gluck, M., & Myers, C. (1997). Psychobiological models of hippocampal function in learning and memory. *Annual Review of Psychology, 48*, 481–514.

Goldstein, D. G., & Gigerenzer, G. (1999). The recognition heuristic: How ignorance makes us smart. In G. Gigerenzer, P. M. Todd, & the ABC Research Group (eds.), *Simple Heuristics That Make Us Smart* (pp. 37–58). New York: Oxford University Press.

Goldstein, D. G., & Gigerenzer, G. (2002). Models of ecological rationality: The recognition heuristic. *Psychological Review, 109*, 75–90.

Gonzalez, C., Lerch, F. J., & Lebiere, C. (2003). Instance-based learning in real-time dynamic decision making. *Cognitive Science, 27*(4), 591–635.

Graybiel, A. M., & Kimura, M. (1995). Adaptive neural networks in the basal ganglia. In J. C. Houk, J. L. Davis, & D. G. Beiser (eds.), *Models of Information Processing in the Basal Ganglia.* Cambridge, MA: MIT Press.

Greeno, J. G., Smith, D. R., & Moore, J. L. (1992). Transfer of situated learning. In D. Detterman & R. J. Sternberg (eds.), *Transfer on Trial: Intelligence, Cognition, and Instruction.* Norwood, NJ: Ablex.

Griffiths, T. L., & Tenenbaum, J. B. (2005). Structure and strength in causal induction. *Cognitive Psychology, 51*, 354–384.

Grill-Spector, K., Knouf, N., & Kanwisher, N. (2004). The fusiform face area subserves face perception, not generic within-category identification. *Nature Neuroscience, 7*, 555–562.

Guthrie, E. R. (1935). *The Psychology of Learning.* New York: Harper.

Halpern, M. E., Gunturkun, O., Hopkins, W. D., & Rogers, L. J. (2005). Lateralization of the vertebrate brain: Taking the side of model systems. *Journal of Neuroscience, 25,* 10351–10357.

Harnad, S. (1990). The symbol grounding problem. *Physica D, 42,* 335–346.

Hauser, M. D., & Carey, S. (2003). Spontaneous number representations of small numbers of objects by rhesus macaques: Examinations of content and format. *Cognitive Psychology, 47,* 367–401.

Hauser, M. D., Dehaene, S., Lambertz-Dahaene, G., & Patalano, A. L. (2002). Spontaneous number discrimination of multi-format auditory stimuli in cotton-top tamarins (Saguinus oedipus). *Cognition, 86,* B23–B32.

Hauser, M. D., & Spelke, E. S. (2004). Evolutionary and developmental foundations of human knowledge: A case study of mathematics. In M. Gazzaniga (ed.), *The Cognitive Neurosciences* (Vol. 3, pp. 1025–1147). Cambridge, MA: MIT Press.

Hazeltine, E., Teague, D., & Ivry, R. B. (2002). Simultaneous dual-task performance reveals parallel response selection after practice. *Journal of Experimental Psychology: Human Perception and Performance, 28,* 527–545.

Heathcote, A., Brown, S., & Mewhort, D. J. K. (2000). The power law repealed: The case for an exponential law of practice. *Psychonomic Bulletin and Review, 7,* 185–207.

Hebb, D. O. (1949). *The Organization of Behavior.* New York: Wiley.

Hikosaka, O., Rand, M. K., Miyachi, S., & Miyashita, K. (1995). Learning of sequential movements in the monkey: Process of learning and retention of memory. *Journal of Neurophysiology, 74,* 1652–1661.

Hikosaka, O., Sakai, K., Nakahara, H., Lu, X., Miyachi, S., Nakamura, K., & Rand, M. K. (1999). Neural mechanisms for learning of sequential procedures. In M. S. Gazzaniga (ed.), *The New Cognitive Neurosciences* (pp. 553–572). Cambridge, MA: MIT Press.

Hinton, G. E., & Sejnowsky, T. J. (1986). Learning and relearning in Boltzmann machines. In D. E. Rumelhart, J. L. McClelland, & the PDP Group (eds.), *Parallel Distributed Processing: Explorations in the Microstructure of Cognition: Vol. 1. Foundations.* Cambridge, MA: MIT Press.

Houk, J. C., & Wise, S. P. (1995). Distributed modular architectures linking basal ganglia, cerebellum, and cerebral cortex: Their role in planning and controlling action. *Cerebral Cortex, 2,* 95–110.

Hull, C. L. (1952). *A Behavior System: An Introduction to Behavior Theory Concerning the Individual Organism.* New Haven, CT: Yale University Press.

Hummel, J. E., & Holyoak, K. J. (2003). A symbolic-connectionist theory of relational inference and generalization. *Psychological Review, 110,* 220–264.

Jacobs, L. F., Gaulin, S. J., Sherry, D. F., & Hoffman, G. E. (1990). Evolution of spatial cognition: Sex-specific patterns of spatial behavior predict hippocampal size. *Proceedings of the National Academy of Sciences of the USA, 87,* 6349–6352.

Jennings, N. R., Sycara, K., & Woodbridge, M. (1998). A roadmap of agent research and development. *Autonomous Agents and Multi-agent Systems, 1*(1), 7–38.

Jones, L., Rothbart, M. K., & Posner, M. I. (2003). Development of inhibitory control in preschool children. *Developmental Science, 6,* 498–504.

Kaelbling, L. P., Littman, M. L., & Moore, A. W. (1996). Reinforcement learning: A survey. *Journal of Artificial Intelligence Research, 4,* 237–285.

Kahneman, D., & Tversky, A. (1973). On the psychology of prediction. *Psychological Review, 80,* 237–251.

Kanwisher, N., McDermott, J., & Chun, M. (1997). The fusiform face area: A module in human extrastriate cortex specialized for the perception of faces. *Journal of Neuroscience, 17,* 4302–4311.

Kaplan, C. A. (1989). *Hatching a Theory of Incubation: Does Putting a Problem Aside Really Help? If So, Why?* Unpublished doctoral dissertation, Carnegie Mellon University, Pittsburgh, PA.

Karklin Y., & Lewicki, M. S. (2005). A hierarchical Bayesian model for learning non-linear statistical regularities in non-stationary natural signals. *Neural Computation, 17*(2), 397–423.

Kehoe, E. J., & Gormezano, I. (1980). Configuration and combination laws in conditioning with compound stimuli. *Psychological Bulletin, 87,* 351–387.

Kimble, G. A. (1961). *Conditioning and Learning,* 2nd ed. New York: Appleton-Century-Crofts.

Kintsch, W. (1974). *The Representation of Meaning in Memory.* Hillsdale, NJ: Erlbaum.

Kirk, R. (1974). "Zombies vs. materialists." *Proceedings of the Aristotelian Society, 48* (supplement), 135–152.

Kirshner, D., & Awtry, T. (2004). Visual salience of algebraic transformations. *Journal for Research in Mathematics Education, 35,* 224–257.

Koedinger, K. R., Anderson, J. R., Hadley, W. H., & Mark, M. (1997). Intelligent tutoring goes to school in the big city. *International Journal of Artificial Intelligence in Education, 8,* 30–43.

Koedinger, K. R., & Corbett, A. T. (2006). Cognitive Tutors: Technology bringing learning science to the classroom. In R. K. Sawyer (ed.), *Handbook of the Learning Sciences* (pp. 61–78). New York: Cambridge University Press.

Laird, J. E., Rosenbloom, P. S., & Newell, A. (1986). Chunking in Soar: The anatomy of a general learning mechanism. *Machine Learning, 1*(1) 11–46.

Lakoff, G. (1988). Smolensky, semantics and the sensorimotor system. *Behavioral and Brain Sciences, 11,* 39–40.

Landauer, T. K., & Dumais, S. T. (1997). A solution to Plato's problem: The latent semantic analysis theory of acquisition, induction, and representation of knowledge. *Psychological Review, 104*(2), 211–240.

Lashley, K. S. (1950). In search of the engram. *Symposia of the Society of Experimental Biology, 4,* 454–482.

Lave, J. (1988). *Cognition in Practice: Mind, Mathematics, and Culture in Everyday Life*. New York: Cambridge University Press.

Lave, J., & Wenger, E. (1991). *Situated Learning: Legitimate Peripheral Participation*. Cambridge, UK: Cambridge University Press.

Lebiere, C. (1998). *The Dynamics of Cognition: An ACT-R Model of Cognitive Arithmetic*. Ph.D. dissertation, Carnegie Mellon University, Pittsburgh, PA. (Also available as Technical Report CMU-CS-98-186, Carnegie Mellon University Computer Science Department)

Lebiere, C., & Anderson, J. R. (1993). A connectionist implementation of the ACT-R production system. In *Proceedings of the Fifteenth Annual Conference of the Cognitive Science Society* (pp. 635–640). New York: Erlbaum.

Lebiere, C., Wallach, D., & Taatgen, N. (1998). Implicit and explicit learning in ACT-R. In F. Ritter & R. Young (eds.), *Cognitive Modeling II* (pp. 183–193). Nottingham, UK: Nottingham University Press.

Lepage, M., Ghaffar, O., Nyberg, L., & Tulving, E. (2000). Prefrontal cortex and episodic memory retrieval mode. *Proceedings of the National Academy of Sciences of the USA, 97*, 506–511.

Lewis, R. L., & Vasishth, S. (2005). An activation-based model of sentence processing as skilled memory retrieval. *Cognitive Science, 29*, 375–419.

Ljungberg, T., Apicella, P., & Schultz, W. (1992). Responses of monkey dopamine neurons during learning of behavioral reactions. *Journal of Neurophysiology, 67*, 145–163.

Loewenstein, J., & Gentner, D. (2005). Relational language and the development of relational mapping. *Cognitive Psychology, 50*, 315–353.

Logan, G. D. (1988). Toward an instance theory of automatization. *Psychological Review, 95*, 492–527.

Lovett, M. C. (2005). A strategy-based interpretation of Stroop. *Cognitive Science, 29*, 493–524.

Luce, R. D. (1959). *Individual Choice Behavior: A Theoretical Analysis*. New York: John Wiley & Sons.

Luchins, A. S. (1942). Mechanization in problem solving. *Psychological Monographs, 54*(248).

Luria, A. R. (1961). *The Role of Speech in the Regulation of Normal and Abnormal Behavior*. New York: Liveright.

MacCorquodale, K., & Meehl, P. E. (1953). Preliminary suggestions as to a formalization of expectancy theory. *Psychological Review, 60*, 55–63.

MacDonald, A. W., Cohen, J. D., Stenger, V. A., & Carter, C. S. (2000). Dissociating the role of dorsolateral prefrontal cortex and anterior cingulate cortex in cognitive control. *Science, 288*, 1835–1837.

MacLeod, C. M., & Dunbar, K. (1988). Training and Stroop-like interference: Evidence for a continuum of automaticity. *Journal of Experimental Psychology: Learning, Memory, and Cognition, 14*, 126–135.

Maguire, E. A., Spiers, H. J., Good, C. D., Hartley, T., Frackowiak, R. S. J., & Burgess, N. (2003). Navigation expertise and the human hippocampus: A structural brain imaging analysis. *Hippocampus, 13,* 208–217.

Marcus, G. F. (1995). The acquisition of the English past tense in children and multilayered connectionist networks. *Cognition, 56,* 271–279.

Marcus, G. F. (2001). *The Algebraic Mind: Integrating Connectionism and Cognitive Science.* Cambridge, MA: MIT Press.

Marr, D. (1982). *Vision.* San Francisco, CA: W. H. Freeman.

McCandliss, B. D., Cohen, L., & Dehaene, S. (2003). The visual word form area: Expertise for reading in the fusiform gyrus. *Trends in Cognitive Sciences, 7,* 293–299.

McCarthy, J., & Hayes, J. P. (1969). Some philosophical problems from the standpoint of artificial intelligence. *Machine Intelligence, 4,* 463–502.

McClelland, J. L., McNaughton, B. L., & O'Reilly, R. C. (1995). Why there are complementary learning systems in the hippocampus and neocortex: Insights from the successes and failures of connectionist models of learning and memory. *Psychological Review, 102,* 419–457.

McClelland, J. L., & Rumelhart, D. E. (1981). An interactive model of context effects in letter perception: I. An account of basic findings. *Psychological Review, 88,* 375– 407.

McCloskey, M., & Cohen, N. J. (1989). Catastrophic interference in connectionist networks: The sequential learning problem. In G. H. Bower (ed.), *The Psychology of Learning and Motivation* (Vol. 23). New York: Academic Press.

McClure, S. M., Berns, G. S., & Montague, P. R. (2003). Temporal prediction errors in a passive learning task activate human striatum. *Neuron, 38,* 339–346.

Medin, D. L., & Schaffer, M. M. (1978). A context theory of classification learning. *Psychological Review, 85,* 207–238.

Meyer, D. E., & Kieras, D. E. (1997). A computational theory of executive cognitive processes and multiple-task performance. Part 1. Basic mechanisms. *Psychological Review, 104,* 2–65.

Meyer, D. E., Kieras, D. E., Schumacher, E. H., Fencsik, D., & Glass, J. M. B. (2001, November). *Prerequisites for Virtually Perfect Time Sharing in Dual-Task Performance.* Paper presented at the meeting of the Psychonomic Society, Orlando, FL.

Middleton, F. A., & Strick, P. L. (1996). The temporal lobe is a target of output from the basal ganglia. *Proceedings of the National Academy of Sciences of the USA, 93,* 8683–8687.

Middleton, F. A., & Strick, P. L. (2000). Basal ganglia and cerebellar loops: Motor and cognitive circuits. *Brain Research Reviews, 31,* 236–250.

Miller, E. K., & Cohen, J. D. (2001). An integrative theory of prefrontal cortex function. *Annual Review of Neuroscience, 24,* 167–202.

Miller, G. A. (1998). Foreword. In C. Fellbaum (ed.), *WordNet: An Electronic Lexical Database*. Cambridge, MA: MIT Press.

Milner, B. (1970). Memory and the medial temporal regions of the brain. In K. H. Pribram & D. E. Broadbent (eds.), *Biology of Memory* (pp. 29–48). New York: Academic Press.

Mirenowicz, J., & Schultz, W. (1994). Importance of unpredictedness for reward responses in primate dopamine neurons. *Journal of Neurophysiology, 72,* 1024–1027.

Moll, M., & Miikkulainen, R. (1997). Convergence-zone episodic memory: Analysis and simulations. *Neural Networks, 10,* 1017.

Myung, I. J., Kim, C., & Pitt, M. A. (2000). Toward an explanation of the power law artifact: Insights from response surface analysis. *Memory and Cognition, 28,* 832–840.

Newell, A. (1973a). Production systems: Models of control structures. In W. C. Chase (ed.), *Visual Information Processing* (pp 527–546). New York: Academic Press.

Newell, A. (1973b). You can't play 20 questions with nature and win: Projective comments on the papers of this symposium. In W. G. Chase (ed.), *Visual Information Processing* (pp. 283–310). New York: Academic Press.

Newell, A. (1980). Physical symbol systems. *Cognitive Science, 4,* 135–183.

Newell, A. (1990). *Unified Theories of Cognition.* Cambridge, MA: Harvard University Press.

Newell, A. (1992). Précis of unified theories of cognition. *Behavioral and Brain Sciences, 15,* 425–492.

Newell, A. (1993). *Desires and Diversions* [video]. Lecture delivered at Carnegie Mellon University, School of Computer Science. Stanford, CA: University Video Communications.

Newell, A., & Simon, H. A. (1961). GPS, a program that simulates human thought. In H. Billing (ed.), *Lernende Automaten* (pp. 109–124). Munich: R. Oldenbourg.

Newell, A., & Simon, H. (1972). *Human Problem Solving.* Englewood Cliffs, NJ: Prentice-Hall.

Newell, A., & Simon, H. A. (1976). Computer science as empirical inquiry: Symbols and search. *Communications of the ACM, 19,* 113–126.

Newport, E. L., & Aslin, R. N. (2004). Learning at a distance: I. Statistical learning of non-adjacent dependencies. *Cognitive Psychology, 48,* 127–162.

Nieder, A., Freedman, D. J., & Miller, E. K. (2002). Representation of the quantity of visual items in the primate prefrontal cortex. *Science, 297,* 1708–1711.

Noelle, D. C., & Cottrell, G. W. (1995). A unified connectionist model of instruction following. In R. Sun & F. Alexandre (eds.), *Working Notes of the Workshop on Connectionist-Symbolic Integration: From Unified to Hybrid Approaches* (pp. 44–49). Montreal: AAAI Press.

Norman, D. A., & Rumelhart, D. E. (1975). *Explorations in Cognition.* New York: W. H. Freeman.

Norman, D. A., & Shallice, T. (1986). Attention to action: Willed and automatic control of behavior. In R. Davidson, G. Schwartz, & D. Shapiro (eds.), *Consciousness and Self Regulation: Advances in Research and Theory* (Vol. 4, pp. 1–18). New York: Plenum Press.

Norman, K. A., & O'Reilly, R. C. (2003). Modeling hippocampal and neocortical contributions to recognition memory: A complementary learning systems approach. *Psychological Review, 110,* 611–646.

Nosofsky, R. M. (1984). Choice, similarity, and the context theory of classification. *Journal of Experimental Psychology: Learning, Memory, and Cognition, 10,* 104–114.

Nosofsky, R. M. (1986). Attention, similarity, and the identification-categorization relationship. *Journal of Experimental Psychology: General, 115*(1), 39–57.

Nosofsky, R. M., & Palmeri, T. J. (1997). An exemplar-based random-walk model of speeded classification. *Psychological Review, 104,* 266–300.

Oaksford, M., & Chater, N. (1994). A rational analysis of the selection task as optimal data selection. *Psychological Review, 101,* 608–631.

Oden, D. L., Thompson, R. K. R., & Premack, D. (2001). Can an ape reason analogically? Comprehension and production of analogical problems by Sarah, a chimpanzee (Pan troglodytes). In D. Gentner, K. J. Holyoak, & B. N. Kokinov (eds.), *Analogy: Theory and Phenomena* (pp. 472–497). Cambridge, MA: MIT Press.

O'Doherty, J., Dayan, P., Friston, K. J., Critchley, H. D., & Dolan, R. J. (2003). Temporal difference models account and reward-related learning in the human brain. *Neuron, 38*(2), 329–337.

O'Kane, G., Kensinger, E. A., & Corkin, S. (2004). Evidence for semantic learning in profound amnesia: An investigation with the patient H.M. *Hippocampus, 14,* 417–425.

O'Keefe, J., & Nadel, L. (1978). *The Hippocampus as a Cognitive Map.* Oxford; Clarendon Press.

O'Reilly, R. C. (2006). Biologically based computational models of high-level cognition. *Science, 314,* 91–94.

O'Reilly, R. C., & Frank, M. J. (2006). Making working memory work: A computational model of learning in the frontal cortex and basal ganglia. *Neural Computation, 18,* 283–328.

O'Reilly, R. C., & Munakata, Y. (2000). *Computational Explorations in Cognitive Neuroscience: Understanding the Mind by Simulating the Brain.* Cambridge, MA: MIT Press.

O'Reilly, R. C., & Rudy, J. W. (2001). Conjunctive representations in learning and memory: Principles of cortical and hippocampal function. *Psychological Review, 108,* 311–345.

Packard, M. G. (1999). Glutamate infused posttraining into the hippocampus or caudate putamen differentially strengthens place and response learning. *Proceedings of the National Academy of Sciences of the USA, 96*, 12881–12886.

Packard, M. G., & Knowlton, B. J. (2002). Learning and memory functions of the basal ganglia. *Annual Review of Neuroscience, 25*, 563–593.

Packard, M. G., & McGaugh, J. L. (1996). Inactivation of the hippocampus or caudate nucleus with lidocaine differentially affects expression of place and response learning. *Neurobiology of Learning Memory, 65*, 65–72.

Papineau, D. (2001). The evolution of means-end reasoning. In D. Walsh (ed.), *Naturalism, Evolution and Mind*. Cambridge, MA: Cambridge University Press.

Park, H., & Reder, L. M. (2004). Moses illusion: Implication for human cognition. In R. F. Pohl (ed.), *Cognitive Illusions* (pp. 275–291). Hove, UK: Psychology Press.

Parle, M., Vasudevan, M., & Singh, N. (2005). Swim every day to keep dementia away. *Journal of Sports Science and Medicine, 4*, 37–46.

Pashler, H. E. (1994). Dual-task interference in simple tasks: Data and theory. *Psychological Bulletin, 116*, 220–244.

Pashler, H. E. (1998). *The Psychology of Attention*. Cambridge, MA: MIT Press.

Paus, T., Koski, L., Caramanos, Z., & Westbury, C. (1998). Regional differences in the effects of task difficulty and motor output on blood flow response in the human anterior cingulate cortex: A review of 107 PET activation studies. *Neuroreport, 9*, R37-R47.

Pavlik, P. I., & Anderson, J. R. (2005). Practice and forgetting effects on vocabulary memory: An activation-based model of the spacing effect. *Cognitive Science, 29*, 559–586.

Pelavin, S. H., & Kane, M. (1990). *Changing the Odds: Factors Increasing Access to College*. New York: College Board Publications.

Peterson, S. B., & Potts, G. R. (1982). Global and specific components of information integration. *Journal of Verbal Learning and Verbal Behavior, 21*, 403–420.

Petrov, A., & Anderson, J. R. (2005). The dynamics of scaling: A memory-based anchor model of category rating and absolute identification. *Psychological Review, 112*(2), 383–416.

Pew, R. W., & Mavor, A. S. (eds.). (1998). Integrative architectures for modeling the individual combatant. In *Modeling Human and Organizational Behavior* (pp. 51–111). Washington, DC: National Academy Press.

Pickering, M., & Crocker, M. (1996, July). *A Rational Analysis of Parsing and Interpretation*. Paper presented at the Conference on Rational Models of Cognition, University of Warwick, United Kingdom.

Pinker, S. (1984). *Language Learnability and Language Development*. Cambridge, MA: Harvard University Press.

Pinker, S., & Prince, A. (1988). On language and connectionism: Analysis of a parallel distributed processing model of language acquisition, *Cognition*, *23*, 73–193.

Pinker, S., & Ullman, M. (2002). The past and future of the past tense. *Trends in Cognitive Science*, *6*, 456–463.

Pirolli, P. (2005). Rational analyses of information foraging on the web. *Cognitive Science*, *29*, 343–373.

Pirolli, P. L., & Anderson, J. R. (1985). The role of practice in fact retrieval. *Journal of Experimental Psychology: Learning, Memory, and Cognition*, *11*, 136–153.

Plunkett, K., & Juola, P. (1999). A connectionist model of English past tense and plural morphology. *Cognitive Science*, *23*, 463–490.

Plunkett, K., & Marchman, V. (1991). U-shaped learning and frequency effects in a multi layered perception: Implications for child language acquisition. *Cognition*, *38*, 43–102.

Porter, A. C. (1998). The effects of upgrading policies on high school mathematics and science. In D. Ravitch (ed.), *Brookings Papers on Education Policy* (pp. 123–172). Washington, DC: Brookings Institution.

Posner, M. I., & Dehaene, S. (1994). Attentional Networks. *Trends in Neurosciences*, *17*, 75–79.

Posner, M. I., & DiGirolamo, G. J. (1998). Executive attention: Conflict, target detection and cognitive control. In R. Parasuraman (ed.), *The Attentive Brain* (pp 401–423). Cambridge, MA: MIT Press.

Premack, D. (1976). *Intelligence in Ape and Man*. Hillsdale, NJ: Erlbaum.

Press, J. H. (2006). *Unknown Quantity: A Real and Imaginary History of Algebra*. Washington, DC: National Academy Press.

Pylyshyn, Z. W. (1984). *Computation and Cognition: Towards a Foundation for Cognitive Science*. Cambridge, MA: MIT Press.

Qin, Y., Anderson, J. R., Silk, E., Stenger, V. A., & Carter, C. S. (2004). The change of the brain activation patterns along with the children's practice in algebra equation solving. *Proceedings of the National Academy of Sciences of the USA*, *101*, 5686–5691.

Qin, Y., Sohn, M.-H., Anderson, J. R., Stenger, V. A., Fissell, K., Goode, A., & Carter, C. S. (2003). Predicting the practice effects on the blood oxygenation level-dependent (BOLD) function of fMRI in a symbolic manipulation task. *Proceedings of the National Academy of Sciences of the USA*, *100*(8), 4951–4956.

Ratcliff, R. (1990). Connectionist models of recognition memory: Constraints imposed by learning and forgetting functions. *Psychological Review*, *97*, 285–308.

Ratcliff, R., Hasegawa, Y. T., Hasegawa, Y. P., Smith, P. L., & Segraves, M. A. (2007). Dual diffusion model for single-cell recording data from the superior colliculus in a brightness-discrimination task. *Journal of Neurophysiology, 97*, 1756–1774.

Reder, L. M. & Kusbit, G. W. (1991). Locus of the Moses illusion: Imperfect encoding, retrieval or match? *Journal of Memory and Language, 30*, 385–406.

Reder, L. M., & Schunn, C. D. (1999). Bringing together the psychometric and strategy worlds: Predicting adaptivity in a dynamic task. In Gopher, D. & Koriat, A. (eds). *Cognitive regulation of performance: Interaction of theory and application. Attention and Performance XVII*, MIT Press, 315–342.

Reed, S. K., & Bolstad, C. A. (1991). Use of examples and procedures in problem solving. *Journal of Experimental Psychology: Learning, Memory, and Cognition, 17*, 753–766.

Reichle, E. D., Carpenter, P. A., & Just, M. A. (2000). The neural basis of strategy and skill in sentence-picture verification. *Cognitive Psychology, 40*, 261–295.

Reisbeck, C. K., & Schank, R. C. (1989). *Inside Cased-Based Reasoning*. Hillsdale, NJ: Erlbaum.

Rescorla, R. A., & Wagner, A. R. (1972). A theory of Pavlovian conditioning: Variations on the effectiveness of reinforcement and nonreinforcement. In A. H. Black & W. F. Prokasy (eds.), *Classical Conditioning: II. Current Research and Theory* (pp. 64–99). New York: Appleton-Century-Crofts.

Restle, F. (1957). Discrimination of cues in mazes: A resolution of the "place-vs.- response" question. *Psychology Review, 64*, 217–228.

Rickard, T. C. (1997). Bending the power law: A CMPL theory of strategy shifts and the automatization of cognitive skills. *Journal of Experimental Psychology: General, 126*, 288–311.

Ritter, F. E., Shadbolt, N. R., Elliman, D., Young, R. M., Gobet, F., & Baxter, G. D. (2003). *Techniques for Modeling Human Performance in Synthetic Environments: A Supplementary Review*. Wright-Patterson Air Force Base, OH: Human Systems Information Analysis Center.

Ritter, S., Haverty, L., Koedinger, K., Hadley, W., & Corbett, A. (in press). Integrating intelligent software tutors with the mathematics classroom. In K. Heid & G. Blum (eds.), *Research on Technology and the Teaching and Learning of Mathematics: Syntheses, Cases, and Perspectives*. Greenwich, CT: Information Age Publishing.

Roitman, J. D., & Shadlen, M. N. (2002). Response of neurons in the lateral intraparietal area during a combined visual discrimination reaction time task. *Journal of Neuroscience, 22*, 9475–9489.

Royer, C., Farahat, A. O., Pirolli, P. L., & Budiu, R. (2005). GLSA Server @ PARC. In *Proceedings of the Twelfth Annual ACT-R Workshop*. Trieste, Italy: Edizioni Goliardiche.

Rubin, D. C., Hinton, S., & Wenzel, A. (1999). The precise time course of retention. *Journal of Experimental Psychology: Learning, Memory, and Cognition, 25*, 1161–1176.

Rumelhart, D. E., & McClelland, J. L. (1986). On learning the past tenses of English verbs. In J. L. McClelland & D. E. Rumelhart (eds.), *Parallel Distributed Processing: Explorations in the Microstructure of Cognition* (Vol. 2, pp. 216–271). Cambridge, MA: MIT Press/Bradford Books.

Russell, S., & Norvig, P. (2002). *Artificial Intelligence: A Modern Approach*, 2nd ed. Upper Saddle River, NJ: Prentice-Hall.

Salvucci, D. D. (2001). An integrated model of eye movements and visual encoding. *Cognitive Systems Research, 1*(4), 201–220.

Salvucci, D. D. (2005). A multitasking general executive for compound continuous tasks. *Cognitive Science, 29*, 457–492.

Salvucci, D. D. (2006). Modeling driver behavior in a cognitive architecture. *Human Factors, 48*, 362–380.

Salvucci, D. D., & Anderson, J. R. (2001). Integrating analogical mapping and general problem solving: The path-mapping theory. *Cognitive Science, 25*, 67–110.

Salvucci, D. D., Boer, E. R., & Liu, A. (2001). Toward an integrated model of driver behavior in a cognitive architecture. *Transportation Research Record, 1779*, 9–16.

Salvucci, D. D., Taatgen, N. A., & Kushleyeva, Y. (2006). Learning when to switch tasks in a dynamic multitasking environment. In *Proceedings of the Seventh International Conference on Cognitive Modeling* (pp. 268–273). Trieste, Italy: Edizioni Goliardiche.

Sanborn, A. N., Griffiths, T. L., & Navarro, D. J. (2006). A more rational model of categorization. In *Proceedings of the 28th Annual Conference of the Cognitive Science Society* (pp. 621–626). Mahwah, NJ: Erlbaum.

Sanner, S., Anderson, J. R., Lebiere, C., & Lovett, M. (2000). Achieving efficient and cognitively plausible learning in backgammon. In *Proceedings of the Seventeenth International Conference on Machine Learning* (pp. 823–830). San Francisco, CA: Morgan Kaufmann.

Schacter, D. L., & Wagner, A. D. (1999). Medial temporal lobe activations in fMRI and PET studies of episodic encoding and retrieval. *Hippocampus, 9*, 7–24.

Schall, J. D. (2001). Neural basis of deciding, choosing and acting. *Nature Reviews in Neuroscience, 2*, 33–42.

Schooler, L. J. (1993). *Memory and the Statistical Structure of the Environment.* Ph.D. dissertation, Department of Psychology, Carnegie Mellon University, Pittsburgh, PA.

Schooler, L. J., & Anderson, J. R. (1997). The role of process in the rational analysis of memory. *Cognitive Psychology, 32*, 219–250.

Schooler, L. J., & Hertwig, R. (2005). How forgetting aids heuristic inference. *Psychological Review, 112*(3), 610–628.

Schoppek, W. (2002). Examples, rules, and strategies in the control of dynamic systems. *Cognitive Science Quarterly, 2*, 63–92.

Schultz, W., Apicella, P., & Ljungberg, T. (1993). Responses of monkey dopamine neurons to reward and conditioned stimuli during successive steps of learning a delayed response task. *Journal of Neuroscience, 13*, 900–913.

Schultz, W., Dayan, P., & Montague, P. R. (1997). A neural substrate of prediction and reward. *Science, 275*, 1593–1599.

Schumacher, E. H., Seymour, T. L., Glass, J. M., Fencsik, D. E., Lauber, E. J., Kieras, D. E., & Meyer, D. E. (2001). Virtually perfect time sharing in dual-task performance: Uncorking the central cognitive bottleneck. *Psychological Science, 12*, 101–108.

Searle, J. R. (1980). Minds, brains, and programs. *Behavioral and Brain Sciences, 3*, 417–424.

Sedlmeier, P., Hertwig, R., & Gigerenzer, G. (1998). Are judgments of the positional frequency of letters systematically biased due to availability? *Journal of Experimental Psychology: Learning, Memory, and Cognition, 24*, 754–770.

Shastri, L., & Ajjanagadde, V. (1993). From simple associations to systematic reasoning: A connectionist representation of rules, variables, and dynamic bindings using temporal synchrony. *Behavioral and Brain Sciences, 16*, 417–451.

Shepard, R. N. (1984). Ecological constraints on internal representation: Resonant kinematics of perception, imagining, thinking, and dreaming. *Psychological Review, 91*, 417–447.

Shepard, R. N. (1987). Toward a universal law of generalization for psychological science. *Science, 237*, 1317–1323.

Siegler, R. S. (1988). Individual differences in strategy choices: Good students, not-so-good students, and perfectionists. *Child Development, 59*, 833–851.

Simon, H. A. (1962). The architecture of complexity. *Proceedings of the American Philosophical Society, 106*, 467–482.

Singley, M. K., & Anderson, J. R. (1989). *Transfer of Cognitive Skill.* Cambridge, MA: Harvard University Press.

Smith, L. B., & Samuelson, L. (2003). Connectionism and dynamic systems. *Developmental Science, 6*(4), 434–439.

Smith, P. L., & Ratcliff, R. (2004). The psychology and neurobiology of simple decisions. *Trends in Neuroscience, 27*, 161–168.

Smolensky, P. (1990). Tensor product variable binding and the representation of symbolic structures in connectionist networks. *Artificial Intelligence, 46*, 159–216.

Smolensky, P. (1995). *Computational Models of Mind. A Companion to the Philosophy of Mind.* Cambridge, MA: Blackwell.

Smolensky, P., & Legendre, G. (2006). *The Harmonic Mind: From Neural Computation to Optimality-Theoretic Grammar,* vols. 1 and 2. Cambridge, MA: MIT Press.

Sohn, M.-H., Albert, M. V., Jung, K.-J., Carter, C. S., & Anderson, J. R. (2004, April). *Pay Now or Pay Later: Preparatory Conflict Monitoring in the Anterior*

Cingulate Cortex and the Prefrontal Cortex. Paper presented at the 11th Annual Meeting of the Cognitive Neuroscience Society, San Francisco, CA.

Sohn, M.-H., Albert, M. V., Jung, K. J., Carter, C. S., & Anderson, J. R. (in press). Preparatory Conflict Monitoring in the Anterior Cingulate Cortex and the Prefrontal Cortex. *Proceedings of the National Academy of Sciences of the USA.*

Sohn, M.-H., & Carlson, R. A. (1998). Procedural frameworks for simple arithmetic skills. *Journal of Experimental Psychology: Learning, Memory, and Cognition, 24,* 1052–1067.

Sohn, M.-H., Goode, A., Stenger, V. A, Carter, C. S., & Anderson, J. R. (2003). Competition and representation during memory retrieval: Roles of the prefrontal cortex and the posterior parietal cortex. *Proceedings of the National Academy of Sciences of the USA, 100,* 7412–7417.

Sohn, M.-H., Goode, A., Stenger, V. A, Jung, K.-J., Carter, C. S., & Anderson, J. R. (2005). An information-processing model of three cortical regions: Evidence in episodic memory retrieval, *Neuroimage, 25,* 21–33.

Squire, L. R., Shimamura, A. P., & Amaral, D. G. (1989). Memory and the hippocampus. In J. Byrne & W. Berry (eds.), *Neural Models of Plasticity* (pp 208–239). New York: Academic Press.

Squire, L. R., & Zola, S. M. (1998). Episodic memory, semantic memory, and amnesia. *Hippocampus, 8,* 205–211.

Stephens, D. W., & Krebs, J. R. (1986). *Foraging Theory.* Princeton, NJ: Princeton University Press.

Sternberg, S. (1966). High-speed scanning in human memory. *Science, 153,* 652–654.

Sternberg, S. (1969). Memory scanning: Mental processes revealed by reaction time experiments. *American Scientist, 57,* 421–457.

Stroop, J. R. (1935). Studies of interference in serial verbal reactions. *Journal of Experimental Psychology, 18,* 643–662.

Sutherland, R. J., & Rudy, J. W. (1991). Configural association theory: The role of the hippocampal formation in learning, memory, and amnesia. *Psychobiology, 17,* 129–144.

Sutton, R. S., & Barto, A. G. (1990). Time-derivative models of pavlovian reinforcement. In M. Gabriel & J. Moore (eds.), *Learning and Computational Neuroscience: Foundations of Adaptive Networks* (pp. 497–537). Cambridge, MA: MIT Press.

Sutton, R. S., & Barto, A. G. (1998). *Reinforcement Learning: An Introduction.* Cambridge, MA: MIT Press.

Taatgen, N. A. (2005). Modeling parallelization and speed improvement in skill acquisition: From dual tasks to complex dynamic skills. *Cognitive Science, 29,* 421–455.

Taatgen, N. A., & Anderson, J. R. (2002). Why do children learn to say "broke"? A model of learning the past tense without feedback. *Cognition, 86,* 123–155.

Taatgen, N. A., & Anderson, J. R. (in press). Constraints in cognitive architectures. In R. Sun (ed.), *Handbook of Cognitive Modeling*. New York: Cambridge University Press.

Taatgen, N. A., & Dijkstra, M. (2003). Constraints on Generalization: Why are past-tense irregularization errors so rare? In *Proceedings of the 25th Annual Conference of the Cognitive Science Society* (pp. 1146–1151). Mahwah, NJ: Erlbaum.

Taatgen, N. A., Juvina, I., Herd. S., & Jilk, D. (2006). A hybrid model of attentional blink. Paper presented at the 2006 ACT-R workshop, act-r.psy.cmu.edu/workshops/workshop-2006/actr-ws-proceedings2006-pn.pdf.

Tenenbaum, J. B. (1997). A Bayesian framework for concept learning. In *Proceedings of the Interdisciplinary Workshop on Similarity and Categorization* (pp. 249–255). University of Edinburgh, Scotland.

Tenenbaum, J. B., & Griffiths, T. L. (2001). Generalization, similarity, and Bayesian inference. *Behavioral and Brain Sciences, 24*(4), 629–641.

Terrace, H. S., Son, L. K., & Brannon, E. M. (2003). Serial expertise of rhesus macaques. *Psychological Science, 14*, 66–73.

Tesauro, G. (1992). Temporal difference learning of backgammon strategy. In D. Sleeman & P. Edwards (eds.), *Machine Learning* (pp. 451–57). San Mateo, CA: Morgan Kaufmann.

Thelen, E., & Smith, L. B. (1994). *A Dynamic Systems Approach to the Development of Cognition and Action*. Cambridge, MA: MIT Press.

Thompson, K. G., Bichot, N. P., & Schall, J. D. (1997). Dissociation of target selection from saccade planning in macaque frontal eye field. *Journal of Neurophysiology, 77*, 1046–1050.

Thorndike, E. (1927). *The Measurement of Intelligence*. New York: Teachers College Press.

Thorndike, E. (1932). *The Fundamentals of Learning*. New York: Teachers College Press.

Tolman, E. C. (1932). *Purposive Behavior in Animals and Men*. New York: Appleton-Century-Crofts.

Tolman, E. C., & Honzik, C. H. (1930). Introduction and removal of reward, and maze performance in rats. *University of California Publications in Psychology, 4*, 257–275.

Tomasello, M. (2000). *The Cultural Origins of Human Cognition*. Cambridge, MA: Harvard University Press.

Tomasello, M., & Call, J. (1997). *Primate Cognition*. New York: Oxford University Press.

Townsend, J. T., & Wenger, M. J. (2004). A theory of interactive parallel processing: New capacity measures and predictions for a response time inequality series. *Psychological Review, 111* (4), 1003–1035.

Treves, A., & Rolls, E. T. (1994). A computational analysis of the role of the hippocampus in memory. *Hippocampus, 4*, 374–392.

Tulving, E. (1972). Episodic and semantic memory. In E. Tulving & W. Donaldson (eds.), *Organization of Memory*. New York: Academic Press.

Uttal, W. R. (2001). *The New Phrenology: The Limits of Localizing Cognitive Processes in the Brain*. Cambridge, MA: MIT Press.

Van Essen, D. C., & DeYoe, E. A. (1995). Concurrent processing in the primate visual cortex. In M. S. Gazzaniga (ed.), *The Cognitive Neurosciences*. Cambridge, MA: MIT Press.

Van Gelder, T. (1998). The dynamical hypothesis in cognitive science. *Behavioural and Brain Sciences, 21*, 615–665.

VanLehn, K. (1990). *Mind Bugs: The Origins of Procedural Misconceptions*. Cambridge, MA: MIT Press.

Van Veen, V., & Carter, C. S. (2005). Separating semantic conflict and response conflict in the Stroop task: A functional MRI study. *Neuroimage, 27*, 497–504.

Van Zandt, T., & Townsend, J. T. (1993). Self-terminating versus exhaustive processes in rapid visual and memory search: An evaluative review. *Perception and Psychophysics, 53*, 563–580.

Vargha-Khadem, F., Gadin, D. G., Watkins, K. E., Connelly, A., Van Paesschen, W., & Mishkin, M. (1997). Differential effects of early hippocampal pathology on episodic and semantic memory. *Science, 277*, 376–380.

Vera, A. H., & Simon, H. A. (1993). Situated action: A symbolic interpretation. *Cognitive Science, 17*, 7–48.

Wagner, A. D., Maril, A., Bjork, R. A., & Schacter, D. L. (2001). Prefrontal contributions to executive control: fMRI evidence for functional distinctions within lateral prefrontal cortex. *Neuroimage, 14*, 1337–1347.

Wagner, A. D., Paré-Blagoev, E. J., Clark, J., & Poldrack, R. A. (2001). Recovering meaning: Left prefrontal cortex guides controlled semantic retrieval. *Neuron, 31*, 329–338.

Wagner, A. D., Schacter, D. L., Rotte, M., Koutstaal, W., Maril, A., Dale, A. M., Rosen, B. R., & Buckner, R. L. (1998). Building memories: Remembering and forgetting of verbal experiences as predicted by brain activity. *Science, 281*, 1188–1191.

Wagner, A. D., Shannon, B. J., Kahn, I., & Buckner, R. L. (2005). Parietal lobe contributions to episodic memory retrieval. *Trends in Cognitive Science, 9*, 445–453.

Wallach, D. P., & Lebiere, C. (1998). Modellierung von Wissenserwerbsprozessen bei der Systemregelung [Modeling of knowledge acquisition processes in system control]. In W. Krause & U. Kottkamp (eds.), *Intelligente Informationsverarbeitung* (pp. 93–101). Wiesbaden, Germany: Deutscher Universitätsverlag.

Washburn, D. A. (1994). Stroop-like effects for monkeys and humans: Processing speed or strength of association? *Psychological Science, 5*(6), 375–379.

Watson, I. (1997). *Applying Case-Based Reasoning: Techniques for Enterprise Systems*. San Francisco, CA: Morgan Kaufmann.

Watson, J. (1930). *Behaviorism*. New York: Norton.

Watson, K. K., Jones, T. K., & Allman, J. M. (2006). Dendritic architecture of von Economo neurons. *Neuroscience, 141,* 1107–1112.

Weiskrantz, L. (1986). *Blindsight: A Case Study and Its Implications*. Oxford, UK: Oxford University Press.

West, R. L., Stewart, T. C., Lebiere, C., & Chandrasekharan, S. (2005). Stochastic resonance in human cognition: ACT-R vs. game theory, associative neural networks, recursive neural networks, q-learning, and humans. In B. Bara, L. Barsalou, & M. Bucciarelli (eds.), *Proceedings of the 27th Annual Conference of the Cognitive Science Society*. Mahwah, NJ: Erlbaum.

Whiten, A., Custance, D. M., Gomez, J.-C., Teixidor, P., & Bard, K. A. (1996). Imitative learning of artificial fruit processing in children (*Homo sapiens*) and chimpanzees (*Pan troglodytes*). *Journal of Comparative Psychology, 110,* 3–14.

Wickens, J. (1997). Basal ganglia: Structure and computations. *Network: Computation in Neural Systems, 8,* R79.

Widrow, B., & Hoff, M. E. (1960). Adaptive switching circuits. In *1960 IRE WESCON Convention Record* (pp. 96–104). New York: Institute of Radio Engineers.

Windes, J. D. (1968). Reaction time for numerical coding and naming numerals. *Journal of Experimental Psychology, 78,* 318–322.

Wise, S. P., Murray, E. A., & Gerfen, C. R. (1996). The frontal cortex-basal ganglia system in primates. *Critical Reviews in Neurobiology, 10,* 317–356.

Xu, Y., & Corkin, S. (2001). H.M. revisits the Tower of Hanoi puzzle. *Neuropsychology, 15,* 69–79.

Yeung, N., Botvinick, M. M., & Cohen, J. D. (2004). The neural basis of error detection: Conflict monitoring and the error-related negativity. *Psychological Review, 111*(4), 931–959.

Young, R., & O'Shea, T. (1981). Errors in children's subtraction. *Cognitive Science, 5,* 153–177.

Zilles, K., & Palomero-Gallagher, N. (2001). Cyto-, myelo-, and receptor architectonics of the human parietal cortex. *Neuroimage, 14,* 8–20.

Zola, S. M., & Squire, L. R. (2000). The medial temporal lobe and the hippocampus. In E. Tulving & F. I. M. Craik (eds.), *The Oxford Handbook of Memory* (pp. 501–520). New York: Oxford University Press.

Author Index

Subject Index